THROWBACKS

THROWBACKS

OLD-SCHOOL BASEBALL PLAYERS IN TODAY'S GAME

GEORGE CASTLE

POTOMAC BOOKS, INC.
Washington, D.C.

Library of Congress Cataloging-in-Publication Data

Castle, George.
  Throwbacks, old-school baseball players in today's game / George Castle.—1st ed.
    p. cm.
  Includes index.
  ISBN 1-57488-453-0 (cloth : alk. paper)
  1. Baseball players—Biography.   I. Title.
GV865.A1C32   2003
796.357'092'2—dc21   2002156571

Softcover ISBN 1-57488-637-1
(alk. paper)

Printed in the United States of America on acid-free paper that meets the American National Standards Institute Z39-48 Standard.

Potomac Books, Inc.
22841 Quicksilver Drive
Dulles, Virginia 20166

10 9 8 7 6 5 4 3 2 1

CONTENTS

CONTENTS

PHOTOGRAPHS

ACKNOWLEDGMENTS

It takes more than a village to grow a book. In this case, a whole host of colleagues and others have to take credit for their assistance in what's always a massive undertaking, the equivalent of writing sixty or seventy magazine-length features.

Start off with a bevy of media-relations and team-publications folks who put in extremely long hours with little credit. They were helpful in providing access and obtaining many of the photos used here. There were Sharon Pannozzo, Samantha Newby, Chuck Wasserstrom, Steve Green, and Jim McArdle of the Chicago Cubs; Scott Reifert and Vivian Stalling of the Chicago White Sox; Brian Bartow and Melody Yount of the St. Louis Cardinals; Jon Greenberg of the Milwaukee Brewers; Mike Swanson and Susan Webner of the Arizona Diamondbacks; Warren Miller and Jimmy Stanton of the Houston Astros; Jim Trdinich and Dan Hart of the Pittsburgh Pirates; Bart Swain of the Cleveland Indians, and Tim Hevly of the Seattle Mariners. Mike Miller, archivist of Little League Baseball's headquarters in Williamsport, Pennsylvania, also dipped into his extensive photo file.

Parents of players were invaluable in sharing their personal keepsake photos for publication: Mattie Glanville, Chuck and Joyce Thome, Nellie Morgan, and Edward Perry. They and other members of the families, such as Kassie Morgan, wife of Mike Morgan, are to be commended for sharing their memories about their favorite ballplayers.

There still exists a bit of collegiality in the dog-eat-dog world of sports media. Paul Hagen of the *Philadelphia Daily News* and Bruce Miles of the *Daily Herald,* based in Arlington Heights, Illinois, shared transcriptions of some interesting locker-room conversations to which I was not originally privy. A number of other baseball writers and broadcasters, too numerous to mention here, shared their observations about the personalities profiled in this book.

Helping track down past articles that provided necessary background were Dave Destler, editor of *Junior Baseball* magazine; Paula Blaine of SportsProfilesPlus.com, and Ruth Smith of the sports department of the *Times of Northwest Indiana.*

Mike Sansone, the former boss of this author and Smith, also gets some thanks. Sansone, doing his usual crackerjack job on the *Chicago Tribune* sports copy desk after moving over from sports editor of the *Times of Northwest Indiana,* turned me loose on the baseball beat a few years back, enabling me to really get to know many of the old-school types you'll be reading about. Chris Freeman, assistant sports editor of the *Times,* carved time out of a crushing schedule to pen a tribute to Jim Thome.

As usual, the staff of the Skokie, Illinois, Public Library were of great assistance in the research work.

The women of the house, wife Nina and daughter Laura Castle, should get kudos for helping round out a still-computer-challenged author's understanding of Word and its assorted features.

And finally, to all the baseball personalities who agreed to be interviewed—on many occasions, multiple times—for *Throwbacks,* my eternal gratitude for submitting to the long-form conversation style. You'll never get the time back, but you'll get proper credit for an old-school attitude that shone through in our talks in person, on the phone and via e-mail.

—George Castle

INTRODUCTION

Facing an uncertain and increasingly terrifying twenty-first century, we often seek solace and escape in institutions that can insulate themselves from the cruel world outside.

Baseball, blessed baseball, with all its faults, is one of them.

The only pro sport that successfully melds past, present and future—the dreamy nostalgia drifting into today's game, which always is framed with the promise of a brighter tomorrow—baseball somehow survives all the assaults on its venerable structure because we can't kick the habit. And we don't want to. When properly introduced at a young age, baseball sticks with you wire to wire.

Indeed, it's the baseball of our youth that we hold so dear. So many memories that we clasp tightly through all the politics, the arrogance, the egos, the venality, the ridiculous concept of privileged men squabbling about dividing a multi-billion-dollar pot. Baseball always had some of these bad qualities, starting in its rough-and-tumble days of the nineteenth century. But its appeal becomes everlasting when all the bad is filtered out through the passage of decades, leaving mostly only fond memories of more innocent times and heroic players. Sort of like the 370-foot fly-ball homer that is inflated to a McGwire-ian moon shot via ballplayers' flawed memories through the years. It's a homer, nevertheless, and it counts the same.

No matter how loving the company of family and friends at the ballgames of our youth, or how tasty the peanuts or Cracker Jack, or cozy the ballpark or inexpensive the bleacher ticket, the basis for our idealized memories are the players to whom we gave unabashed loyalty. They always play better in retrospective, always seem bigger. The Cubs, for instance, had a hell of a mid-1970s outfield in Jose Cardenal, Rick Monday and Jerry Morales; we forget the team never won more than 75 games with that trio patrolling the gardens. Even legitimate stars' achievements were further magnified through the dual prisms of youthful innocence and historical revisionism.

We're in a constant search for present-day baseball figures who are "throwbacks" to the "old school" of players we treasured, who helped grow our love of the game in the first place. No way could the present generation of millionaires be as dedicated as the $80,000 stars of our teen-age years.

They may be bigger, stronger, faster and better conditioned, but are they as dedicated? Will they adeptly sacrifice their own numbers to take two and hit to right, behind the runner? Will they snarl at the manager to complete the game even though their fastball is 6 mph slower than in the early innings? Will they pitch on guts with a sore shoulder or limp to their destination, Kirk Gibson–style? Will they sit in the clubhouse before games poring over the *Sporting News'* stats to get every last edge on opponents, and then repose by their lockers after the game dressed only in dirty skivvies, well-supplied with beer and cigs, replaying with a host of teammates the good, the bad, and the ugly of the previous few hours?

After they depart the ballpark, will they belly up to the bar with the fans—well-paid workingmen, but workingmen nevertheless? And in the off-season, will they still be a pillar of the community, slogging through the snow to work at a local job, keeping the team together via a charity basketball team and gladly speaking at "hot stove league" dinners?

In reality, negatives have dogged the game from its professional inception in 1869. Players slowed down to save their strength at the end of doubleheaders on 100-degree afternoons in St. Louis' old Sportsman's Park. Not every ground ball has been run out full-tilt. Outfielders loafed after fly balls. Stubbornness and sheer stupidity have been in display in the same proportion as in the general population. Ballplayers are eminently human; they're merely more talented in one skill than the rest of us and, after building up a little service time in the big leagues, have been paid better than the median family income level or in some instances greater than entire countries.

Of course, our view of players from the middle part of the twentieth century and earlier was idealized. We didn't have clubhouse access as young fans, so we didn't see them up close, warts and all. Their images were filtered through a corps of baseball writers who traveled on team planes (and trains before that), who viewed their jobs as Supreme Court–style lifetime appointments, and who in many cases were extensions of the team's official lines.

The newspapers were the main conduit for baseball information in the pre-*SportsCenter* era, and we know that the whole truth is held back from the sporting public through the intricate, and interwoven, network of writers, players, managers, media relations officials and team executives. Baseball Confidential stayed just that way—confidential. For every scandal or collection of sordid personal-life events publicized, four times that number were swept under the rug.

No matter that from the hindsight of history, we know that our heroes sometimes had feet of clay. We'd still like every player today to hustle like Pete Rose (minus his dark side off the field) or be a fiery, take-no-prisoners pitcher like Bob Gibson. We'd prefer them to be smart and enduring like Warren Spahn and dedicated to an all-around game like Willie Mays. We'd cherish them if they were studious, observant and analytical like Ted Williams, or tough but affable lugs like Roy Campanella. We'd love it if they were talented ambassadors of the game like Stan "The Man" Musial or downright flakes like Bill "Spaceman" Lee.

But we're disappointed when few find it humanly possible to attain such ideals. Players as a whole couldn't fit our perfect-world image of them back then, and certainly can't now. Society has changed, the players' compensation system has changed, and they have largely achieved elite entertainer status, at least those at the top rung of salaries.

Yet more often than not, the millennial player still possesses a basic desire to win, tries to do everything fundamentally sound to achieve that goal, and has fun in the process, in the same manner as when they played the game for fun as kids. As long as they do, we'll continue to discover the throwbacks to the good ol' days whose memories we keep alive, that keep baseball alive. A number of these archetypes are profiled in this book.

Journey through our most traditional game and find some comfort. We still have living role models like those who played when the "unis" were made of baggy flannel, the players were hungry, the tickets were cheap, the TV was black and white, the newspapers came out in the afternoon with the final markets and day-game line scores, and baseball reigned supreme as the national pastime.

Plenty was wrong with that old world, from duplicity in the White House to rank discrimination against too many stratas of society to unenlightened social mores. But there's nothing wrong with retaining what was good and comforting. And even if some of what we carry through the ages is illusory, it hurts no one. So we want to have an idealized view of an "old-school" ballplayer. Nothing wrong with some grounding when society is so fragmented and pulling apart, fighting for scraps of success and nervously tiptoeing through its paces after September 11, 2001.

If ballplayers can fit the mold of that glorious past, so much the better. There's nothing wrong with being a throwback. We have precious little continuity in life. Baseball at its most basic can provide a bit of that desired quality.

Spoilers of the illusion need not show their face around here.

1

THROWBACKS, WEBSTER'S
UNABRIDGED

Just what and who is a baseball throwback? And what qualifications enable players to graduate from the game's "old school"?

Explanations are as varied as the different ways to score from third base without a base hit: sacrifice fly, error, steal of home, balk, catcher's interference . . .

"It comes down to respect for the game and playing the whole game the way it's meant to be played," said former pitcher Kevin Tapani, as plain a speaker as existed in baseball through the 1990s and into the new millennium.

"Not an [emphasis on] offensive or defensive game. Do all the things required, different kinds of slides, taking guys out, hitting the ball the other way, hitting the ground ball with the infield back. Pitchers who try to do something with the bat, bunt, move the guy over, back up bases, field their position, cover first base and give effort as required.

"That's the ideal player. Guys hopefully will take being a throwback player as a compliment and try to emulate the people who came before him and go on to play the game right."

Switch from Tapani's Upper Michigan fact-of-the-matter speech to the elegance of Bob Costas's sculpted broadcast tones, originated on Long Island and refined through two decades of national prominence.

"It's somebody who plays the game for the joy of it," the NBC-TV sportscaster said of throwbacks and old-school types. "A player who has some sort of perspective, who respects its traditions. There's a certain way in which you play the game if the score is 12-0 on a Tuesday night in August with both teams fifteen games out of first, or whether it's the World Series. It's a certain respect for the game, a certain regard for its history."

Now consult with a man who spoke softly, but carried a big stick. Andre Dawson was a man of his word—and made every word he uttered count after growing up in a loving family in a Miami just shedding its Jim Crow prohibitions.

"Old school to me is being around veteran ballplayers who take you under their wing," Dawson said, "teach you the ropes, show you what the game is all about, educate you about the history of the game. They're always there for you. That's what it means to me. I came up in a time when I was playing with an expansion team [the mid-1970s Montreal Expos] with a lot of veteran ballplayers. Being a young player, I depended on those veterans to help me out."

A throwback goes about his business uncomplainingly and buries his ego. If he's a star pitcher, he need not fuss if he gets into the game on a day he doesn't take the mound.

"Old school is a guy who's willing to play with some aches and pains," said Yankees broadcaster Jim Kaat, the model of the quick worker when he pitched during a twenty-five-year career. "Before the DH, our goal was to be a better hitter than the other guy, a better fielder. I got used as a pinch runner, got hurt a bit—a knee, a wrist—and it cost me a couple of wins. But I always thought I was a baseball player who just happened to be a pitcher."

Former Kansas City Royals manager Tony Muser, who exudes "throwback" from every pore, suggests the concept was part of life when he was growing up in the 1960s.

"I didn't hear anything about 'old school' when I was growing up," he said. "That's the way it was. You were expected to show up on time. If you were late, you were off the team. It was a collection of laws and rules you had to live by. The whole idea is to pass those on and make somebody's life better, make them a better person, a better player, make them more respectful about the game, and make them understand how fortunate we are to be doing what we're doing for a living.

"The old school for the most part did it right."

Arizona Diamondbacks owner Jerry Colangelo, who believes the old school once was the dominant institution, agrees.

"It was a time and place in America where you understood what a good foundation was regarding values, commitment and morals," he said. "Now it's a culture looking for instant gratification. That's society today."

So then if models for throwbacks to the old school are now pretty much defined, how many big leaguers can fit in that model?

"If I ran an inventory of all the rosters, I probably could name 100 of them," said Costas, naming The Master, Greg Maddux, right off the bat along with Derek Jeter.

Cubs president Andy MacPhail, the third-generation baseball executive in his family, believes throwbacks are widespread in the game today.

"I think a larger percentage than what people normally assume," MacPhail said. "Human character hasn't changed, but money has a way of distorting our perspective on things. My experience has by and large been that the vast majority of players play the game hard, they want to win, they have drive to succeed and be productive players. I don't think that's any different.

"The economics change. But I don't think the character has changed. I think there's a large percentage of players who would have fit in back in the sixties just as well as they do today. Even in the context of the game forty years ago, there were some guys who played the game harder and got the uniform dirtier than others."

Kaat volunteers the candidacy of veteran infielder Randy Velarde for his all-around hustle. Larry Walker is another on his list. Paul O'Neill also got a vote, with a caveat. "He's old school except for one bad habit, and he knew it—not running out every ground ball," said Kaat. "He'd hit a ball, get mad, throw his helmet and trot. Other than that, putting his ego aside and his team first, he was terrific."

Baseball raconteur Joe Garagiola, now loyal to the Arizona Diamondbacks for whom he broadcasts and who are general-managed by his son, Joe Garagiola, Jr., names the heart of the lineup as throwbacks: Luis Gonzalez, Matt Williams, Mark Grace, Steve Finley, and Tony Womack.

Muser mentions Pirates outfielder Brian Giles, who he calls a "grinder, a tough kid who plays every day, doesn't do a whole lot of complaining and doesn't ask a lot of questions. He just looks at the board [lineup] where he's supposed to be."

A quartet of modern baseball mainstays were praised by former long-time catcher Mike Stanley, who served for a while as a Red Sox coach.

"[Jeff] Bagwell and [Craig] Biggio," he said. "They've got the dirt on their jerseys and sweat running down. Roger Clemens also is old-school. I lockered next to Roger and lockered next to Nolan [Ryan], and I never saw them. They weren't out messing around. They were in the weight room, they were climbing stairs, they were doing whatever they could to make themselves the best."

Many obvious names from the last generation are cited as throwback models. Pete Rose is mentioned by almost everyone. Cal Ripken, Jr., and Tony Gwynn, seemingly the last of the one-team, two-decade players, are other overwhelming choices. Costas reminds us not to forget Don Mattingly.

Cardinals first baseman Tino Martinez is overjoyed that he made it to the majors in time to rub shoulders with all-time old-school types.

"I came up when guys from the '70s were still playing, throwback-type players," Martinez said. "Guys like George Brett and Robin Yount. That's the way I learned the game, the way they taught it. They played hard every day without any flash. I'm not a very flashy player. I take it serious. I consider myself like those players."

Kaat also brought up a name from the latter twentieth century that you wouldn't normally call a throwback or old-school guy. "Dick Allen was in that category," he said of his former White Sox teammate from 1973–74. "If he had played in the era of sports psychologists and better media handling, he would have been able to handle the pressure better. He was just such a great fundamentally-sound ballplayer."

But why aren't the pundits' lists of throwbacks overly long? Why do they struggle to name more than a handful? Why would Costas stop at around 100, just one-sixth of all big leaguers?

"More guys are worried about MRIs than ERAs," said Garagiola.

"TV has a lot to do with it," Kaat said. "A lot of guys get out of the box, look at the ball, wonder what it will look like on *SportsCenter*, and it's already in the gap. They've got to suddenly turn it on at that point."

At one time, players policed one another, partly due to the bonds they formed traveling together on the old Pullman sleeper cars between the cities in the country's northeast quadrant. Elden Auker, the sidearming right-hander who starred for the Tigers in the 1930s, wrote about that lifestyle in his 2001 book, *Sleeper Cars and Flannel Uniforms.* That kind of camaraderie, promoting old-school values, can scarcely be duplicated today among the millionaire businessmen of the clubhouses today.

"I don't think there's any doubt about it," Auker said. "We played together all day. On the train, we slept together, we ate together, we played cards together, we talked together. We were together like a family. Being on the Pullman cars between cities was a wonderful life. It was all first class."

The change in attitudes along with an apparent slacking off in overall dedication to the game made Dawson decide by late in his career, around 1990, that he would not want to manage the present generation of players.

Dawson had set standards for himself, not just in performance, but also in preparation for games. He became well acquainted with the surgeon's tools after injuring a knee playing high school football in Miami in the early 1970s. Dawson endured ten more operations on both knees during his baseball career, requiring hours of pregame and postgame preparation and work-outs just to get the balky knees in shape. His desire to play flamed so brightly he put up with the pain, surgeries, and constant knee drainings for a total of twenty seasons.

"You look around, see that a lot of guys don't play as hard," Dawson said. "A lot has to do with guys being rushed here, or being financially rewarded for having mediocre years. I could never go along with mediocrity.

"If I was going to be in charge, there would be certain standards I'm going to have to enforce and expect. I would not want to put myself under a microscope, and let the game be dictated to me in a different fashion."

Another critic is Stanley.

"Now guys don't need to be the best because they're making a pretty healthy living," he said. "The change in attitude has to do with guys being secure with the way things changed monetarily. They didn't have to fight too hard.

"It took me six full years in the big leagues before I made over $150,000. Toward the end of my career, the minimum was $200,000. You had to scratch and claw and do everything you could to make a living. Now, after a couple of years, guys are making $2 million, $3 million. It took me my whole career to start making that kind of money. The long-term contracts that kids get these days are absolutely ridiculous. I don't think kids understand what the guys had to go through for them to make the kind of money they're making."

Not everyone is down on the overall attitude of today's major leaguers. Surprisingly, one of the biggest advocates for recognizing the throwbacks in today's game is the one man who can't enjoy the full benefit of an association with baseball.

Banned from a job in the game and Hall of Fame consideration due to alleged gambling activities in the 1980s, Pete Rose sticks up for players striv-ing to imitate his "Charlie Hustle" playing style.

"I think there's a lot more who play harder today than don't play hard," Rose said. "We don't like to recognize those guys today. We look at today's players as hitting home runs and lumbering around the bases.

"I don't think it's really fair to say that the [present] players don't play hard. They do, but they have a different way of showing it. It's not when the cameras are on them during a game."

Rose gets some surprising backing from a couple of old baseball tradi-tionalists.

"Many of my peers tell me, 'Frank, they don't make 'em like they used to,'" former slugger Frank Howard said. "I say, 'You're absolutely right, they don't make 'em like they used to.' They make them bigger, faster, stronger. They're better educated. They have access to all that data. With the money structure, why wouldn't they be dedicated?

"Today's guy, because of the year-round conditioning, they're a new, improved version of Ivory soap. We had guys forty or fifty years ago who might be indifferent to the game on a particular day. The effort to do well is there [today]."

Seconding that notion is Hall of Famer Robin Roberts, who never encountered a nine-inning stint on the mound he'd willingly refuse.

"I think they're all old school, but it's a different school," Roberts said. "I have nothing but the greatest respect for them. They travel. They're arriving [in the next city] at oddball hours. The games are lasting three hours.

"You don't have to gut it out for nine innings to prove you're good. If you've got a guy like [Mariano] Rivera, why wouldn't you want him to come in the last inning? Four days' rest and using eleven men on the staff is much better for baseball. You pitch a complete game and get beat, it's not a real good thing to do. Pitch seven innings and win, it makes more sense."

Perhaps the art of communicating one's desire to hustle and win to the consuming public is a problem. Media-player relations haven't exactly been improving in recent decades as the gulf widens between millionaire athletes and modestly-paid writers and broadcasters, under the gun to beat increasingly worse deadlines to fill news holes and feed attention-getting sound bites.

"A lot of guys are kind of intimidated by the press and are scared of talking to the press," Rose said.

Maybe the players don't talk to another enough to get in practice. The art of hanging around the clubhouse for an hour or more after the game for a post-mortem analysis seems to be dying out.

"To sit around and hash out the game, they don't have to do that anymore," former catcher Stanley said.

"No question about that, Michael's right," Howard said. "You sit around and have a couple of beers, talk about the game, talk about the pitcher you faced tonight, talk about the great play your guy made."

But society as a whole always changes, sometimes for the better. Baseball traditionally moves at a glacial pace to keep up. Perhaps a player can be old school without the usual veneer of scratchin', spittin', and chewin'.

Some of the old-school behavior came from players who had to always look over their shoulders and didn't get their fair share of baseball's income.

"Your motivation was the weekly *Sporting News,*" critic-funnyman Garagiola said of his 1940s days with the Cardinals. "As a catcher, the first thing I did was look to see how the guy at Rochester or Columbus was doing. If he had a big week, 'Oh, oh, I'm going down to the batting cage and work on something else.'

"When I played, we had no leverage. The winner's take-home share of the 1946 World Series was $2,700. It was ridiculous. The owners had too much power. Now the players have too much power."

"There's no fear among players about being sent to the minor leagues or being demoted," said Bob Uecker, like Garagiola another catcher-turned-baseball comedian-turned-announcer. "Back in those days, it always was a hammer in management. You were gone, and sometimes the manager wouldn't even tell you."

Other old-school aspects of the game were too hide-bound with ossified tradition and faux toughness.

"When I broke in during the 1950s, seeing how guys operated without helmets, it proves how bad we were judgment-wise," said Uecker.

"We thought wearing a helmet was sissy. I remember the Pittsburgh Pirates organization in the minors was the first to wear helmets in the minors in 1959. We were with Jacksonville, and when those guys came out on the field we were amazed. We used those inserts, they were made of cardboard. They just left a bigger dent in your head if you were hit by a baseball.

"I look at catchers who wear the protective piece below the mask. How stupid were we? Same with shinguards above the knee."

Whether operating in a vintage 1953 reserve clause–structured game or a 2003 players-rights sport, a personal value system can't be taught between the white lines. It has to come from within, or from the family.

"I've often said, sure, there's guys who can run faster than me and throw better than me," said Rose. "But they didn't have the work ethic I had. That's a God-given talent. They didn't have the enthusiasm that I did, that's a God-given talent. Certain things you're born with. Hustle and determination, you're born with. When I played the game, I wasn't going to get embarrassed. I knew what my opposition could do. It was a four at-bat battle every night."

Rose thus had all that he needed within him to serve as a model player. But he slipped up badly when he didn't heed the philosophy of an Andre Dawson.

"I just know that I try to surround myself with influential individuals," Dawson said, "[who] pat me on the back, or slap me on the rear when that was warranted, who I could trust, depend on to not mislead me."

Those who feel they are throwbacks, who are old school, who are well-grounded, believe they have to somehow propagate that kind of mentality in a sport they concede should experience natural change.

"All we are is a total sum of our life's experiences," said hard-bitten former manager Tony Muser. "It's a value system that never leaves you.

"Our job is to pass them on and make the players aware of it."

Judging from the stories of the baseball figures in upcoming pages and others throughout the game, the existing throwbacks are making a dent in that effort.

2

THE PESKY LEADOFF MAN

The game's musclemen may lay down a perfunctory bunt at the start of their turn in the cage during batting practice before they start swinging with all their might and enthralling early-bird fans.

In contrast, Fernando Viña has no thoughts about reaching the seats and beyond during his time. His devotion to perfecting the little man's game is almost maniacal.

The first three pitches the Cardinals' second baseman sees in the cage are bunted to the left side. Then he swings away, slashing the next four serves to left field. A grounder to shortstop follows. Nothing has been pulled so far.

Finally, in his second set of swings, Viña pulls some pitches—toward second base, down the first-base line. But that's seemingly just for show. In his third and final set of hacks, there's another three bunts and more opposite-field liners to left. Tough and savvy, Viña will not be pigeon-holed by pitchers. He will not have holes or tendencies. He will hit the ball all over the field against anyone, and be in a position to do just about anything in an at-bat to get on base.

But Viña doesn't stop with his bat-handling virtuoso. He will try to work on the nuances of baserunning after he finishes his swings. And in infield practice, devotion to his position at second base goes without saying. No reason for him not to achieve Gold Glove–caliber prowess while there's time to practice.

Plain and simple, Viña, all of five-foot-nine, 174 pounds, strives to dominate a game, but in a different way than the monster-man bashers and fire-balling pitchers. He won't do it with brute strength or sheer speed. Viña will accomplish his feats via determination, grit, hustle and a desire to wear down his opponents. He'll outthink and outlast them. He'll aggravate 'em. But, in the end, he'll also gain their admiration.

"I just go up there and battle and do whatever you can to get on base," Viña said. "I think that goes a long way. You just go up there with the confidence that the pitcher has. Hitting's hard enough when you go up there with a weakness. You've got to go up there with confidence, go up there and believe you can get a hit, get on base.

"I don't go up there with any fear. If you go up there with fear, you're finished. You've got to go in there positive without any weaknesses. You definitely can affect them [pitchers]. It definitely affects them, when they have to keep throwing pitches and be a pest or whatever you might need to do to bother them. You've got to have that mentality and go hard."

You can't tire out Viña. What he does best, though, is tire out the pitchers who have to work so hard to retire the smallest, spunkiest man in the Cardinals lineup, a man first among equals. He's the pesky leadoff man—his official Cardinals biography uses the adjectives "feisty" and "spunky"— who on any given day can be his team's most valuable player. A former Cardinals teammate, Craig Paquette, now with the Tigers, had yet another description. "There's no doubt he's stubborn," he said.

The pitcher may have to give in to Viña. But he doesn't return the favor, not while he has his wits about him.

"When somebody competes as hard as he does, it really sets a good tempo," Cardinals manager Tony La Russa said. "That's what you ask for. The starting pitcher has to work so hard for an out [against Viña]. At some point, whether it's that inning or later in the game, it will take something away from him."

"The real good leadoff man, the one thing he needs to have—Fernando's terrific at that as well as Rickey [Henderson in his prime]—they don't throw at-bats away. They know how to set the table. They grind out every at-bat every day. Viña's one of the best I've ever seen at just refusing [to give up]—I don't care if it's the ninth inning of a three and a half-hour game and you're up by 10 or down by 10. He's such a great example that way."

"He's a tough guy," said the White Sox's Jose Valentin, Viña's old Brewers double-play partner. "He wants to get on base no matter what. That's the way you're supposed to play the game—hard."

Viña won't easily give up in any aspect of play, no matter what the odds. In the sixth inning of a game at Wrigley Field on July 26, 2001, he slashed a ball to right field that the Cubs' Sammy Sosa quickly retrieved, wheeled and fired a true throw to second. The strike should have nailed Viña by ten feet. But he barreled into Cubs shortstop Ricky Gutierrez, knocking the ball loose. Viña was safe, credited with a single while the usually sure-handed

Gutierrez was charged with an error. That kept the inning going. Moments later, Viña scored the lead run on Albert Pujols's double. The Cardinals went on to win 3-1.

"I'm just digging to get in there. My whole thing is winning," Viña said afterward.

"I'm not going to slide like that," Gutierrez retorted. "But he plays hard. You have to admire someone who plays hard."

Viña's tough play suggests other Cardinals of another, legendary time—

Fernando Viña's play evokes memories of the Gashouse Gang.
St. Louis Cardinals

the early 1930s. At 33, he's scarcely heard of Pepper Martin, Ducky Medwick and other members of the "Gashouse Gang," players whose uniforms got dirty the moment they poked their nose out of the dugout, players who'd kill to win. But Viña need not be a baseball historian. His very being suggests a direct spiritual lineage to those Redbirds of old and every other gritty player who gleefully performed the game's dirty work.

"My style—I think it's just the way I was brought up and raised," Viña told Thomas R. Raber of the *Cardinals GameDay Magazine.* "I've never been handed anything. I've always had to go get it and prove myself at every level. In Little League, I wasn't always the biggest guy, but the way I played just really had me stand out.

"Thank God, I've always been pretty active and played well all the way up. That's just the way I go about my business. I have to go hard at it all the time. And I love playing the game that way."

No wonder it's easy to link Viña with Cardinals of the good ol' days.

"He's just a hard-nosed, gritty ballplayer," Cardinals general manager Walt Jocketty said. "He'd have been good with the Gashouse Gang."

The Cardinals' resident elders agree, and throw in a tough-guy representative of a slightly later era for comparison.

"He plays hard, he comes out to play," says seventy-nine-year-old Hall of Famer Red Schoendienst. "Eddie Stanky, even though he couldn't run with Viña and didn't have the talent, he took pitches and got hit by the pitch. He took every advantage he had and knew what was going on at any time."

"He's a typical 'Gashouse' type of guy," eighty-year-old Cardinals coaching legend George Kissell told *Cardinals GameDay Magazine.* "He's real hard-nosed. He comes to play. He's a manager's player. That's what he is. If you had twenty-four like him, you wouldn't have to worry much."

Contemporary baseball figures also see Viña's old-school qualities.

"He's definitely a throwback, no question about that," said former outfielder Bobby Bonilla, a teammate of Viña's in 2001.

Viña doesn't want to be special. He doesn't desire to be old-fashioned. He just wants to be able to do what he does at the same level, all season.

"The big thing is just being consistent," he said. "It comes to a point when you can do the offensive game and play defense. If you can be consistent for 162 games and play at a high caliber every day, that's what gets you to the next notch. It's just being an everyday, complete player. If you're that, you can help your team. When you can do that for a whole long season like that, it makes it special."

Most importantly, Viña understood early on about what kind of player he could not be. Once he accepted his role as a little guy who stirs things up at the top of the lineup, he then could concentrate on mastering his own little corner of the game.

"As you keep getting higher and higher into bigger and better leagues, you start realizing what your role is," he said. "If you want to keep going to the next level, you better figure out what your role is pretty quick. Otherwise, you won't keep going if you don't."

♦ ♦ ♦

Fernando Viña can flat-out hit. That has been proven beyond a shadow of a doubt. Between 1998 and 2001, he batted .300 or better three out of the four seasons. In 2001, he had 191 hits, a career-high 9 homers and 56 RBIs, and was the second-toughest man in the majors to strike out with 35 whiffs in 690 plate appearances. His bunting prowess and hustle paid off with 14 bunt hits and 29 infield hits.

But it's the concept of risking his health to get on base where Viña inherits the mantle of a modern Gashouse Gang guy. He will put his body in the way of pitches and dash off to first base, dealing with the consequences of the resulting pain or even injury later.

"How many guys are willing to get hit by a 95-mph fastball to get on base?" Craig Paquette asked. "He's the perfect guy to do it and he doesn't care if it hurts or not."

Viña seemed to develop the hit-by-pitch talent during his first extended big-league service with the Mets in 1994. He was plunked twelve times, one short of the club record, while playing just seventy-nine games. With St. Louis, he was hit a National League–high twenty-eight times in 2000 despite playing in only 123 games due to a right hamstring injury. The hit-by-pitch total was the most by a Cardinal since Steve Evans's thirty-one in 1910, the National League record for a left-handed hitter. Viña followed that up with twenty-two hit-by-pitches in 2001. Six times he led off a game by being hit.

"I do cringe every time he does get hit," Cardinals general manager Walt Jocketty said. "It's phenomenal how often he gets hit. I don't know how he does it. He is quick enough to get out of the way to where he shouldn't get hurt."

Viña will hang as close to the plate as he can stand it—and pitchers allow him.

"I'm on the plate a little bit," he said. "You've got to cover both sides of the plate. I don't really jump out of the way too much. I stay in there and stay quiet, and that's what it takes to be a good hitter. I try to do that and sometimes, unfortunately, you get hit.

"It's nothing that's magic, it just happens. It isn't something that you want to look to do. In your role as a leadoff hitter, you've got to take it for the team sometimes. I've been hit in the ankle a couple of times and it took me out. You're nothing without your legs. God willing, you don't get hurt and you keep playing hard.

"If the ball hits me, it hits me. So I go up there with the attitude that it's not going to hurt me. I don't go up to the plate with any fear."

Viña actually played for a college coach who taught the concept of getting plunked.

"In junior college [Sacramento City College], our coach had us practicing it a lot of with Wiffle balls," he said. "Kind of taking it for the team and really standing in there and not moving out of the way. And it really stuck with me. Sometimes it can be tough, but you want to get on base any way you can."

Lou Brock, the greatest Cardinals leadoff man of all time, had the same philosophy. He paid for it with pain at times, too.

"Sandy Koufax hit him in the shoulder blade and it was fractured, but Lou stayed in the game," Red Schoendienst said. "Viña is a good scrapper the same way."

As if getting hit—sometimes while the pitcher was ahead on the count—wasn't enough of a morale-buster for the man on the mound, Viña would further peck his foes to death through his bunting skills.

Of course, he consulted the master bunter of modern baseball, Brett Butler, a few years back in spring training.

"I always bunted in high school," Viña said. "I always had speed. As I got into junior college, I mastered my bunting even more. You bunt buckets of balls each day. You do repetition over and over again as you would hitting the ball. As you keep doing it, you get a better touch and get confidence with it.

"There's limitations, so you have to know the pitchers, where he likes to throw the ball. You don't want to bunt the ball toward second base if a guy likes to throw the ball away from you a lot. If you get your pitch where you want it and your mechanics where you want it, you should be able to bunt it. I think you've got to pick your spots and see where they're playing you. And figure if you can help your team if you bunt this pitch for a base hit."

The devotion to the black-and-blue brigade and "little ball" always have been a part of Viña's personality. Patience was a virtue, too. He had to wait the better part of a decade to earn status as one of the game's elite second baseman, a status that still goes hand-in-hand with his scrappy style. The way he grew up in the game, there wouldn't have been any other way.

Viña was born April 16, 1969, in Sacramento, but his real roots were three thousand miles away in Cuba. His parents were among the country's most grateful new immigrants when their son was born. They had just escaped Fidel Castro's clutches.

"They came from Cuba and had a tough time getting out of there. My mom was pregnant with me when they left," Viña told Rick Sorci of *Baseball Digest*. He rated his parents the top influences in his life.

Another role model was brother Jorge Viña, who steered his sibling to hit left-handed even though he was a right-handed thrower.

"My brother is a left-handed thrower and hitter," Viña said. "I was a little guy always watching him play, and I started hitting left-handed 'cause I wanted to be like my brother. Even when I was real young, with the tee and Wiffle balls and stuff, I used to hit left-handed and it kind of grew on me. I never did switch-hit."

Viña graduated from Valley High School in Sacramento, then attended Sacramento City College. He was able to see his family's roots as part of Team USA's trip to Cuba in 1989.

Viña went on to baseball powerhouse Arizona State. There would be no long-ball feats in Tempe. In 1990 he ranked third in the nation among college hitters with 108 hits, capturing the Pac 10 batting title. Viña struck out only seven times in 279 at-bats. But hitting was not as easy as the results suggested.

"It just takes time and work and repetition," Viña said. "Jeff Pentland was my hitting coach at Arizona State, and taught me to be a better hitter."

"Better" may have been putting it mildly, according to the recollection of Pentland, who went on to a long run as Cubs hitting coach after scouting and coaching duties in the Marlins organization.

"Actually, when he first came up, he wasn't a good hitter at all," Pentland, now with the Royals, said. "He could do all the other things. He could play defense and he was a smart baserunner. But he was a dead-pull hitter who hit a lot of fly balls. We spent a lot of time hitting balls down and let him hit the ball that [left-field] way.

"It didn't take long. With his intensity and the way he went about his business, he picked it up quick. He really worked at it. Nobody was as hardworking and wanted it worse than he did. You had to get the ball down and learn to use the whole field. He could always make contact. You couldn't strike him out."

Viña signed with the Mets after being selected in the ninth round of the

15

June 1990 draft. But the Mets let him go two years later in the Rule V draft. He would begin a crazy-quilt period in which he bounced around between different organizations, moving up and down from cups of coffee in the majors.

The Mariners picked up Viña and put him on the roster as a second base-man–shortstop for the first two months of the 1993 season. He learned from budding star shortstop Omar Vizquel. "He helped me out a lot my first year," Viña said. But his time to soak up Vizquel's infield savvy was limited. He was sold back to the Mets on June 15, finishing the season in Triple-A.

Making the Mets as a utility player in 1994, Viña saw service at third base and the outfield in addition to the middle infield. Although he was tied for the club lead with six pinch hits, he couldn't get into a great rhythm over 124 at-bats, hitting .250. One day before the strike began on August 12, he was optioned back to Norfolk. But his additional time in the minors was cut short on August 17 when he was injured by a pitch, this one nailing him in the ankle. Viña missed the rest of the Triple-A season.

In the middle of the strike on December 22, 1994, Viña received a big break. He was shipped to Milwaukee along with catcher Javier Gonzalez as the players to be named later for reliever Doug Henry, who had earlier been dealt to the Mets. Viña finally cracked the lineup as a regular for the always-struggling Brewers late in 1995, hitting .257.

The following season would turn out to be eventful for Viña for reasons other than establishing himself as a legitimate big-league hitter. By now Viña was a lineup sparkplug with a .283 average, ten triples and a career-high five-hit game with two homers and a triple on September 12 at Texas.

"My situation was the same as Fernando's," said the White Sox's Jose Valentin, then Viña's teammate. "We went to that organization. We were happy to be there. We found a place to be everyday players. He made himself a better player."

But playing for the mid-1990s Brewers usually condemned a big leaguer to obscurity. Viña became known not for his gritty play, but for tangling with Albert Belle.

On May 31, 1996, at County Stadium, Viña was part of a long series of negative incidents involving the moody, antisocial Belle. In the eighth inning of the Brewers-Indians game, Belle was hit by a pitch. About to be tagged out by Viña on a grounder moments later, Belle flattened the second base-man with a vicious forearm to the chest. The bloodied Viña, giving away five inches and perhaps sixty pounds, got up and started jawing at Belle, but no punches were thrown.

The crowd booed Belle as he walked off, causing several Milwaukee

County sheriff's deputies to converge behind the Indians' dugout while the fans still were throwing verbal brickbats at Belle.

The incident got inflamed in the ninth. Brewers reliever Terry Burrows threw three inside pitches to Belle, then hit him in the left shoulder. At the end of the inning, Belle talked to Indians reliever Julian Tavarez before he took his position in left field. Tavarez's first pitch in the bottom of the ninth sailed behind the back of the Brewers' Mike Matheny, who then charged the mound. In the melee, Tavarez picked up first-base umpire Joe Brinkman, throwing him to the ground. Joining the brawl, Belle ran over Brewers pitcher Steve Sparks.

"I wasn't going to get mad. We're going to get even," Belle said afterward.

Viña was puzzled by Belle's behavior. He thus joined a vast majority of baseball watchers.

"He broke my nose," Viña said. "It ain't right for a guy to come at your face like that."

The two teams picked up right where they left off the following game. Seven pitches into the June 1 contest, Indians center fielder Kenny Lofton, who had led off with a double, gave Viña a shove after pitcher Angel Miranda tried to pick him off second. The benches cleared again, but no punches were thrown.

"We started jawing and we almost went at it," Viña said after the game. "I was upset from last night. But I always play hard."

Viña ended on the high road in connection to the mess. American League president Gene Budig suspended Belle for five days. Tavarez and Matheny also drew identical punishments.

The physical and emotional toll on Viña had long since healed. More than half a decade after his brush with Belle, he refuses to talk about the incident, putting it behind him. He was at the peak of his career with St. Louis, while Belle was anonymous in retirement.

Viña was fortunate to not be seriously hurt by Belle's forearm. However, other injuries cut into his desire to be a consistent, 150-games-a-season performer.

"If there's any disappointments, I'd say it would be some of the freak injuries I've had in my career, but it's something that happens," he said.

In addition to the sore ankle from the hit-batsman in 1994, Viña lost time the same season due to a bruised right heel. Early in the 1997 season, he broke his left ankle stealing second in a game in Cleveland. He lost nearly three months. Then, in 1999, he played only 37 games due to tendinitis in his right knee and two injuries to his left quadriceps muscle. And despite a successful debut for the Cardinals in 2000—he tripled off the Busch Stadium center-field wall in his first St. Louis at-bat—Viña played in just 123 games due to injuries to his right hamstring and left rib cage.

Despite the time missed due to injuries, Viña's hard-nosed veneer appealed to other teams. Then–Brewers GM Sal Bando was always seeking to dump salary off his cash-strapped team. After Viña's spectacular 1998 season (.311, 198 hits, 101 runs scored, 39 doubles), St. Louis GM Walt Jocketty began making overtures to Milwaukee.

"It took us over a year to make that deal," Jocketty said. "I started talking with Sal Bando about it and then was finally able to complete the deal with Dean Taylor when he took over as GM. At one point we had a three-way deal with Colorado."

Viña finally arrived in St. Louis on December 20, 1999, in exchange for pitcher Juan Acevedo and two minor leaguers to be named later. At around the same time, Taylor traded Viña's double-play partner, Jose Valentin, to the White Sox. Both Viña and Valentin became stars in their new big league homes, while the Brewers got little bang for the pitchers they got in return for both players.

"He's happier now because he's on a better team," said old chum Valentin, who echoed his sentiments about the White Sox. "He's a better player than he used to be before. He's glad to be out of Milwaukee."

Sometimes you throw too much out when you clean house. But Viña couldn't be concerned with front office ineptitude too much. There were too many more games to play and more than enough pitchers to wear down.

◆ ◆ ◆

Viña has become a complete ballplayer, a .300 hitter and Gold Glove second baseman. He lacks only two qualities as a hitter. He has little power, which doesn't hamper him as a leadoff man. And, strangely enough, he manages to get on base without walking much.

Viña's top walk total was 54 in 1998, contributing to a career-best on-base percentage of .386. In 2001 he was at .357, good but somewhat under the ideal for a leadoff man. Mind you, his Cardinals bosses aren't complaining.

"I think he's better than we expected," Jocketty said. "He's an outstanding leadoff hitter."

Viña grew up swinging and is not going to change. He learned patience at the plate wasn't necessarily a virtue.

"It's tough. As a young guy coming up, it doesn't pay to walk 100 times a year," he said. "It pays to get hits, to get doubles and triples, that's the only way they notice you. When you get settled at the big-league level in your role, that's when you can try to draw more walks. It's tough, with different pitchers you do different things. If they're throwing strikes, you can't sit there and take it all day."

Instead, Viña has the ability to be a bad-ball hitter. A prime example was on May 13, 2001, at Busch Stadium. The Cardinals were busy routing a wild Kerry Wood from the game. In the process, Wood—whom Viña has frustrated in the past—threw an eye-high pitch to the second baseman. Rather than taking, Viña tomahawked the pitch down the right field line for a triple.

"I'm sure he doesn't want to do that all that often, but he can go outside the strike zone," said Jeff Pentland, his old hitting coach at Arizona State.

"Fernando does a good job getting on base in every way," Red Schoendienst, Cardinals Hall of Famer and former manager, said. "I had Lou Brock, who hit home runs, but he did not walk a lot. He could run, of course."

Viña compensates for his relative lack of walks. He has learned to hit left-handers. His ability to slash the ball to left field served him well against southpaws. Lifetime through 2001 Viña was a .287 hitter against left-handers, compared to .289 against right-handers. In 2001 the numbers were even better: .311 against left-handers compared to .299 against right-handers.

But one left-hander is almost unsolvable: Randy Johnson. Viña's good against southpaws, just not that good. Viña said facing Johnson was a "battle." He's his toughest mound opponent.

"You gotta go up there and if he throws something good to hit, you hit it," Viña said. "You can't mess around and wait. If you get behind him, you're done. You've got to be aggressive with him. You try to hit it where it's pitched. Hit something solid, so it's tough to make that decision [to go the other way]. He throws so hard and his ball moves, that it makes it tough to bunt on, also."

Viña also has come through with men in scoring position. Lifetime through 2001, he was a .303 hitter with runners in scoring position. In 2001 alone that mark was .311.

While Viña gets almost all the credit for his leadoff-man talents, the defensive part of his game is vastly underrated. He's not generally known as one of the game's best defensive second baseman despite his first Gold Glove award in 2001.

Viña had quietly built up his defensive portfolio through his natural aggressiveness after becoming a regular with Milwaukee. He led American League second basemen with 116 double plays in 1996, then led National League second baseman (following the Brewers' switch to the NL) with 884 total chances and 135 double plays in 1998. With the Cardinals, he led NL second basemen in fielding percentage in both 2000 (.988) and 2001 (.987), while leading his position in total chances (705), putouts (313) and double plays (100) in 2001. Lifetime, his fielding percentage at second base was .985.

"He's the best second baseman I've seen since I've been with the Cardinals, and that goes way, way back [1940]," team warhorse Kissell said, ranking him ahead of the likes of Red Schoendienst, Julian Javier, Tom Herr, and Jose Oquendo.

"He has excellent hands, excellent, excellent. Good range. And he really makes the double play outstanding."

Schoendienst and Jocketty like what they see, too.

"He can make the double play as good as anybody," Schoendienst said. "He's got a good arm."

"I don't think there's a better second baseman at turning the double play," Jocketty said.

Kissell became a kind of defensive mentor to Viña when he came to St. Louis.

"I take a ton of ground balls in every direction before the game with George Kissell," Viña told *Cardinals GameDay Magazine*. "He helps me tremendously, 'cause we do the same thing every day. It's not only about the techniques, but about the repetition, repetition—turning double plays again and again. George has a routine where he can hit every type of ground ball that's possible. Every angle. He gets me ready to roll. And I think I've been gifted, thank God, with the ability to play that position.

"He's my dad away from home, I would say," Viña said of Kissell. "He really takes care of me, I mean after every game we win we give each other a hug, and he has really taken me under his wing. We go over the games and talk about different situations. I can't tell you how much baseball I've learned from him."

In turn, Viña will have a lot of experience, knowledge and passion to give to those who follow him. His post-career goal is to work with youths and stay in the game as a coach. He also will follow Kissell's symbolic role with a real-life one: devoted father to Fernando, Jr.

By the time the younger Viña is a teenager, he'll finally be able to brag about a dad who's recognized as one of the best in the game at his position. Praise is coming relatively late in Viña's career, but now the kudos are making up for lost time.

"He's the consummate baseball player," Pentland said. "He really loves doing what he's doing. His skills are very average. But he's turned them into above-average because of his hard work and aggressive nature."

"Most of the time in this league, you have to do something over a period

Hall of Famer Red Schoendienst once said Fernando Viña turns the double play "as good as anybody." *St. Louis Cardinals*

of time to really earn that kind [of recognition]," La Russa said in 2002. "He had two solid seasons with us, and he's on his way to a third one. After what he did in Milwaukee, I think slowly but surely people are realizing how good he is."

Viña will take the praise when it comes.

"You definitely want to be recognized for the things you do," he said. "If it happens, it happens. You want to be a complete player, and people will notice. When people give you a lot of accolades for that, it makes you feel better."

Even a modern-day Gashouse Gang type likes a pat on the back once in a while.

3

THE SMARTEST MAN
IN BASEBALL

Greg Maddux doesn't have to throw his glove on the field to gain the upper hand. The great master need not waste even that much effort. He merely has to step on the mound to get halfway home to a victory.

Maddux's mere presence on the field is the ultimate distraction, an all-encompassing illusion, to batters who need all the fine tuning of mind and body in sync to accomplish sports' hardest task—hitting a baseball. Where the Randy Johnsons of the world are physically intimidating, Maddux by contrast looks like the average man/suburban dad that he really is when he takes the mound. He doesn't give off one iota of the world-wise athlete in his appearance; an eternally boyish face can allow him to shave off a decade and pass for his mid-twenties. And when he sported horned-rimmed glasses in the dugout, Maddux looked almost professorial. He hardly appears to merit the tag "Mad Dog," a career-long baseball nickname.

And Maddux practices some subtle verbal misdirection when anyone suggests he's truly special. Sometimes he even appears to play dumb.

"I'm just trying to make pitches, dude," he told columnist Barry Rozner of the *Daily Herald* of Arlington Heights, Illinois, on August 30, 2001. "You've known me, what, like fourteen, fifteen years? I'm just trying to make good pitches."

Rozner's interpretation of Maddux-speak? "For print, that's about all you'll get from Maddux . . . He doesn't give away secrets, and he doesn't care how boring it sounds. Maddux likes the idea that people think he's a little strange because—like his librarian glasses—it just adds to the mystique."

There's no mystique on the radar gun, though. Unlike the potential lethality of Johnson's or Kerry Wood's 99-mph fastballs, Maddux's sub-90-mph stuff wouldn't hurt a fly. That is, unless he accurately aimed it at a hitter, which he has potentially greater ability to do than anyone else in baseball.

His control-fiend reputation, razor-sharp execution of jumping-bean fastballs, cutters and changeups, and sheer mental acuity defeats hitters before they even get started. Johnson or Wood overpower you with their repertoire; Maddux overpowers you with his mind. He sees all and knows all. The Braves' Yoda of pitching will notice every last twitch of a hitter's hips, his subtle shift of stance or foot placement, and other kinds of body language.

"He picks up things in hitters that would never cross ordinary pitchers' minds," said former Atlanta teammate Jason Schmidt, an accomplished hurler in his own right. "The way they move their shoulders, the way they approach the plate, the way they take their swings in the on-deck circle. Things you'd never think to look for."

Maddux himself verbalized that strategy in Rozner's column.

"The book on the hitter is, what is he doing right now? Where are his feet? Where are his hands? How is his bat speed? How did he react to that last pitch? What does that tell me about what he was looking for? Where is he trying to hit it? What is the situation?"

Texas Ranger outfielder Doug Glanville provided a telling example of Maddux's powers of observation.

"Every time I started off [in the batter's box], the pitch was in the air," Glanville said. "I wasn't set. He quick-pitched me. When I'm doing all this stuff [getting set to bat], he's throwing."

But Maddux may not even stop at noticing every last bit of body English by his opponents. He seemingly can enter the hitter's psyche, starting with doubting eyes and probing further. If anyone is baseball's foremost mentalist, it's this strike machine who would always deny he possesses ESP. Yet try telling that to a horde of frustrated, mentally-beaten hitters shaking their heads after slapping infield nubbers or harmless pop flies from all the strikes Maddux feeds them.

"I remember a game he pitched against the Pirates," Giants starter Schmidt, also an ex-Bucco, said. "I heard one player after the game banging his hands on the table and saying, 'Maddux, it's like the guy can read my mind at the plate.' He was absolutely going nuts. And why not? He can read your approach to the plate off every pitch."

"I think he can read the physical part of whether they're pulling him or trying to go to the opposite field," Braves pitching coach Leo Mazzone said.

"He recognizes it better than any other pitcher. He's one of the few pitchers who recognizes things before the fact."

Any kind of mind games, Maddux will never refuse. Any kind of misdirection, distraction or illusion, he'll quietly accept. One day in 1995, still burning over Maddux's free-agent defection from Chicago two years earlier, Cubs shortstop Shawon Dunston was asked what he thought of another brilliant performance against his team by the greatest pitcher they ever let get away.

"When you look at him out there, all you see is Larry Himes," Dunston said of the unpopular former Cubs general manager who, along with former Tribune Company chairman Stanton Cook, presided over Maddux's departure from the Windy City. And yet seeing the image of the often-taciturn Himes only played into Maddux's hands even further.

Even Hall of Fame–bound Tony Gwynn, who practically owned Maddux earlier in his career, finally gave up on Maddux's speciality pitch, a fastball that starts out far inside to left-handed hitters, then dances and breaks over the corner for a strike. Gwynn feared no pitcher or pitch, yet this offering in his mind could only be approached defensively. Try to foul it off, Gwynn advised, and then hope Maddux brings the next pitch further over the plate.

Gwynn was not hallucinating. Another skilled left-handed hitter, Rafael Palmeiro, agreed.

"You try to hit a mistake," Palmeiro said. "You don't try to hit that pitch."

The evidence thus is strong that Maddux has goofed up an entire league of hitters—and some American League opponents in interleague play—since his dominant 1992 season, when he had a 2.18 ERA and allowed just seven homers, winning his first Cy Young Award pitching in cozy Wrigley Field. But even though a questioner has known Maddux since he was a skinny, twenty-year-old rookie in 1986, even though he professes to know something about his makeup, bringing that evidence—especially Gwynn's testimony—directly to the source sheds little light on Maddux's own mental power base. If anything, you get caught up in his special style of mind games.

"You can't read the hitter's mind," Maddux insists from his favorite corner of the dugout, from which he'll discuss his craft, within strict limits. "Everybody's a creature of habit, we all know that. You just go out there and if you locate pitches, your pitch selection doesn't have to be all that great. And vice versa, if your pitch selection is good, you don't have to locate as well. It's a combination of the two things."

"I don't know," he said when asked if he distracts and misdirects hitters.

"It's not something I'm concerned with. I'm concerned with my part of it, selecting the pitch to throw and trying to make the pitch."

But what about Gwynn's rare mental yielding to Maddux? Isn't that that litmus test of his ability to psych out hitters?

"It's not my concern what the hitters are thinking," said The Master. "You have to figure out what strength you have as a pitcher. One of the strengths is locating the fastball with movement. I don't care what they think. As a pitcher, you have to have good pitch selection and locate your fastball."

Maddux will repeat that mantra year after year, all the way through his eventual 300th victory. Pitching is so simple, so basic. When asked how he developed his razor-sharp control, Maddux had a most succinct answer: "Practice." Or he might respond when asked about his motivations: "I just pitch. Pitching is fun."

Spookily, Maddux has started to call his own shots. Braves manager Bobby Cox told Bob Nightengale of *Sports Weekly* on August 15, 2001, that he went to the mound a few years ago when Maddux was in a jam with runners on second and third and one out. Was Maddux going to walk the next hitter, a left-hander, to load the bases and set up a force at any base?

Cox recalled Maddux's response: "No, that's all right. I'm going to get him to pop up to third base on the second pitch, and then get a grounder, and get out of this thing."

Cox told Nightengale that scenario of events is exactly what transpired.

What's at work here is more distraction and misdirection, mixed in with a heavy dose of quiet confidence. Magicians don't reveal how they perform their tricks. And if you probe too closely to this mound magician's secrets, he'll throw up a verbal wall. You will go no further.

"He's very mysterious in his craft," said Rick Kranitz, Maddux's first pro pitching coach at then-rookie-level Pikeville (Kentucky) in the Cubs farm system in 1984.

Because he keeps his modus operandi close to his vest, it forces you to go about your business Maddux style, working around the edges, setting up others to give hints about how the Great One operates.

"Pitchers do get in hitters' heads," said Mazzone, who doubles as Maddux's proverbial second-opinion guy. "We're in the Mets' heads. But at the same time, the Cardinals are in our heads."

"He's in their head before the game starts," former Maddux teammate Mike Bielecki, an ex-pitcher himself, said. "When the opposing manager pencils his name into the lineup, part of the battle is won. The manager says, 'I've got to manage to win today because I got Maddux tomorrow.'"

"Sure," responds Mets coach Don Baylor, who was Braves hitting coach in 1997, when asked if Maddux messes with hitters' minds. "You always think it doesn't happen, but it happens to about 95 percent [of hitters]."

You've worked the corners well enough with Mazzone's next admission.

"His knowledge [of pitching] exceeds mine, and I don't mind him saying that one bit," he said. "I can help him in some areas. But our relationship is an exchange of ideas. He taught me a great deal that I've passed on."

"He thinks as good as any pitcher I've ever been around," Cox said. "He's way ahead of me in the game."

Only those who have walked in Maddux's shoes, all the way to enshrinement in Cooperstown, have an insider's understanding of the magician's craft.

"He doesn't overthrow," Hall of Famer Robin Roberts said. "He throws one pitch, and he determines what his next pitch will be. He doesn't confuse the issue. He's uncomplicated. He's relaxed on the mound and handling just one batter at a time. He's not worrying about down the road."

It's incredible, but true. Greg Maddux, the kid from Vegas with just a high school education, is probably the smartest man in baseball. Many will want to qualify that with just the "smartest pitcher," but Maddux is an expert in all facets of the game. An all-around athlete, he has a passion for everything. He fields his position better than any pitcher. He's one of his team's best bunters, and he loves to take his hacks at the plate. Going back to the start of his career, he hung around with hitters to extract the contents of their minds even when he didn't have to face them. He soaks up information "like a sponge," said former Cubs and Braves teammate Bielecki.

If Maddux paints while on the mound, well, that's a good comparison, too.

"He's an artisan when he's standing on the mound," Braves general manager John Schuerholz said. "He creates his own music, he creates his own canvas. He's a Rembrandt of pitching."

"While other guys are playing musical instruments, Maddux is playing a concert," said Hall of Fame pitcher Don Sutton, now a Braves broadcaster.

His style is oh-so-basic. Control the location of the pitch and make the hitter hit your pitch. Nothing more, nothing less.

Maddux is compared throughout the game as a throwback to the great aces, control artists all, of baseball history: Catfish Hunter, Fergie Jenkins, and Robin Roberts. More names come to light: Bob Gibson, Jim Bunning, Whitey Ford, Randy Jones, Rick Reuschel. Baseball Valhalla–dweller Christy Mathewson is offered up for comparison. And why shouldn't the man for whom the top award for pitching excellence be linked with Maddux after he won four Cy Young Awards in the 1990s and ranked as the only pitcher since Young to win fifteen or more games fourteen consecutive seasons?

Around 2010, when Maddux has retired to the golf course for good, there will probably be a change in that viewpoint. They will be comparing every pitcher before and after to Maddux. Even without a twenty-five-victory or 300-inning season, he may be better than any of them. He already has an intellectual capacity and powers of observation beyond that of any other pitcher in history.

◆ ◆ ◆

The "second sight" that Maddux apparently possesses may stem not from innate psychic abilities, but from a keen competitive fire honed in a sports-minded household in Las Vegas. Maximum concentration and observation were needed to gain any kind of an edge on father Dave Maddux and older brother Mike, who went on to become a journeyman big-league pitcher.

Dave Maddux had been a high school center in basketball-crazed Indiana, then pitched on Air Force softball teams as he moved his young family to bases around the United States and in Taiwan and Spain before settling into Vegas after retirement from the service. Dad then introduced his sons to baseball and basketball, and competed against the kids.

One day Dave fired a 79 on the links. Greg had never previously broken an 80. Challenged, he shaved his score to 78.

Golf always has been a sport in which Maddux has sharpened his concentration. Playing on the links against Maddux years later, Kranitz—now a Cubs minor-league manager—noticed how Maddux kept looking at the hole, not downward at the ball and club. Always, always, the eyes were on the target.

"He rises to the occasion. What can I tell you," Dave Maddux told *Vine Line Magazine* in June, 1988.

Keeping up with an older brother who was a highly-rated athlete provided further motivation.

"Greg said a long time ago that his idea of the perfect game [against brother Mike] was to beat him 1-0, with Greg hitting the home run to win the game!" his mother, Linda Maddux, said in the *Vine Line* interview.

"He was four years ahead of me," Greg Maddux said in 1991. "And growing up, that's a lot. Now that doesn't seem like that much, but as we were growing up, he was always eighty pounds heavier and four years older. There was no question he was better than me."

The brothers did not limit their competition to baseball and golf. Practically every activity which could fill spare time was accounted for, according to Mike, now pitching coach of the Double-A Round Rock (Texas) team, owned by Nolan Ryan, in the Astros organization. Mike told Bob Nightengale of *Sports Weekly* the pair battled it out in tennis, bowling, throwing Frisbees, paper football, checkers, chess and cards, the latter a natural for a Vegas family as Dave went to work as a poker dealer in the casinos.

The sibling rivalry did affect Greg, who had a youthful temper that contrasted to the more mild-mannered Mike.

"Mike and Terry [their sister] picked on [Greg] continuously," Linda said in *Vine Line*. "No wonder he got mad."

In addition to proving himself to his brother, Greg had to overcome his slight build. Never a studly physical specimen—he's presently listed officially as six-feet, 185 pounds—Maddux also may have developed what has long been termed the "little man's mentality."

"He was always the littlest kid on the team. We had no idea he'd be a professional ballplayer," Linda Maddux told *Vine Line*. "Even later, in junior and senior high school, he was small for his size."

Longtime Maddux buddy Rodney Beckwith, now a Las Vegas businessman and aspiring filmmaker, remembered first bumping into Maddux—literally—on the basketball court in junior high. The skinny runt's desire burned brightly even then.

"I was going up for a jump shot," Beckwith recalled. "All of a sudden, I felt something pull my arms back. I turned around and, honest to God, it was this five-foot-two, sixty-five-pound kid. I was looking around for the guy who swatted me, and it was Greg."

Years later, Maddux was so boyish in appearance that he had a hard time convincing others he was a big-time baseball prospect.

"We had a party on day at our [team] doctor's house," Kranitz said of a 1984 soiree in Pikeville. "I don't think anyone thought he was the second-round pick. I thought he was the batboy." Bill Harford, then an administrator in the Cubs' farm system, recalls Maddux weighing all of 145 pounds when he was drafted. And even in his second big-league season in 1988, Bielecki said Maddux "looked like a baby."

Yet he was far from a lightweight and immature in brainpower and passion for baseball. Although Maddux always will soft-pedal his analytical skills, he'll always admit to a love for the game as it was meant to be played.

"Growing up, I played the game because it was fun," he said. "That was it. I didn't really try to figure anything out. I enjoyed playing it. I thought if you played the game right, you had a chance to get better at it."

Despite his statements to the contrary, Maddux paid close attention to baseball, even though he grew up hundreds of miles from the nearest big league market. He could recite the lineup of the Big Red Machine and the Willie Mays/Willie McCovey–era Giants practically before he learned his alphabet. Despite his slight appearance, he gave off the aura of an athlete who somehow would go far.

Linda Maddux recalled another prediction of the future: "The lady who lived next door to us, who I hardly knew, came over one day and she said to me, 'That kid of yours is truly going to be a professional ballplayer one day.'"

The prophecy came true after Maddux starred for coach Rodger Fairless at Valley High School in Las Vegas. There was some consideration that despite his rail-thin build, his overall athleticism, smarts and very respectable stuff might even merit status as a first-round pick.

Maddux already was trying to imitate the game's finest mound craftsmen.

"Even then, he usually was the best at what he does," buddy Beckwith, who pitched at Valley High along with Maddux. "At fifteen, he was trying to hit spots. By seventeen, on a legit gun he was throwing 88, 89, 90 [mph]. One of the most special things about Greg was he'd be 3-and-2, have the bases loaded, and it was the bottom of the seventh. He'd have no problem throwing a changeup. He started with the circle change in high school. He was one step ahead of everyone."

Maddux's entrée into pro baseball was provided by the Cubs, through area scout Doug Mapson and regional supervisor Gene Handley, who had a long track record of snaring quality pitchers in the western states. Maddux originally planned to attend the University of Arizona, but was dissuaded by his father when the pitcher admitted he'd go to college just to play baseball. He might as well sign a pro contract, was the elder Maddux's reasoning. The Cubs did not pick Maddux in the first round in 1984, instead taking college left-hander Drew Hall.

Signing quickly, Maddux was bundled off to the sticks in Pikeville. Rick Kranitz, whose own minor-league pitching career had just ended, was also a rookie, as a coach.

Feeling his way at first, Kranitz didn't alter Maddux's delivery or repertoire when he first worked with him. But after a month, Maddux came up to Kranitz to ask, "When are you going to teach me something?" The budding student of baseball was eager to learn.

"I don't think either one of us knew a whole lot about what we were doing at the time," Maddux said. "It was a learn-as-you-go type thing. But he helped me a lot. He made my rookie-ball experience a lot better than it had to be."

A story has long circulated that supposedly originated around this time.

The Cubs minor league pitchers were all gathered by their instructors to go over fundamentals and signs. From the back of the room came a question posed by what appeared to be someone young enough to be the batboy; Kranitz wasn't the only one who was struck by Maddux's baby face. "What's the sign for the brushback pitch?" was the question attributed to Maddux.

Word was spreading to the front office at Wrigley Field that the organization had a pitcher who would stick out from the crowd in ways other than physical appearance and speed of fastball.

"He was a great competitor," said Bill Harford, now a scout. "What I saw when I was traveling [through the minors] was a kid who had no fear. Reports that we got back said this kid was something special."

Minor league teammates were astounded to learn Maddux was far from a one-dimensional pitcher. He coveted the entire baseball experience. He soaked up information about the art of hitting.

Longtime outfielder Davey Martinez, a teammate of Maddux at Triple-A Iowa in 1986, the Cubs the next two seasons, and the Braves starting in 2001, agreed that Maddux was a student of the game, and more. "He thought he was a hitter," Martinez said with a laugh. "He asked me about hitting. I didn't think it was weird. He just wanted to learn everything about the game. He studied the game. The thing with 'Doggie' was he had fun while he did it. Some guys would kill themselves to do everything. He was just like a little kid."

Amazingly, as Maddux established himself as a rotation starter with the Cubs by the end of the 1987 season, he broke down the barriers that typify pro sports rosters. Pitchers consort with pitchers and hitters with hitters in baseball, while the offensive and defensive groups are usually segregated in football. His quest for knowledge led him to sit with veteran hitters to pick their brains. And the hitters didn't mind, since they realized a young all-around athlete was in their midst.

"He was always seemingly sitting next to the Hall of Famers," said Bielecki, who in 1988 was in his first season with the Cubs. "He was always talking to the hitters—Shawon [Dunston], [Andre] Dawson, Jerry Mumphrey. It made a lot of sense."

"I enjoy talking to the hitters," Maddux said. "I wanted to see what it was like, to see what these guys know about hitting, for no other reason than the enjoyment of it. I like baseball. I like hitting. Guys make comments sometimes that are interesting. If one of your teammates hits a certain way, there's probably a good chance someone on the team you're facing the next week hits the same way, too. If you get something out of it, great. But for the most part, you're just killing time."

The advice must have paid off. Maddux, who impressed early on with his wiry, limber athletic build, led all NL pitchers with nineteen hits in his first full season in 1988. The following year, he had seventeen hits, one behind league leader David Cone. He would never get cheated coming to the plate.

But it was his willingness to learn that impressed the most. Coming off his 1987 National League Most Valuable Player season, Dawson lauded Maddux's all-ears stance of the time.

"I saw a kid who had composure out there," he said. "He believed in the guys behind him. He wasn't afraid to pitch. I could gradually see it all come to the surface that he could have a heck of a career."

"One thing you did notice was that he could grasp things and hold on to it. He could talk to you intellectually about the game."

Even now, Maddux spends time in refresher courses on hitting fundamentals and psychology.

"He spends a lot of time talking with our hitting coach," Mazzone said. "He gets into the mind of what the hitters are looking for."

Maddux insisted all along he played the game for fun. But as a nonvoluble guy, he was all eyes and ears as he won thirty-seven games in his first two full big-league seasons with the Cubs in 1988 and 1989. The learning curve had some bumps along the way as Maddux endured a few pratfalls through the 1991 season. But by '92, he had blossomed as baseball's leading guru of pitching, eager to discuss anything except his own personal mound tricks.

As an example, Maddux could tell you how lefty reliever Chuck McElroy was more effective against right-handed hitters due to the way his ball broke. Any analysis of pitching that was needed required only a stop by Maddux's locker for a quiet, but thorough discourse as he headed toward his first Cy Young Award.

Still only twenty-six, he became much more than a passive commentator. He was now the savant of the Cubs staff. And he extended his expanding fount of knowledge to actively help at least one other starter during games.

"We'd be on the bench, watching whoever was pitching, and I'd ask what would you throw here?" said Boston right-hander Frank Castillo, in his first full big-league season as a Cub in 1992. "He was always talking pitching. He'd also ask me what would you throw in a situation?"

But Castillo, a quiet, self-effacing kid, was far from Maddux's class in '92 in the confidence level. An El Paso, Texas, native, he was gifted enough to throw a curveball at thirteen, and had developed an effective changeup.

But his fastball on its best days was only of average velocity. Castillo had to be fine with his pitches or else he'd get pounded. He endured the struggles and doubts of a young pitcher until he asked for help one day in mid-season '92.

"I remember being in a jam and not having that much confidence in what I was throwing," Castillo said. "But I had 'Mad Dog.' After the game, I asked him is there any way I could look over at the bench [for help]? I was struggling and I had the best pitcher in the game on my team."

The two came up with a secret set of signs, relayed directly from Maddux in the dugout to Castillo on the mound. In his sixth big league season, Maddux would call parts of Castillo's game as if he was a manager or veteran pitching coach.

"He said touching his chin would be the change-up," Castillo said. "Right ear, fastball away. Left ear, fastball in. Touch his nose, it would be a breaking pitch.

"Whenever I was in doubt, I'd look over and he'd touch his chin. A typical situation would be if I had a guy 1-and-2, and he'd keep fouling it off, I'd need some help. After the All-Star break in '92, he knew when I look in there to the dugout, he'd be ready. He helped me in a number of games. I talked to him between innings and in between starts. He helped me on the mental aspect of pitching."

The advice eventually took hold. Castillo won four of his final five starts in '92 to finish 10-11 with a good 3.46 ERA. Opponents hit just .232 against him. He allowed 179 hits in 205⅓ innings while walking two or fewer batters in 20 of his 33 starts.

Castillo admitted during the '92 season that he received help from Maddux. Then-teammate Mike Morgan, a longtime Maddux buddy from Las Vegas, also revealed the secret-sign system; he sat right next to Maddux on the bench. But true to his baseball magician's code of secrecy, Maddux refused to confirm he performed the de facto coaching. "That's ballclub business," he said back in '92.

But when Maddux departed as a free agent after the season, Castillo had lost his guidepost. He slumped badly in 1993, going 5-8 with a 4.82 ERA. He did not win after July 30. Not until the 1995 season did Castillo return to form, and then only for that year before ineffectiveness and injuries turned him into a journeyman.

"I definitely missed him," Castillo said. "You could see in a three-game series, that if he was pitching on a Friday and I was going Sunday, I'd follow his pattern."

Mind you, Maddux did not walk around the clubhouse in evangelical fashion, forcing his philosophy on more impressionable pitchers. If actively recruited by a teammate, he'd help. Otherwise, he would keep some distance.

"I think one of the biggest problems young pitchers have when they come up is they get too much advice," Maddux said in 1991. "I got way too much advice. You've got ten different guys telling you ten different things.

"I can't try and teach somebody to pitch like me because they don't throw like me. The best thing I can do is if they ask me about a hitter's weakness, and if I know that hitter pretty well, then I'll tell them. The young pitchers have got the pitching coach, they have the manager, they probably have two or three other pitchers telling them about pitching—and they're probably getting confused."

But even Maddux did not realize how much he would continue maturing mentally through the 1990s—and how much his counsel would be prized by pitchers, coaches and even managers.

Leo Mazzone knew the game's best control pitcher was being delivered gift-wrapped to him for the '93 season. "Greatest free-agent signing in history," he crowed. But Mazzone never fully realized how much of an athletic genius he had acquired until he began working with the pitcher.

Mazzone, who had never pitched above Double-A in his own career, had risen from the minor league coaching ranks with some of the top home-grown young arms at the cusp of the 1990s. He is a good baseball technician, charged with maintaining the longtime Braves philosophy of throwing more frequently between starts, emphasizing "touch and feel" instead of sheer velocity.

But the teacher-pupil roles became blurred where Maddux was concerned. By the mid-1990s, the pitcher's brainpower simply expanded beyond belief. One day, visiting Wrigley Field, Maddux set himself up in his favorite dugout seat cradling a bat. A couple of longtime Maddux observers were the audience. Pointing to different parts of the bat, he explained that the object of pinpoint pitching was to hit any spot but the fat part. The desired result, Maddux said, was to avoid hard contact and induce routine grounders and pop-ups.

"He lives on the handle and the end," said ex-Cub teammate and buddy Mark Grace. "Living on the handle is a smart thing. It's a pretty good goal. His fastball, he tries to run inside and get in on your hands. His changeup, he wants to get you on the end of the bat. The less balls that are centered are going to be outs."

"He always told me one thing: the goal is to hit on the handle or on the end," Mazzone said.

Maddux kept on soaking it up. He now could calculate the exact time a routine fly ball should reach the outfielder.

"I remember a comment he made about a fly ball," Baylor said. "He's counting in his mind on the mound that the ball should be caught by now. Five seconds gives an outfielder enough time to run under balls.

Mazzone recalls the optimum Maddux hang time as seven seconds, relating to *Sports Weekly*'s Bob Nightengale a 1997 incident when a pop-up between left, center and short was snared with a diving catch by left fielder Ryan Klesko. Maddux came back to the dugout angry, insisting a fly ball that hangs in the air for seven seconds was an easy catch. Four seconds is a line drive, while three seconds is a single to the outfield.

Finally, witnessing the sheer power of his intellect and intuition, Mazzone and the Braves would simply ask Maddux for a final say-so on strategy and pitching mechanics.

"We were going through the Yankees scouting report for the 1996 World Series," Mazzone said. "Greg said the report on Bernie Williams was not correct. I stood up and said, 'Fuck the advance report. Go with what Greg says.'" (Williams batted just .167 in that series.)

Braves pitchers young and old kept beating a path to Maddux.

"When Jason Marquis went in to look at film, he wanted Greg to come in and look at it with him," Mazzone said. "Jason sat between Maddux on the left and [John] Burkett on the right."

"As a [Braves] rookie coming up, I had so much information coming from him, a lot of it didn't make sense at first," the Giants' Jason Schmidt said of his 1995 season, when he stayed at Maddux's home upon his callup from Triple-A Richmond. "It was over my head and it was things I hadn't experienced in the game yet. Terry Mulholland, who was very knowledgeable as a veteran himself, went over things he got from Maddux."

"You come out of the minor leagues with good stuff, but you don't know how to get out major league hitters consistently," former Braves starter Kevin Millwood, now with the Phillies, said. "That's where I benefited the most from being around Greg. I don't know if I'd let him call pitches for me during a game. But before or after a game, I'll go to Greg, go over the other team's lineup and ask what I should have done in a certain situation. I haven't found anyone as smart as him. It's pretty unbelievable how he can read hitters."

Lefty Tom Glavine, who should be in Maddux's ballpark in intellect, one day asked Mazzone for help. *Sports Weekly*'s Bob Nightengale said Mazzone in turn asked Maddux, who recommended that Glavine should change his release point.

"Glavine comes up to me and says, 'Leo, Leo, you're a genius. That works. That really, really works,'" Mazzone told Nightengale. Apparently, Glavine did not immediately know the source of the new advice.

After a decade at his side, Mazzone figures Maddux could handle any of the Atlanta field jobs—his own, Cox's, whoever. And anyone else's in the game, for that matter.

"He could manage a game," the coach said. "Figure out a lineup, positioning defense, everything.

"I don't think so, I know so."

Cox agrees. "He'd be good at managing, being a pitching coach, hitting [instruction]," he said.

For now, though, Maddux just wants to pitch. That's the ultimate good news for teammates, but bad news for opponents who just can't figure out how Maddux has, well, figured them out. Maybe it's just second nature for him.

"I had to study the game to survive," Hall of Famer Don Sutton said. "Maddux does it because it's natural for him."

◆ ◆ ◆

If Maddux can probe into the psychology of his foes, then turnabout is fair play.

For full disclosure, a profiling of the Hall of Fame–bound right-hander is in order. And the master of control is at once simple and complex. Outwardly, he's buried his ego, his personality very much the same as a decade ago.

"He's the same guy," said Dave Martinez, a minor league and Cubs teammate in 1986–88 before reuniting with Maddux in Atlanta in 2001. "When I saw him in [2001] spring training, I told him you haven't changed a bit. He said, 'Why change?'"

Still non-voluble, Maddux hates to stick out in the crowd, enjoys being able to move about in public without being mobbed and has no pretensions of going beyond his Everyman off-the-field persona. He's never gotten arrogant about his success in baseball, either. Maddux truly believes he's playing the game for fun in the same manner as he did in those beloved days at Valley High School. He towers over almost everyone else in the game, yet you wouldn't pick up one air of that status hanging around Maddux. Nintendo in the hotel and golf on off days were as fancy as he got. He appreciates where he's been and where he's going, and has placed that in healthy perspective.

"When we met not long ago, I talked to him briefly about the type of careers we each had," 1986–88 Cubs teammate Rafael Palmeiro said. "And he said, 'Can you believe what we've done?'"

Never at any point did Maddux believe he was invincible. He'd always retain just enough self-doubt to keep him on edge.

"I wouldn't say I feel confident I'll dominate every time out," Maddux once said. "I have my doubts as a pitcher, and I think I pitch better when I have doubts. I think I get in trouble the times when I'm overconfident; also when I'm under-confident. It works both ways. I try to find that certain level I like to pitch at."

At Maddux's core is a red-hot vortex of competitiveness and passion. He will tear your heart out to win. Why else would his nicknames suggest destruction: "Mad Dog" and "The Baby-Faced Assassin"? The last shreds of that youthful temper combined with that fierce desire to win result in a few "f-bombs" being thrown around, grist for the lip readers, when he stalks about the mound after an uncommon in-game setback.

Hardened by the childhood competition against brother Mike and focused by an old-school desire to play the game right, Maddux is the most unlikely-looking tough guy in the game. But he'll mess with you before you can get him, and he'll make you look foolish doing it.

He's endeared himself to teammates and even opponents by adhering to the game's old rules and pecking order, not trying to play outside it. Frustrated hitters can't begrudge the generous strike zones he receives from many umpires, simply because he has outworked all other pitchers in mastery of location to get corner strikes, and then some, called.

Despite his childhood temper, Maddux learned soon enough that it's preferable to say two words where three words normally would do as he broke into baseball.

"When you first come up, I was kind of told by other people to just lay back and be quiet and try to go unnoticed," he said in 1991, his fifth full big league season. "That will take the heat off you if you're going well or doing bad. The things you do will go unnoticed with the media, and the fans, and everything. But the front office knows what's going on, because it's their business.

"Very few players come up and are the loudest ones in the clubhouse. Usually, the loudest are the ones who have been around. I don't think I'm a loud person now. I think I'm pretty much the same as I was then [his rookie year in 1987], only more sure of myself."

At the time he voiced this train of thought, Maddux was about to endure his transformation from follower to leader. Red-bearded giant Rick Sutcliffe was in his final days as a Cub. But as long as Sutcliffe, the 1984 National

League Cy Young Award winner, was on the roster, Maddux adhered to the pecking order of the pitching staff on which Sutcliffe had long been the leader. By 1989, it was clear the twenty-three-year-old Maddux, with thirty-seven victories over the past two seasons, had surpassed the oft-injured, aging Sutcliffe in ability. Any attempt to tag Maddux as staff ace was given the brushoff.

"I consider myself one of the five starting pitchers," he said in '91 with a reverberation that would echo more than a decade into the future. "Whoever's pitching the best at that time is the ace. I think that ace business is overrated. We've all got a job to do. Starting pitchers are going to pitch every fifth day. You can't concern yourself too much with what the other four pitchers are doing on days you're not pitching. It's not going to help you as a pitcher."

The admiration of Maddux's teammates only grew when he patiently waited his turn to lead while Sutcliffe's Cubs tenure played itself out.

"I think it's one of the old-school rules that people probably don't adhere to any more," said Mike Bielecki, whose 18-7 record trailed only Maddux's 19-12 on the 1989 National League East champion Cubs. "It used to be you waited your turn when I came up and Greg came out. Now you've got guys straight out of college thinking they're going to go to the Hall of Fame.

"But once 'Sut' left, then Greg had become the ace of the staff. He was the guy to go talk to, and took control of the reins."

Even before Maddux formally became the staff leader in 1992, he picked up points with his ability to protect his hitter's backs. The story about the batboy-like Maddux asking for the knockdown sign in the pitchers' meeting already had circulated. Now Maddux would put it to good use.

On September 5, 1992, the right-hander was on a second-half hot streak that would eventually net him his first Cy Young Award. Locked in a 3-3 game against the San Diego Padres at Wrigley Field, Maddux seemed a good bet to notch victory number seventeen if he could hang on long enough for the Cubs to scratch out another run.

But the basic law of baseball interfered. Padres reliever Jose Melendez almost hit Cubs star Ryne Sandberg in the head with a fastball in the seventh. No warning was issued by plate umpire Ed Montague.

The chips began whirring in Maddux's internal computer. Padres catcher Dan Walters was up with two outs in the eighth and nobody on. With his first pitch, control-artist Maddux hit Walters in the back.

Montague immediately ejected Maddux, without the obligation of having to toss him had a warning been in place.

Greg Maddux in the late 1980s, early in his career. In addition
to admiring his ability, teammates admire Maddux's adherence
to the "baseball code," even at the expense of his own statistics.
Stephen Green/Chicago Cubs

"Maddux is such a strong competitor," Montague said afterward, "that
in my mind I know he's going to retaliate. I was hoping he wouldn't. But if
it's flagrant, I've got to get rid of him."

Montague was asked by reporters why he didn't also give reliever Melendez the heave-ho.

"Melendez just doesn't have the control of a Maddux," the umpire said.
"Maddux was on the plate all day. The ball got away from Melendez."

The ejection cost Maddux and the Cubs dearly. Reliever Jeff Robinson

38

was summoned. Padres left fielder Jerald Clark immediately slugged a two-run homer to give San Diego the margin of victory in the eventual 5-3 win, with the loss charged to Maddux. Instead of staying in to be in position to win what would have been his seventeenth of the season, he was charged with his 11th (and final) defeat of the season.

Publicly, Maddux denied any intentional beanball activity or retaliation for Sandberg's low-bridging afterward. But, then again, the budding magician wasn't going to reveal the real story.

"It doesn't make sense to me," he said. "If he thought I was going to defend Sandberg, he should have issued a warning right there. Anyway, why am I going to hit a guy [Walters] who hasn't proven he can hit up here? He's a guy who pitchers want to face."

But it was apparent to any witness to the incident that Maddux was protecting Sandberg, even at the cost to his personal statistics. He couldn't retaliate against Melendez, who would not have batted. The catcher was as good a target as anyone.

Andre Dawson, who went 3-for-5 in the loss to the Padres playing right field for the Cubs, knew Maddux had long passed the test of old-school, throwback toughness in being ready to back up his hitters. No wonder the Cubs played so hard behind him in his then-dream 20-11, 2.18 ERA season.

"One thing you did know was that he had your back," Dawson said. "He would protect his ballplayers. As a teammate, you really enjoyed going out to play behind that individual because you know you were protected."

"He's also got large balls, for a lack of a better phrase," said the Diamondbacks' Mark Grace, who played first base for the Cubs in the same game.

Maddux was truly fearless on the mound. Around this same time, he was asked about the epidemic of hitters charging the mound to start brawls. He replied he would back away from no one. "If a guy has to come out to the mound to prove he's a good hitter, let him come," he said, knowing that with the ball in his hand and possessed of the game's best control, he'd probably have the last word in almost all instances.

"It says a lot about the team concept, but also the courage he has as a pitcher," Mazzone said. The Braves pitching coach discovered first hand how tough Maddux was when he went south in 1993. Maddux would display his considerable *cojones* at times other than the Walters/Sandberg affair and his famed intimidation of the Indians' Eddie Murray in the 1995 World Series.

In a one-run game at Tropicana Field in Tampa in 2000, the Devil Rays nailed ball-magnet Andres Galarraga a couple of times. Maddux was on the mound for the Braves. "He said, 'Leo, I have to get somebody,' " Mazzone recalled of Maddux's response. Maddux hit Jose Canseco in the knee with a one-run lead. Of course, he retired the next batter.

"Brian Jordan comes into the dugout and tells Greg, 'I've got to hand it to you, Mad Dog, you picked the biggest SOB in the league to hit,' " Mazzone said with a chuckle.

An even larger, more prominent target was a recipient of a Maddux dead-eye offering. He almost had to apologize for doing what he had to do.

"He hit [Mark] McGwire one time," Mazzone said. "McGwire was hanging out over the outside corner. We saw Maddux going over to first base. We asked him what the hell are you doing? Greg said he asked him if it hurt. McGwire said no."

Maddux's own pain threshold is enormous, emerging as a key tenet of his throwback personality. From time to time rumors have swept through the game that he suffered from a sore arm, but kept on pitching. One line of thought had Maddux leaking out a phony injury elsewhere to cover up an arm injury in the classic manner of tough-but-proud football players who don't want the opponents to zero in on the afflicted body part.

In the good ol' days, most pitchers tried to conceal minor-to-moderate injuries out of competitive zeal, fear of the doctor's needle and scalpel and, above all, insecurity about losing their rotation spot. Too many baseball executives, wielding the ready-replacement sword of Damocles over their heads, encouraged this overly macho attitude. Oddly enough, even in the days of guaranteed contracts and watchdog agents, that philosophy has not died out. And certainly not with Maddux.

"There are a lot of pitchers who do that [conceal injuries]," Mazzone said. "Many times he goes out there and does not feel 100 percent. They think he can still go out there and win. He's so mentally tough.

"Once he got hit by a line drive on the elbow. I thought his arm was broken. It swelled up like a balloon. He didn't miss a start. His recuperative powers are great. There are times he felt like shit and came out to play."

Maddux has said he has been lucky to never have suffered a season-busting, career-threatening injury. But if he breaks down in that manner, he'll have no problems walking away from the game, his reputation secure.

"He told me one time if he ever hurt his arm, he wouldn't go through rehab," Mazzone said. "He'd pack his bags and go home."

Loyalty is another trait that runs strongly through Maddux's life. It starts with family and expands through his clubhouse relationships and views of his employer. When the concept of two-way loyalty was fractured for no good reason with the Cubs starting in the winter of 1991–92, Maddux proved he could take resolute action in response, changing the history of two franchises for the next decade.

Maddux and wife Kathy have been a twosome since their senior year at Valley High. Early on, he said he felt fortunate he did not have to sow his wild oats as a young player.

"I've never been single," he said in 1991. "I've never been wild and out of control where I needed someone to settle me down.

"I think it kept me out of trouble. I've seen a lot of guys in the minors that came in at three or four in the morning. It *can't* help their baseball careers. Every now and then, it's not going to do too much damage. But there are guys doing it three, four times a week."

The Madduxes settled down into an unpretentious life in suburban Vegas. A visit to his house on a Friday night in January 1993 to determine his motivation for defecting to the Braves found Maddux chuckling as Kathy and several friends arrived to use the hot tub. "Bikini central," he mused with a lifted eyebrow. After ninety minutes of conversation and munches of pizza, it was time to head back to the hotel on The Strip. No problem getting a cab, though. Maddux and a buddy had to make a beer run, and he offered a ride on the way to procure the suds. You were not in the presence of a man who took his exalted baseball and financial status, with a fresh $28 million, five-year contract too seriously.

Maddux did not let ego-feeding interfere with the stability of his family life during the All-Star Break in 2001. By then the Madduxes had two children, Amanda, seven, and Chase, four. The kids had asked Dad if they could go on a vacation at the All-Star break when he started off the season 4-5. But a ten-game winning streak made Maddux a prime Midsummer Classic candidate. He turned down the automatic berth in favor of keeping the family's plans to go to the Bahamas.

The family likely would have been spending much of their summers of the 1990s in Chicago had Maddux's first and most passionate choice of teams not gone unexpectedly sour on him. The fact he did not stay a Cub at least another five seasons was the result of corporate arrogance and ignorance about baseball talent by an over-the-hill Tribune Company lifer named Stanton Cook.

Maddux's loyalty to his original organization had never wavered, in spite of the requisite management blunders of Cubs history, through the early summer of 1991, with his free-agent season looming the following year. He fully planned in his own mind to stay in Chicago.

"Longevity and security are probably the most important things," Maddux said then. "Two years ago, when they guaranteed my money for this year, I told them I would talk to them. I would negotiate with them openly and freely. That was part of the deal two springs ago, so I'll hold up my end of the bargain."

The Cubs, through Cook and hired-gun attorney Dennis Homerin, didn't hold up theirs. Placed in charge of overseeing the Cubs after he simply wouldn't walk away with his golden parachute after retiring as Tribune Company CEO, Cook seized control of the team's baseball operations from GM Jim Frey in the fall of 1991. Maddux did not agree quickly enough to a five-year deal placed on the table by Homerin. Going against the advice of agent Scott Boras, Maddux agreed to drop the no-trade clause and was ready to settle for five years and $25 million. But Cook and Homerin suddenly yanked the deal off the table. You didn't move fast enough, kid, and besides, a newly enriched deal for icon Ryne Sandberg was the priority. Never mind that you can hardly find an ace, that you have to develop your own, and the Cubs had one in Maddux. That kind of baseball concept went over casual fan Cook's head. He could also beat down his Tribune production workers in a protracted strike in the 1980s, so what's the problem with one skinny kid pitcher who hasn't yet won twenty games?

Obviously, Cook didn't bother to read Maddux's smoking-gun quote of midsummer 1991: "If I don't sign anything by next spring [1992], there's a very good chance it will be my last year in Chicago," he said. "However, if I do sign something by the spring, then I'll probably look to buy a place here in Chicago."

And like many of his predecessors at the financial and artistic helm of the Cubs, Cook—by experience a newspaper production department manager—could not fully understand the need to keep a sinkerballing ace who knew how to pitch in Wrigley Field. In fact, an ace who liked pitching in Wrigley Field with the wind blowing in.

"This infield definitely has the highest grass in the league," Maddux said at smoking-gun-quote time. "When the wind blows in, there's not a better pitcher's park in the league." On another occasion, Maddux said Wrigley Field with the wind blowing in played bigger than Houston's Astrodome.

"I try not to worry too much about the field," he added. "I try to throw ground balls whether on grass or turf. You may give up three or four more homers here that you don't give up in parks on the road. But we're going to hit homers here that we won't hit on the road, so it works out both ways. I liked the ballpark from the beginning. . . . Wrigley Field definitely blows away the other ballparks."

Despite the hardening of Maddux's and Boras's positions due to the bungling by Cook and Homerin, the pitcher still tried to re-sign with the

Cubs, albeit for more than $25 million, at several junctures in 1992. But now new GM Larry Himes was in the contract mix. Grateful that Cook had rescued him from underemployment after being fired by the White Sox in 1990, Himes was not going to push his patrician boss to ante up a few million more for Maddux. Himes's unique personality, in which he embraced few people and believed he had most of the answers, allowed no room for schmoozing. He admitted he was not a political animal, crucial for long-term success in baseball. He had no emotional way to reel Maddux and Boras back into the fold after the initial damage of the Homerin-tabled contract.

Even after he accepted his 1992 Cy Young Award, with dizzying contract offers from the Braves and Yankees enveloping him, Maddux tried one last-ditch backchannel approach to re-signing with the Cubs. Claiming his free-agent money had been apportioned to former Texas Ranger right-hander Jose Guzman, Himes would not hear of any appeals. The most disastrous player departure—and there have been wagonloads—in Cubs history was officially under way as Maddux accepted the Braves' deal.

"It wasn't my choice to go," Maddux told Barry Rozner of the *Daily Herald* of Arlington Heights (Illinois) in 2001. "I just know Chicago is a great town, and the fans treated me like a king. I hope they get a World Series someday."

That will be long after Maddux enjoyed the Braves' World Series championship in 1995 and two other visits to the Fall Classic. Maddux's loyalty was about in the same ballpark as Cubs' fans' never-say-die loyalty to their team. The worst of modern American business management practices stuck its gilt-edged nose between the two to prevent a very logical relationship from continuing.

◆ ◆ ◆

If Greg Maddux truly is the master at work, then the line between leisure and toil has been blurred forever.

One day in the working life of the smartest man in baseball showed that if you really enjoy your job, then it's truly not work.

That's the pleasant fact that could be deduced from watching Maddux prepare for and execute his duel with the Cubs' Kerry Wood on Friday, September 7, 2001, at Wrigley Field a few days before the world turned upside down.

Start to finish, Maddux absorbs the total baseball experience, then becomes the centerpiece of the same.

More than three hours before the 2:20 P.M. start, Maddux could be found leaning back by his cubicle, his feet up on a chair, totally relaxed and not enmeshed in some psyched-out zone into which other pitchers enter before their starts. As card games and clubhouse chatter ensued nearby, Maddux talked with an equipment manager and longtime teammate John Smoltz, then was handed a crossword puzzle. Two words into it, he told a visitor that he's not as good at working words as he is both sides of the plate.

The friendly neighborhood shoe distributor, Dana Noel of Nike, then came by to join the conversation. But the subject quickly shifted from footwear to golf, another Maddux specialty. By now the entire Braves team had filtered into the clubhouse, and pregame stretch time was approaching. At 12:15 P.M., Maddux briefly stretched on the floor, then walked out the door, stopping at a rack of bats to select his batting-practice companion, and proceeded to his favorite seat at the far end of the visitors' dugout.

Maddux never let go of the bat the entire time he sat in the dugout. Talking briefly to reliever Rudy Seanez, Maddux sat there with wide-open eyes and mind, soaking in the atmosphere of a Wrigley Field he always loved. Cradling that bat, he could have passed for an awfully young coach, not the man who seemingly pulls a string on every pitch.

After talking briefly to manager Bobby Cox in the dugout, Maddux was the first one in the cage when visitor's batting practice started at 12:50 P.M. He sprayed line drives to the wall, then chatted with Cubs announcer Joe Carter and several teammates by the side of the cage while others hit. And when he was alone, he kept watching the hitter in the cage, soaking up more morsels of information and color as an original baseball junkie.

When the lineup regulars arrived to hit, Maddux grabbed a glove and headed toward the outfield to join his fellow pitchers. Most starters would take it easy at this point prior to the first pitch, but Maddux always shags in the outfield with his start looming. No matter that it was mid-day and energy-draining sultry. Every moment Maddux could spend on the field, even during batting practice, is like an elixir to him.

After a break to change his shirt, Maddux returned to warm up. He knew what had to be accomplished with the wind blowing out at 15 mph. On the mound against his old team, he took advantage of the high Wrigley Field grass. The first seven Cubs were retired on infield grounders. He walked Sammy Sosa in front of Fred McGriff's wind-blown fourth-inning homer, then held serve in a 2-2 tie against Wood. Strangely, Wood—still struggling at this point of his career with command and control—threw a higher proportion of strikes than Maddux. Wood's count was 45 strikes in 66 pitches; Maddux, 41 strikes in 72 pitches.

Fourteen ground-ball outs in six innings was the only way to survive with the hot gales blowing. He got a no-decision, but was instrumental in the outcome when Andruw Jones's fly ball piggybacked on a gust to just reach the left field bleachers in the ninth. Braves 3, Cubs 2, no small thanks to Maddux for keeping all but one baseball in the park.

Afterward, Jones held court near Maddux's locker, analyzing the good fortune of what he called the cheapest homer of his career. While reporters listened, Maddux quietly returned from the shower and dressed quickly, almost as fast as he pitches. Noticing his arrival, the assembled media shifted from Jones to form a tight semi-circle around the Master. They would hear a combination of direct, pithy answers with some dry wit mixed in.

Maddux almost never walks anyone, so what about one free pass to Bill Mueller on a 3-and-2 pitch?

"I threw the pitch I wanted to," he said. "He didn't swing at that. Take your base."

Do you try not to walk batters, especially if the wind is blowing out?

"Pitchers who try not to walk guys don't last long. They wouldn't get past the fifth inning."

How 'bout keeping the ball on the ground on a day like today?

"This is a good place to throw ground balls. It's the best infield in the league to throw ground balls."

Do you change your style due to the wind?

"You do. You try to throw it lower. When the wind blows in, you throw it higher. The wind here can be your friend."

What about Wood's performance?

"Woody's throwing frickin' cheese. Plus he's sneaky."

Do you like John Smoltz coming in as the closer?

"I'd rather have him pitching in my games instead of before my games."

Do you like playing in Wrigley Field?

"I enjoy playing here. It's a great atmosphere. It's a good city. It's a good sports town, not just for the Cubs."

The conversation petered out. Maddux began walking toward the equipment room. He didn't record another "W" on his inexorable march toward 300 victories. No matter. He kept the Braves in the game. And he had fun. There were worse ways to make a living.

◆ ◆ ◆

Waking up on any game day in the late 1990s, Maddux did not just suddenly find himself the master of control, able to pull the string on most of his pitches.

In reality, the evolution of Maddux from a skinny, would-be power pitcher to a fellow rated by many the greatest pitcher of modern times was not linear. It was an often bumpy process, with some frustration and false starts, and required a change of philosophy on Maddux's part and incessant between-starts bullpen sessions.

And, if the truth be known, the transformation needed Maddux to alight in the stable, pitching-oriented Braves organization, where he could flourish as an ace among aces on a team still on the ascent in 1993. Remaining with the Cubs would have been a just outcome, yet Maddux may not have become the consummate pitcher amid the constant management upheavals, clubhouse dissension, continual losing seasons and the aura of the franchise as "lovable losers."

"When he came up, he was throwing in the low- to mid-90s [mph] with a curveball," said Mark Grace, who was the Cubs' rookie first baseman in Maddux's second big-league season in 1988. "Now he's in the mid- to high-80s with a changeup and slider. Greg realized he had to change something to be successful.

"He realized he couldn't rear back and blow the ball by people to remain successful. He made too many mistakes with his fastball. He learned how to work the corners. That's why I admire him so much."

Maddux was lucky early on. For a pitcher who lives and dies on movement, he was blessed with a fastball that only needed its location harnessed to craft the best control in the game. Too many pitchers' heaters come in straight and predictable to hitters. Maddux's always had movement.

"He threw all four-seamers," said Rick Kranitz, his first pro pitching coach at rookie-league Pikeville (Kentucky) in 1984. "The ball jumped the last five feet and sometimes handcuffed the catchers. Greg also had a very good curveball."

But endurance and stamina were the key issues for the eighteen-year-old, who earned a second-round nod by the Cubs in '84 despite his skinny 145-pound frame.

"He'd dominate the whole league until the fourth or fifth inning," Kranitz recalled. "Then he didn't have the stamina to go further. As the year went on, he had a hard time putting hitters away."

Nevertheless, Maddux finished his first pro season 6-2 with a 2.63 ERA. All the reports filtering up to Wrigley Field were positive. Maddux proved himself a winner in the front office's eyes with a 13-9 season in 1985 at low-Class A Midwest League Peoria. Moving further up the chain, he was 4-3 at Class AA Eastern League Pittsfield starting out the 1986 season, then earned a promotion to Triple-A Iowa on May 28, 1986. He punched a ticket to Chicago with a 10-1 record and 3.02 ERA through the rest of the Triple-A season, earning a berth on *Baseball America*'s Triple-A all-star team.

The batboy was now pitching in the majors. He was promoted to the Cubs on September 1, 1986, just four months past his twentieth birthday, and made his big-league debut a day later in relief, getting charged with the loss against the Astros at Wrigley Field. Maddux became the youngest pitcher in the majors that season to win a game and throw a complete game in an 11-3 victory over the Reds in Cincinnati on September 7. Three more losses in as many starts followed until he got psyched up for the first big-league matchup against his brother, Mike, a Phillies rookie. On September 29, 1986, at Veterans Stadium, Greg evened a lot of the score from his childhood by giving up three runs in seven and two-thirds innings, striking out seven, in an 8-3 victory.

The triumph over his brother would be the last positive development in Maddux's career for the next year. Although he earned a berth in the Cubs' rotation in 1987, he was inconsistent, making all the youthful mistakes in locating his fastball. The increasingly fractious atmosphere in the clubhouse was not conducive to getting the most out of a rookie pitcher, listed by the Cubs at all of 150 pounds. Cubs manager Gene Michael found himself increasingly miscast as a National League manager and chafed under the dictums of often-bellicose GM Dallas Green. Pitching coach Herm Starrette, in his only year in that role with the Cubs, was hardly a help. Ace relief stopper Lee Smith was dissatisfied and loudly demanded a trade. Worse yet, 1987 featured an apparently juiced baseball with offensive numbers skyrocketing all over the game.

Struggling in the first half with a 4-7 record, Maddux did not win a game after July 24, had a 13.91 ERA in four August starts, and earned two demotions to Iowa during August. He finished with a horrific 6-14 record and 5.61 ERA, displaying none of his future trademark control with seventy-four walks and 181 hits allowed in 155²/₃ innings.

Once he got past the chaos of 1987, though, Maddux began a slow progression upward to eventual Master status. Over the next four seasons starting in 1988, he'd amass quality stretches that hinted at the brilliance to come, punctuated by spectacular pratfalls that only dulled the Cubs' corporate overseers' awareness of the budding talent they easily could have wrapped up for life.

Maddux benefited immediately from the sweeping management changes in the offseason of 1987–88. Green was ordered to leave by Tribune Company overseer John Madigan. Successor Jim Frey made the automatic appointment of childhood chum Don Zimmer as manager. Dick Pole was promoted from Iowa to succeed Starrette as pitching coach. Pole's appointment was good for Maddux; many believed he had been instrumental in helping him at Pittsfield in 1986.

The often-gruff Pole and the quiet Maddux often butted heads, but overall they were a good tandem. The coach began working with his pupil on a cut fastball to counteract the days when the wind would blow out at Wrigley Field. Maddux's changeup gradually improved through side work and repetition.

"It seems like you're always learning how to throw pitches in the minor leagues, and when you get to the major leagues is when you learn how to pitch," Maddux said.

"Dick was great because we had the same goal. The goal was to try to become a better pitcher. Personalities didn't matter. We both had that common goal. We both did everything we possibly did to make it better."

The Pole-Maddux pairing immediately paid off. Maddux was baseball's pitching sensation in the first half of the 1988 season. He hurled twenty-six and two-thirds scoreless innings from May 6 to 17, amassed a nine-game winning streak from May 22 to July 10, was named NL Pitcher of the Month for June (5-0 record and 2.22 ERA), was 15-3 overall at the All-Star break and became the youngest Cub to ever be named to the Midsummer Classic.

But the sturdiness that was a Maddux's trademark was still off in the future. He tailed off in the oppressiveness of the record-breaking hot summer of '88. He was only 3-5 with seven no-decisions and a 4.92 ERA in 93$^1/_3$ second-half innings.

Maddux almost inverted the pattern for 1989. Beset by poor run support at the start, he began the season 1-5. Cubs hitters weren't helping, having scored just four runs while he was in the game during his first five defeats. But on May 19, he started a hot streak that would turn around his season. He won thirteen of his next sixteen decisions while lowering his ERA to 2.77. Maddux was 9-3 in July and August as the Cubs overtook the Montreal Expos for first place in the NL East. He also won his nineteenth game, going eight and one-third innings on September 26 in the Cubs' division-clinching 3-2 victory over the Expos in Montreal. That would be the last time the Cubs finished first. The Cubs then passed up a chance to get Maddux his twentieth victory to better prepare him for a Game 1 start against the Giants in the National League Championship Series.

His first postseason was a disaster that batted down an otherwise positive image he had crafted for himself. In two starts, Maddux allowed eleven runs in seven and one-third innings, including Will Clark's infamous towering grand-slam homer far out onto Sheffield Avenue in Game 1. Maddux had to immediately live down that failure, and he never completely did in the unsophisticated baseball mindset of Tribune Company honchos.

"We were playing basketball that winter at an outdoor court [in Las Vegas] with a bunch of ten- and twelve-year-olds," longtime Maddux buddy Rodney Beckwith said. "This little kid after our game starts running away and screams, 'Will Clark roped you.' It was funny."

Maddux's upward progress was by no way linear. On May 5, 1990, he beat the Padres 3-2 to boost his record to 4-1. But over the next thirteen starts, he couldn't buy a win. He was 0-8 with a 6.15 ERA. Even though Maddux was being dragged down by a team slump in which the entire Cubs pitching staff crumbled, critics wondered if he had felt pressure from a new contract that had boosted his salary from $275,000 in 1989 to an eventual $2.4 million in 1991.

"You think I think about my bank account on the mound?" Maddux told *Chicago Tribune* columnist Bob Verdi. "I'd rather be poor than be humiliated, and that's what I am now, professionally. I've been lousy."

"This kid's gone through hell," then–Cubs manager Don Zimmer said.

But Maddux managed to right himself after finally picking up a victory against the Padres on July 18, 1990, his record having fallen to 4-9 with a 4.74 ERA. He won his next four starts to even his record. He'd end the season 15-15, 3.46. And he kept working on his total game, earning his first Gold Glove Award by fielding 1.000 with a league-leading 94 chances.

Earning another Gold Glove in 1991, Maddux began to gain notoriety for endurance in 1991. He started out relatively slowly, pitching a little better during another Cubs team meltdown, with an 8-6 record and 3.65 ERA on August 1 settling in to a final 15-11, 3.35 mark. Maddux led the NL in starts (37) and innings pitched (263) and was second in strikeouts (198).

By now the pitching coach's baton had been passed from Pole, fired early in the 1991 season, to Billy Connors in his second stint on the job. At this point, Maddux concentrated on fine-tuning his stretch mechanics and location on his specialty pitch—the fastball that breaks back over the inside corner against left-handers.

Leo Mazzone swears Maddux had the pitch finely-tuned by the time he came to the Braves. It behaves as if it has a mind of its own, boring in on a left-hander's fists until it darts over the inside corner for an unhittable strike.

"It looks like it's going to hit you, and it ends up a strike," said Davey Martinez. "He didn't throw that pitch in the 1980s. He threw more curveballs and changeups [to left-handers]."

Maddux seems to will the ball to move on its eccentric path, but he insisted the action is not magic.

"It's all mechanics," he said. "It has to do with how you hold the ball in your hand, the size of your hand, arm angle and delivery. You always look for ways to tinker with your mechanics, your grip, to increase your movement.

"You can always do things to improve on it. Some pitchers' balls just move more than others. I was fortunate to have a fastball that moves. If you have a fastball that moves enough, you can throw it over the center of the plate. You don't want to, but that's how you get away with mistakes."

Few mistakes are made on this tricky pitch, which Mazzone said emanates from Maddux getting properly aligned on the mound.

"You can't have an open delivery," Mazzone said. "You line yourself up like a golfer to make sure you take a direct route to the corner to which you're going. Greg showed me how he does it. Everybody can do it to a degree, but not to the degree of consistency he does. [Orel] Hershiser used it, but he didn't use it as good as Greg."

Maddux's ability to make this pitch move from side to side was astounding. Most great pitchers taught themselves to make pitches drop.

"The main thing is I wanted it to sink," Hall of Famer Fergie Jenkins said of his vintage fastball. "I was a down-and-away pitcher a lot, with a slider and running fastball. I'd throw the slider in on [left-handed] guys and jam them up. Getting movement is all finger grips and pressure. But the knack Greg has gotten with that pitch against lefties is the best in the game."

Hitters can remember when they've made any kind of contact against the pitch.

"I swung at it [early in the 2000 season], and I got a jam double over [Andres] Galarraga's head," recalled Martinez. "But usually he locks you up. You buckle. You can't do much with that pitch."

The famed Maddux changeup also was being readied for prime time in the early 1990s. The pitch was so impressive when located properly that the all-time greats took notice.

"I had an old coach up in Vermont who was involved with Christy Mathewson," said Hall of Famer Robin Roberts. "He said Christy had this famous pitch called a 'fadeaway.' Well, Greg Maddux came up with this pitch with the Cubs. People call it a changeup. But I've never seen a pitcher who can get batters to swing at that pitch that he does. For an old pitcher to watch this guy pitch is enjoyable."

All the Maddux pitches worked to perfection in his first Cy Young Award season in 1992. Most impressive were two numbers that backed up Maddux's claim about being able to thrive in Wrigley Field. For the season, he allowed just seven homers—two in the September 5 game in which he was ejected after protecting Ryne Sandberg against the Padres. Only one clout was to a right-handed hitter. That was an incredibly low total even during a cool summer in which the wind blew in the vast majority of times at Wrigley Field. He also sported a 2.18 ERA, second-lowest by a Cubs starter since World War II. He was 12-4 with a 1.91 ERA and seven complete games in the Friendly Confines. The only full-time Cubs hurler who undercut Maddux's 1992 ERA was lefty Dick Ellsworth with 2.11 in 1963. Next after Maddux was Bill Hands's 2.49 during a twenty-victory season in 1969.

Thirty of Maddux's thirty-five appearances in 1992 were considered quality starts, including nineteen of his last twenty and fourteen straight from June 25 to August 31. He could have won twenty-five or more games with any run support. The Cubs scored eight runs in his eleven defeats and were shut out seven times.

After Maddux shut out the Dodgers 2-0 in one hour, fifty-six minutes on August 31 to boost his season record to 16-10, then–Cubs manager Jim Lefebvre was moved to proclaim, "If we had scored more runs for him, he'd have twenty-three wins by now."

He had to make do with the likes of Rey Sanchez, Kal Daniels, Steve Buechele, Derrick May, Dwight Smith, and Rick Wilkins filling out the 1992 Cubs batting order behind him. But Maddux had few regrets over not being able to push the statistical envelope even higher in that dream season.

"You try not to get too caught up in that," Maddux said of the non-support at the time. "I don't want it to affect the way I approach the game. I can't control the runs my teammates score. I just need to pitch well enough to keep us in the game."

Watching from the Braves' dugout, Mazzone could only admire Maddux. He had no clue that he'd be dropped from the sky right into his lap in a matter of months. He was the best pitcher not already on the Braves in the summer of '92.

"After the All-Star Game that year, I made it a point to tell him he was a great, great pitcher," Mazzone said. "When he was on the other side, you hated him. You wanted to beat him. He was a killer, he could eat you up."

Soon the books were closed on his 20-11 season, he collected the Cy Young Award and he made the fateful move to Atlanta. Teeth were gnashed en masse once again in Chicago, while the rich became richer in Dixie. Within a few years, Maddux wouldn't have any regrets. He had made the right move at the right time.

Atlanta had benefited from its poor finishes in the mid- and late-1980s to land a mother lode of young talent. The Braves became a pitching-oriented organization while developing a winning atmosphere. Slipshod management and off-the-field controversies were minimized. The team's clubhouse chemistry was among the best in the game. Atlanta was a big city that still possessed a slow-enough Southern pace. A baseball wonk/young family man like Maddux could thrive there.

"Without a doubt, going to the Braves was a good move for him," Mark Grace said.

At Fulton County Stadium, Maddux found an even higher performance plane to which to aspire. The motivation was being the best of the best after standing head and shoulders above his rotation mates in Chicago.

Maddux became fast friends and golfing partners with established aces Tom Glavine and John Smoltz. But the friendly competition among the trio played right into Maddux's competitive spirit. And as stellar as many of the numbers from 1988 to 1992 might have been, Maddux outdid himself with fewer walks, even lower ERAs, and that special spellbinding dominance that had hitters talking to themselves all over baseball.

Glavine already had become the NL's best left-hander with 20-11 and 20-8 records in 1991 and 1992, respectively, capturing the '91 Cy Young Award. Smoltz was starting to come on with 14-13 and 15-12 records in '91 and '92, respectively, along with the league's best pure stuff that netted him the '92 NL strikeout crown with 215. Now Maddux made that group even better, even though there was a period of adjustment while their personal chemistries took time to mesh.

"When Greg came here, I sensed not an animosity, but a real high level of competition," said Mike Bielecki, who had preceded Maddux from Chicago to Atlanta by a full year.

"Everyone there was real excited about having another great arm there. But they were also concerned about what type of guy Greg was. Once he was there three, four days, they realized that. I sensed that each guy going out for his next outing was trying to one-up the next guy, which was good."

Glavine confirmed that each of the pitchers began feeding off each other. And Maddux, the sponge of information, could only benefit by having craftsman Glavine and stuff-king Smoltz as chatter partners in and out of the clubhouse.

"Being around great pitchers makes you a better pitcher," Glavine said. "Number one, you learn what those guys are doing. Number two, when you're around great players, it motivates you to do well. In our rotation, you don't want to be the guy not in the race for the Cy Young. When you have that kind of talent surrounding you, it pushes you to try to go to that level and not be the weak link.

"We've been fortunate in that regard. We're friends on the field, friends off the field. We do a lot of things in common on the baseball field. We spend a lot of time playing golf. When we get together like that, we end up talking about baseball, talking about pitching. Every one of those conversations, we file in the back of our brain and find something to use.

"We're fortunate we're with an organization that has gone with the mindset we'll build a team around pitching and do everything financially possible to keep us together. The three of us have liked being around with each other and pitching with each other, and that's part of the reason we wanted to stay here as well."

Mark Grace said Maddux's situation was comparable to that of Curt Schilling and Randy Johnson's complementary arrangement for the World Champion Diamondbacks of 2001.

"It was friendly fire there, competition," Grace said. "It's the same way with Randy and Curt here. They feed off each other."

Maddux's development built even more confidence in Glavine and Smoltz. In 1998, Smoltz said the Braves would stay in contention as long as the terrific trio could pitch effectively as a unit.

Maddux went to the front of his new class in the categories other than victories. Of course, he paid immediate dividends for Atlanta, winning another twenty games and his second Cy Young Award in 1993, falling short only in the postseason when an entire team of throwback players, the NL East champion Phillies, upset Atlanta in the National League Championship Series. A big improvement over his Cubs seasons was his total dominance in control.

"I thought he had the best control I had ever seen when he first came over to the Braves," Mazzone said. "Maybe he was more relaxed."

Maddux had walked one too many batters at times with 81 in 249 innings in 1988 and 82 in 238$^{1}/_{3}$ innings in 1989. He walked a respectable 70 in 268 innings in 1992. But he cut the walks down to 52 in 267 innings with Atlanta in 1993. The following two seasons were strike-shortened campaigns in which his innings pitched totals fell to just over the 200 mark. But in 1996, in the first full season in three years, Maddux allowed an astounding 28 walks in 245 innings. That total plunged further to 20 walks in 232$^{2}/_{3}$ innings in 1997.

Carrying the control-freak status to the extreme, Maddux went on to set the National League record for most consecutive innings without a walk—72$^{1}/_{3}$ innings between June 20 and August 12, 2001. On the former date, Maddux walked the Marlins' Charles Johnson, then went 289 hitters before Bobby Cox ordered him to intentionally walk the Diamondbacks' Steve Finley at Turner Field in the third inning of a 9-1 Braves loss. Between the walks, Maddux had thrown 639 strikes in 894 pitches, going to three balls in the count just twenty-two times.

"It never meant that much to me," Maddux said after the game. "Walks are a big part of pitching. You've got good walks and you've got bad walks. That's why the streak doesn't matter."

But in amassing the streak, Maddux surpassed the control feats of Christy Mathewson and Randy Jones. He was not merely obliterating the all-time control pitchers; he was the precedent setter placed squarely in modern times at the turn of a millennium.

While Maddux turned into baseball's finest strike machine, he had also shaved his ERA to 1960s-style lows, if not a throwback to the actual dead-ball era. In twenty-five games in strike-shortened 1994, he had a 1.56 ERA, setting a record by finishing 1.09 runs lower than the majors' runner-up, Oakland's Steve Ontiveros. The difference between Maddux's ERA and the National League's average ERA was 2.65, also ranking as the greatest differential in history. Maddux also garnered another record with his third straight Cy Young Award.

To prove '94 was no fluke, Maddux led the universe with a 1.63 ERA to win an unprecedented fourth Cy Young Award the following season. He was the first pitcher to have back-to-back sub-1.70 ERA seasons since Walter "Big Train" Johnson in 1918–19. His 19-2 record earned him renown as the first big-leaguer in history to post at least a .900 winning percentage with at least twenty decisions.

Watching Maddux up close, Mazzone had one throwback wish: to have seen Maddux pitch prior to 1969, when the mound was high, the strike zone was wider, and pitchers had up to forty or forty-one starts a year in the old four-man rotation.

By the late 1990s Maddux had so befuddled hitters that a debate ranged in clubhouses all over: Do you swing at Maddux's first pitch to prevent him from setting you up, or do you work the count like any other pitcher? Nothing seemed to work, as Maddux was continually able to outthink and out-anticipate most hitters. Theories abounded, but none were too successful.

"The approach that I would use against him is to get out of the batter's box as soon as possible and get the first, second or third pitch," said Rafael Palmeiro. "He'll make mistakes like anyone else. He is human. You have to capitalize on that mistake. But when he was two strikes, that's when you're in trouble because he can do so many things with the ball. You try to get him early in the count, and if he falls behind in the count, you have a little bit of an advantage."

On a few occasions the batters seemed to gain significant advantages. In

1999 he surrendered 258 hits in 219⅓ innings with a 3.57 ERA, the most he had been cuffed around since his rookie season in 1987. Reporters swarmed around his locker asking about the source of the problem. Maddux's typical response was to shrug his shoulders and explain he had been pitching the same way as always.

"His stuff was the same," Mazzone said.

Maddux has a perceived weakness in the postseason, starting with his implosion against Will Clark and the Giants in 1989. He has pitched well in three World Series, going 2-3, but sporting a 2.09 ERA in five games. But Maddux had more trouble in recent years in both the Division Series and the National League Championship Series. His last victory had been in Game 1 of the 1999 NLCS against the Mets. Since then he had gone 0-4 in six post-season starts with a 4.50 ERA. Maddux admitted an 11-4 loss to the Diamondbacks and Albie Lopez in the 2001 NLCS was "embarrassing."

Mazzone is his chief defender. "That's just a statistic," he said of the recent postseason failures. "He should be 6-1 in those starts. At the worst, 5-2.

"It's a joke. Check his numbers across the board. In the postseason, he's going against the other [top] guy. Check between the total runs and earned runs."

In fact, many in baseball regard a matchup against Maddux as the game of a pitcher's life. Maddux's opponents had elevated their games going up against The Master. They turned it up even more in the postseason. Pitching in more low-run games than most of his contemporaries in the regular season, Maddux himself found himself with no margin of error in the playoffs.

"You don't have any room for error yourself, and that makes you a better pitcher," Giants starter Jason Schmidt said. "Against Maddux you're more conscious of what's going on, that if you're down 1-0 that might be it. Everybody wants to beat him so bad. Every pitcher knows it's going to be the toughest games of the season. Guys have their career games against him.

"It's amazing he's won as many games as he has under those conditions. He's one of the most mentally strong guys I've ever met."

The magician had slipped only a little in the 2001 postseason. But almost all of his competitors would gladly change rotation spots and postseason assignments with him.

♦ ♦ ♦

Maddux may be better than any of them. Still, the game's wise men like to make comparisons between him and the greats of the past.

As an all-around athletic pitcher, Mets coach Don Baylor nominates Jim

Palmer as equivalent to Maddux. "He was pretty incredible," Baylor said. "He was a good baserunner before the DH. A good hitter and can field his position."

What about a pitcher who can move a ball on the corner like Maddux's special fastball to left-handers? "Frank Tanana, the ball looked in, and you'd see it come back over," Baylor said. "You'd see that natural movement. A lot of times players think they'd scuff the ball. But you look on the tape, it has late movement."

Images of the all-time control pitchers are evoked by Hall of Famer Don Sutton.

"He has Catfish Hunter's control and Jim Bunning's movement," Sutton said. "Fergie Jenkins would be a better comparison than any of the others, though."

Bobby Cox offers up the name of two southpaws. "Whitey Ford had great control," he said. "Randy Jones probably compares more than anybody to me. On the knees and down, every pitch. Check Jones's game pitches, and they probably were low counts like Maddux."

Bunning's name is seconded by one of his old catchers, Braves coach Pat Corrales. "Jim had great control with four pitches—fastball, curve, slider and change," he said. "He could throw the ball where he wanted to throw it, when he wanted to throw it. But Greg's number one, really a master to make the ball move where he wanted."

Maddux is easily passing most of these pitchers' lifetime victory totals. The 300-win mark that Maddux once said he'd only pursue if he continued to have fun is within reach. And yet the man who can make the baseball bend to his will professes not one word about being the best ever.

It's like losing weight. You can't lose fifty pounds without dropping that first pound. Maddux approaches his craft similarly: batter by batter, inning by inning, each game its own little season. The numbers eventually add up after all the little battles are won.

"I never had a goal," Maddux said. "I pitch. I just want to pitch. If it's something that happens today that will help me tomorrow, I'll try to take advantage of it. I never really had goals. My goal was and is to find something today that will help me tomorrow."

Obviously, Maddux has found enough nuggets to make sure he's one day first among equals in the Hall of Fame.

4

THE SUPER SLUGGER

The early summer afternoon of Monday, June 22, 1998, was pleasant for any baseball watcher filing into Wrigley Field for the first-ever interleague visit by the powerful Cleveland Indians.

But for Jim Thome, the emotion was almost too good to describe. Start with heavenly. The surroundings overwhelmed the Indians slugger. Finally, he was an invited guest on the field at Clark and Addison, part of the visiting act with all the privileges of a big leaguer coming into a road ballpark. At around 3:30 P.M., more than three and one-half hours prior to the game, Thome sat alone in the near corner of the visitors' dugout, normally the manager's in-game perch. Cradling a bat, dressed in his T-shirt and uniform pants, he soaked in as much of the bucolic atmosphere as humanly possible. He gazed at groundskeepers and other ballpark workers off in the distance. He watched a few Cubs sauntering across the field to the batting cage underneath the right-field bleachers. Mostly, though, it was the kind of quiet and peaceful scene associated with the calm before the storm.

Amazement filled Thome's face, for two good reasons. He had realized a childhood dream of playing in his favorite ballpark, a dream that seemed so far away when the Indians drafted him in the thirteenth round of the 1989 draft while his favorite team, the Cubs, ignored him. He'd always drive up to Wrigley Field when the Indians came to town on the South Side to play the White Sox. But Thome's thoughts no doubt drifted a decade further back than '89, to a time when his eyes really bulged with childhood wonder. He doesn't remember the exact date, but it was probably midsummer 1979, at a time when Wrigley Field was jumping due to the presence of a tall, titanic slugger named Dave Kingman. The typical noise of the ballpark would come to a hush when Kingman strode with his lanky six-foot-six frame to the plate, aiming at houses 500 feet away on Kenmore Avenue, running north-bound perpendicular to the outside left-field bleacher wall.

One hundred-fifty miles away in Peoria, a nine-year-old Thome exulted in every Kingman at-bat he could catch on TV or radio. Kingman was his idol. What kid wouldn't want the ability to hit the ball 100 or 150 feet beyond the outfielders' furthest reach?

"Baseball was everything to me," Thome would say two years after his silent session of gazing in the Wrigley Field dugout. "We played with the tennis ball against the brick building, and I was Kingman. I liked the way Kingman hit the ball out of the ballpark. Dave Kingman was one of those guys who was all or nothing. My dad loved him. I had this obsession with Kingman."

Sitting in the dugout in '98, Thome easily could remember the trips up to Chicago to watch the Cubs and Kingman. His father, Chuck Thome, and mother, Joyce Thome, didn't have to be convinced to pack the family up in the car at 5:30 A.M. and make the three-hour drive in time to see Cubs batting practice. With the exception of Jim's brother, Randy, and uncle Art, both Cardinals fans and thus the family's black sheep, the Thome clan in the central Illinois city were avid Cubs fans.

"We'd drive up Lake Shore Drive [toward Wrigley Field] and I heard Kingman had a boat [in Belmont Harbor]," Jim Thome said. "I'd pick out all the boats and asked, 'Dad, is that Kingman's?'"

On one excursion to the Friendly Confines, the young Thome had seen Kingman enter the home dugout. The kid had an idea. When his parents briefly turned their back on their eager son, he made his move.

"I decided to go down into the dugout [in search of Kingman]," Thome remembered. "My mom and dad are standing around and I'm nowhere to be found. [Cubs catcher] Barry Foote ended up carrying me out [of the dugout]. It was a great story. It's like any kid—when they have a player they admire, they'll do anything to get their favorite player's autograph. That's how I was."

"He came out with two signed baseballs," Chuck Thome recalled of the daring dugout excursion.

Years later, Chuck noticed that Foote was working as a White Sox coach on September 1, 1991, when the South Siders played the Indians. Jim Thome was first called up to the majors three days later. Foote and Thome did not meet.

Neither did Kingman and Thome. But the roles had changed. Kingman should ask for Thome's autograph, because the idol-worshipper now has far outdone, in every way, what his old hero ever accomplished on and off the field.

Thome has now beaten Kingman's best power season in numbers, his forty-nine-homer output in 2001 exceeding Kingman's glorious 1979 campaign by one. Then he outdid himself with fifty-two homers in 2002. He has matched and in many cases passed Kingman in sheer raw power, with the ability to hit homers to dead center further than anyone else in baseball. And Thome has spread his good name throughout the game, his down-to-earth personality winning friends and influencing people in a way the often anti-social Kingman could never dream of doing.

Thome fulfilled the dreams of his friends and any baseball-playing kid nationwide. Kingman was Thome's model, but there were more prolific bashers that embryonic sluggers could emulate. Everybody wanted to be Mickey Mantle, Frank Howard, Willie Stargell, Willie McCovey, Harmon Killebrew, and a host of others in summoning up the tape measure to record their ICBM trajectories. Mark McGwire outdid them all in distance. He was like a robo-slugger come to life.

But then injuries finally got the best of Big Mac after the 2001 season. That left the likes of Sammy Sosa, Barry Bonds and, yes, Jim Thome, as his

With his high stirrups and baggy uniform, Jim Thome brings to mind the power hitters of old in both game and looks. *Cleveland Indians*

worthy successors as producers of distance classics. Factor in his high stir-rups and blousy uniform that's needed to cover his massive torso, and Thome truly looks like the throwback to the muscleman slugger that has captured the public's imagination since Babe Ruth.

Yet look beyond Thome's production and massive force placed into every swing. Kingman barely sniffed contention on any of the teams for which he played. On June 22, 1998, the Indians beat the Cubs 3-1 behind veteran Doc Gooden as 39,556 fans, including a large Cleveland contingent roaring from their seats down the lines in the upper deck, looked on. Thome already had been the veteran of two World Series at this juncture. Cleveland would go on to win yet another American League Central title in '98, a feat that had seemingly become the formerly downtrodden Indians' birthright in the 1990s.

He was now a mainstay on a contender, a feared Indians club that was diametrically opposite of the *Major League* stumblebums of Hollywood fame. Thome has garnered the respect that wasn't always a given to him, and he's known as a winning ballplayer. You could have never said the same thing about Dave Kingman.

"I think in this game you're always questioned about your ability," he said. "Maturity has made me realize you can't please everybody. There will always be someone who will say Jim Thome can't do this or that. The bot-tom line is when the year is over, I want people to say he had a solid year. How can you say all these negatives when he had a solid year?

"But I don't want to capitalize on myself. I want my team to win the World Series."

Eventually Thome had to get up from his dugout seat that afternoon in '98 and return to the clubhouse to get ready for batting practice. The memo-ries flashed by, but you could be sure he didn't just time-trip that day. He soaked up every last second of baseball experience in the dugout, and it was like an elixir. He had to fight his way to the top in the game. Now, he wasn't going to waste one moment. The special gifts that were frittered away by Kingman were going to be clasped oh-so-close to Thome and not let go without a fight.

Only a select few in history get to be a super slugger. Thome will sure savor every moment of that special tag.

◆ ◆ ◆

On July 3, 1999, at Jacobs Field, Jim Thome took one of his patented mon-ster cuts and got one of his best-ever results, if not the all-time best.

Royals pitcher Don Wengert could only make a 180-degree turn and gape. Thome launched the bomb way, way back, clearing the ballpark picnic area. The ball bounced through an iron gate onto Eagle Avenue, getting close to East Ninth Street as startled Cleveland passers-by must have wondered what fell from the sky. The blast has ranked as the longest homer ever in the history of Jacobs Field, which opened in 1994.

"That one I remember like yesterday," Thome told Bill Needle in an article in the Indians team magazine. "My back had been hurting real bad before the game, but I played, and that at-bat I kept getting real good pitches to hit. And I said to myself, if I get another pitch like the ones I'd been getting, I was going to hit it hard.

"I'd have to say that was the best ball I ever hit in my whole career."

That was saying something for Thome. While Mark McGwire took everyone's breath away with his extreme bashing, the strong boy in Cleveland was developing his own tape-measure track record. With Thome's own natural hitting style in his younger days oriented toward the opposite field, his ability to blast homers in the mid–400-foot range to center field and long blasts to left like a right-handed pull hitter began to earn raves throughout the American League.

"He's just as strong as anyone in the game. He's just naturally strong," then–Indians manager Charlie Manuel said.

There would be no performance-enhancing substances ingested or maniacal sessions in the weight room to put the extra thirty or fifty feet into his blasts.

"No supplements, not for me," Thome said. "I have my routine. I've never used creatine or power shakes. I just have a routine I have followed. And I'm not into weightlifting where it's free heat and out of whack, every day.

"Obviously you work very hard, to make sure your legs are very strong. Your legs are your firm base. Look at Mark McGwire, even Henry Aaron, their legs all were a big, solid base."

At nature's pace, Thome became as strong as players like McGwire's former Oakland "Bash Brothers" partner Jose Canseco, who has authored more than a few tape-measure blasts himself. One of those who took notice, Canseco believed Thome is one of the game's leaders in raw power.

"Consistently, I've seen him hit some tremendously long homers," Canseco said. "He's probably the most powerful left-handed hitter in the game, that's for sure. He's tremendously strong. He's a big man who has quick hands when he hits the ball. I've seen him hit a few 500-footers.

"He hits the ball to the opposite way as far as any left-hander I've seen.

He probably hits the ball to center the furthest I've ever seen for a left-hander."

Canseco has expressed his wonder to Thome himself after witnessing a gargantuan blast at Toronto's SkyDome.

"Canseco told Jim that when he hit a ball into the restaurant in Toronto, the ball was more than 510 feet," Chuck Thome, Jim's father, said.

Former teammate Ellis Burks is another believer in Thome's dominance over distance.

"Distance-wise, he hits them pretty much as far as anybody," Burks said. "[Mark] McGwire hit them out of sight; you have him in a category by himself. But Jim's right there with his natural strength. Center field, opposite way, left-center, wherever it's pitched he's going to hit it that way. He has that natural strength, that Harmon Killebrew stuff."

Thome's own attitude about his tape-measure blasts has matured through the years, along with his own role as a lineup mainstay.

In midsummer 2000, he still expressed some awe. "There are some times when I'll hit a ball and I'll be amazed," he said then. "I think that can work for me and it can work against me at times. I'm at the stage where I'll hit two or three home runs, and you get into a rhythm where you think you can hit more."

But by early 2002, he took his best blasts more in stride.

"At a younger age, I might step back after a long home run and think about it for a couple of days," he said. "Now I realize it's just another at-bat. I can't go in after hitting a long home run and say I've got it figured out, I'm going to do it again. This game is a mentally grinding game. You have to be on top of your game every single at-bat. When I hit a home run or drive in a run, I say, 'OK, it's over with, it's time to do it again.' Maturity has helped me do that."

Thome's favorite childhood ballpark also enters into his long, longball talk. He remembered a rooftop sign for the Torco oil company across Sheffield Avenue from Wrigley Field. Thome would ask his father after a vintage blast, "Was that a Torco homer?"

Chuck Thome fantasizes about the ultimate distance classic. The famed Wrigley Field scoreboard is close to 600 feet from home plate. Homers have been hit as far as halfway up the center-field bleachers, below the scoreboard. But no batted ball has ever hit the scoreboard. Roberto Clemente hit one out on the left-field side, parallel to the famed green-and-white structure in 1959. Bill Nicholson, a Cubs slugger of yore, blasted one to the right field side more than a decade earlier. As part of a promotion in 1951, Sam Snead, positioned at home plate, slammed a golf ball off the scoreboard with his best drive.

Thome, once a hopeful lifelong Indian, now will get the chance to reach the scoreboard as a visiting Philadelphia Phillie. And the wind would have to be blowing out a gale.

"It's going to be sad for me if he never hits one out there with the wind blowing out," Chuck Thome said.

Shed no tears for Jim's old man. He's got plenty of chances each season to watch his big kid conquer the far reaches of any big-league ballpark of his choosing.

◆ ◆ ◆

The fact that Jim Thome's parents, brothers and twin sister, Jennifer, make up his biggest cheering section is no surprise. He truly is a product of his family and upbringing. His values and outlook are quintessentially Middle American. Remember the old adage—if it can play in Peoria, it can play anywhere.

"I guess it's my Midwest upbringing," he once told Bill Needle in the Indians team magazine. "Those are my values. That's just who I am, nothing special. I come from a great family. But they never sat me down and said, 'This is how you should act.' They just acted the right way. I know we're role models. I know it means a lot to people if you can just give them a smile, or a hello. It could make their day better."

Thome's days were made better by the family athletic tradition that dated back two generations and the inherited athletic genes that enabled him to develop into one of baseball's top strongmen.

Three generations of Chuck Thomes went to great lengths to play sports, starting with Thome's grandfather, Charles Arthur Thome.

"He played minor-league ball for Peoria in the Three-I league," said Jim's father, Chuck (Charles Gene) Thome. "He was a third baseman. Phil Cavarretta and my dad were supposed to leave at the same time to go to Pennsylvania [a higher minor-league stop], but he hurt his back and didn't make the trip. He said Cubs fans wouldn't have heard of [third baseman] Stan Hack if he hadn't been hurt."

A little bit of Charles Arthur Thome is carried with his grandson in every game he plays for the Indians. His trademark high socks/stirrups are not some old-school fashion statement in an era when many players' uniform pants seem to drag on the ground. Rather, they honor the family forebear.

"That's for my grandpa," Thome said. "It's not try to prove anybody different. Grandpa played in Peoria. He wore his socks up. I said, 'He never got to see me play in the big leagues, and for him I'll do that my whole career.' Every day he's with me, good and bad. That's my gig, that's my deal with my grandpa."

The original Chuck Thome raised a family of softball-lovin' players who played in a popular Sunday morning league in Peoria. "It was the softball capital of the Midwest in the 1960s," the second Chuck Thome said. Older brother Art Thome was a third baseman, but Navy service cut short his athletic advancement. Chuck was a shortstop who worked the day shift as a foreman at the giant Caterpillar tractor plant in Peoria, then drove 100 miles northwest on Interstate 74 to play softball in the evening in the Quad Cities—Rock Island, Moline, and East Moline, Illinois, and Davenport, Iowa.

"It was quite a challenge to work at Caterpillar all day and then drive up there," Chuck Thome said. "Everyone in the area wanted to play up there. They had the best pitchers in the country. I did it three times a week."

Chuck's older sister, Carolyn Thome, also played for Caterpillar's women's softball team. "She had an opportunity to play in the women's pro baseball league through a tryout around 1950," he said. "She was offered a contract, but it was less than they paid at Caterpillar." Eventually, Carolyn was inducted into the Softball Hall of Fame.

Jim Thome's siblings preceded him in sports, following the family tradition. One brother, Chuck (Charles Eugene) Thome, eventually got a basketball ride to Western Illinois University. "But he didn't take it because of a girl," his father mused. Another older brother, Randy, was a left-handed hurler who along with his father pitched to the youthful Jim Thome, who at nine served as batboy for his brothers' softball team.

"Randy is the most competitive, hard-nosed guy I know, probably more competitive than my older brother [Chuck] and myself," Jim Thome said. "If my brother Randy wanted to get something done, he'd do it, no matter if he's working in his garage or whether he goes to my [hunting] lodge and does something for me. If he's going to do it, he's going to do it the right way and to the best of his ability.

"My brother Chuck had the size [six-foot-five] and the ability to be a great player. I have a little bit of both in me. I have the competitiveness and drive that Randy had, and I have the God-given ability that my brother Chuck had, along with my dad, my grandfather, and my uncle. There's a little bit of a mix of them all."

Randy Thome also taught his brother to bat left-handed. He was looking far, far ahead with the utmost confidence in the kid.

"I knew most of the parks in the majors were shorter to right field and there weren't a lot of great left-handed hitters in the majors," Randy said.

You had to project Jim Thome's passion to project him as a future big leaguer in the mid-1980s. He was a shortstop with "good, soft hands," according to his father.

"He didn't have the physical size," Randy said. "He was very little. He didn't have the frame my older brother, Chuck, had. He filled out later."

When he wasn't playing Little League and high school baseball, Thome engaged in the age-old two-man baseball game of pitching to a batter standing by a chalked-off strike zone on a school or playground wall. "I'd wear my Cubs helmet and throw the ball against the brick wall," Thome said. "I'd act like I was Andre Dawson or Ryne Sandberg. That's the game everybody calls 'fast-pitch' or 'strikeout.'"

Thome was skilled enough to become an Illinois All-Stater in both baseball and basketball at Limestone High School in Bartonville, a Peoria suburb. Basketball was a good sport for him. An off-guard, he tallied thirty-six points in a conference championship game as Limestone went 60-13 his final two seasons. He continued playing basketball at Illinois Central College, but baseball was his first love. He earned junior college All-American status. The scouts had moderate interest. The Cincinnati Reds looked at Thome. Tom Couston of the Indians began tracking him. So did the St. Louis Cardinals and Seattle Mariners. But his beloved Cubs were not hot on his trail at all.

Thome's hitting style was different as a high schooler and collegian.

"You could see the raw strength, but he was an off-field [left-field] hitter, a shortstop but slow afoot," said Rockies general manager Dan O'Dowd, who in 1989 ran the greatly-expanding Indians scouting program. "I don't see how you could have missed him. His mother and father are big people. He had strength potential. Jim was 190 pounds then, now he's 235, 240 pounds."

"He was known for opposite-field hitting," Randy Thome said. "A lot of people did pull the ball at that age. One thing scouts do miss is the drive and desire of a player. Jim had those qualities."

The Cubs, thirsting for power at then–general manager Jim Frey's behest, took Earl Cunningham, a very raw high schooler out of rural South Carolina as their first draft pick in 1989 while ignoring the kid right under their noses. Jim Thome would have practically paid the Cubs to play for them. But he never got the call, and had to wait for the thirteenth round for the Indians to finally pick him. Cleveland drafted outfielder Calvin Murray number one.

"I never thought I'd be drafted," Thome told Bob Dolgan of the *Cleveland Plain Dealer*. "I was happy. I wanted to play baseball."

Years later, Chuck Thome laughed when the Cubs' oversight was chronicled from a man with the bully pulpit.

"I got a kick out of [announcer] Harry Caray, who found out Jim was from Peoria," the elder Thome said. "He said, 'How'd that kid get away from us?'"

But perhaps it was best that Thome was not drafted by his childhood heroes. The Cubs were entering a chaotic period in management, with their farm system soon to collapse, becoming one of the worst in the game. Meanwhile, the Indians were shifting considerable financial resources into player development, both domestically and in the Caribbean. Cleveland would groom its own players, nuture them and bring them up in large numbers, ending decades of losing.

Thome would be one of those players, and he would get all the instruction he needed to make it to the majors from that revived farm system.

◆ ◆ ◆

His early seasons in the minor leagues did not give the Indians a good hint at Thome's future power potential. In fact, his ability to hit the ball the other way made him a potential batting champion—minus the speed usually required for such status.

Thome hit twelve homers in just 34 games while batting .373 at short-season Class A Burlington of the Appalachian League in 1990. Promoted to Class A Kinston, he batted .308 with four homers in 33 games. The batting feats earned Thome the Lou Boudreau Award as the minor league player of the year in the Indians organization.

Promoted to Class AA Canton-Akron, a short drive from Cleveland, in 1991, Thome continued slashing the baseball all over with an Eastern League–leading .337 mark and just five homers in 84 games before he was promoted to Triple-A Colorado Springs. There he batted .285 with just two homers in 41 games before finally reaching the majors on September 4, 1991. He played third base in Cleveland the rest of the season, waiting until the very end—October 4—to connect for his first big-league homer at Yankee Stadium. He blasted a two-run shot into the upper deck in the top of the ninth to give the Indians a 3-2 victory.

Two injures—a strained right wrist suffered in spring training and a right shoulder strain in May—hampered Thome's attempt to stick in the Indians' lineup in 1992. In two minor league stints, though, he continued to hit well over .300.

Thome's power breakthrough finally took place at Charlotte in 1993. The immortal Carlos Martinez opened the season at third for Cleveland while Thome was dispatched to Triple-A for a little more seasoning.

Former Indians manager Charlie Manuel, Charlotte's manager in '93, took an intense interest in working with Thome to unleash his long ball potential.

"The biggest change was in his hitting, and he made the adjustment at Charlotte," Manuel said. "Going from rookie ball to Double-A, he was an opposite-field hitter. He was inside-outing the ball. In Charlotte, he went 100, 125 at-bats, and he did not pull the ball.

"Many start out as straightaway hitters. Rod Carew hit the ball to left field all the time. A lot of great hitters, ones that become big hitters, start out hitting to the opposite field."

Manuel engaged in a little dispute with then–Indians player development honcho Dan O'Dowd on how to best handle Thome's development. But no disagreement existed on the player's passion for baseball.

"What we saw in Jimmy was he was a good worker, strong and power-ful," Manuel said. "We took him out to the park one day and opened him up [stance]. We had situations like man on second, nobody out, pull the ball. But at the same time, I did not want to take the fact he hits the ball to left field away from him. We'd get him up in the count, 2-and-0, 1-and-0, 3-and-0, 3-and-1, and started pulling the ball and using his strength more. We changed his style, put his back foot closer to the plate and opened up his front side."

The changed worked almost to perfection. Thome didn't lose anything in the batting average category, leading the International League in batting with .332. But he also slugged twenty-five homers in 115 games while adding a league-leading 115 RBIs. Then–Indians general manager John Hart had seen enough. Thome was recalled on August 13, 1993, homering off Texas lefty Craig Lefferts the same night. He hit six more homers in Cleveland the rest of the season.

Manuel, who was soon to join the Indians as hitting coach, would not let Thome forget his natural style even as he flexed his muscles.

"When he first came up, I'd talk to him about hitting .300," Manuel said. "He can get caught up in hitting home runs. His big years in the big leagues was when he was hitting .300."

Thome finally took over the third-base job for the resurgent Indians early in 1994. He still had some growing-up to do as a hitter, even though his 20 homers in 98 games led all American League third basemen and 41 of his 86 hits went for extra bases. Thome's overall batting average of .268 was depressed by a .167 mark (with two homers) against left-handers. Against right-handers, though, the results could be devastating to the opposition. On July 22, 1994, he slugged three homers against the White Sox at Jacobs Field, one off Jason Bere and a pair against Scott Sanderson.

Early in his career, the Indians opened up Jim Thome's batting stance, adding power while still keeping a high average. *Joyce Thome*

The strike that fractured both the 1994 and 1995 seasons hardly hurt Thome's upward momentum. Manuel's hitting advice kicked in as he climbed back to his accustomed level with a .314 average along with 25 homers. Combined with 97 walks, Thome's .438 on-base percentage ranked third in the AL.

But Thome was not at the heart of the powerful Indians' lineup, the strongest in baseball by this point. He drove in just 73 runs in 1995. Yet positioning him sixth or seventh in the lineup would turn out to his advantage. The likes of Albert Belle, Manny Ramirez, Carlos Baerga, and Eddie Murray took care of the bulk of the copious run production, taking the focus off Thome as he polished his game.

"No doubt," he said of the relieving of pressure. "I learned from tremendous players. Albert was a tremendous hitter. He was right with Manny Ramirez as the best RBI producer in the game. And you can't forget Juan Gonzalez [in 2001]. I've been fortunate to be around three legitimate top RBI guys in baseball.

"I always hit behind those guys. To be honest, it prepared me, I think, just by learning from those guys, watching those guys. It's helped prepare me for the everyday grind, for sure. What impressed me is those guys wanted to make sure they got one RBI, instead of all of them. Their mindset was get that first guy in and if I get all three or four of them, it's a bonus. I learned that style. I'll at least try to give myself up [hitting to the right side]. Will I do it every time? No. Will I get it accomplished, say, half the time? Probably."

Thome's run production would rise to nearly the level of the Belles and Ramirezes in the latter half of the 1990s while the Indians became a perennial playoff team. But the regular appearance of October baseball at Jacobs Field would not turn out to be the Promised Land as envisioned by long-frustrated Indians fans.

◆ ◆ ◆

It was only six years from the popularity of the movie *Major League*, displaying the typically woebegone stumblebums who suddenly become winners, to the advent of the real-life Indians powerhouse of 1995.

During that truncated season, Cleveland crushed all comers with a 100-44 record, leading the league in homers (207) and stolen bases (132). Albert Belle went wild in the second half to amass the then-astounding total of fifty homers. The American League Central champion Indians easily swept the Red Sox three games in a row in the Division Series. They faced a tougher task in the American League Championship Series, rallying from a two-games-to-one deficit against Seattle to win the final three games. Thome's two-run homer in the sixth inning of the pivotal Game 5 stood up as the winning run in the 3-2 victory.

But their power was short-circuited by the vaunted Braves pitching in the World Series, the first for Cleveland since 1954. Atlanta took a three-games-to-one lead, eventually winning Game 6 1-0 as Tom Glavine and Mark Wohlers limited the Tribe to one lone Tony Pena bloop single in the sixth.

"In 1995, the Braves were destined to win it," Thome said. "For us, it was all something new. Come September or October, you're in a pennant race, you're so excited, but you're so young, you don't know how to handle it. You don't know getting into the postseason what the media is like, what you have to do, what you have to turn down. You've got to remember your job is to win games. In 1995 we got caught up in the fact that we were there, instead of the fact we were going to win it."

The Indians fell short in 1996 in the Division Series against the Orioles. They were hampered by a broken hamate bone in Thome's right hand, suffered on a swing against Baltimore stopper Randy Myers in the ninth inning of Game 1. Thome managed to play the final three games with the injury, but was hampered with no extra-base hits after leading the Indians with forty homers in the regular season. Cleveland hit just .245 in the four-game series as future Indian Roberto Alomar's twelfth-inning homer in Game 4 off Jose Mesa clinched the 4-3 victory.

Despite Albert Belle's free-agent departure and the trade of Kenny Lofton to Atlanta, the stars seemed to be aligned just right for an Indians World Series victory in 1997. Thome shifted to first base as Matt Williams took over at third. The Indians had their poorest regular-season record (86-75) of their contending years, but appeared battle-hardened by now for the playoff run.

Cleveland squeezed by the Joe Torre–led dynastic Yankees three-games-to-two in the Division Series by rallying in the eighth and ninth innings to win 3-2 in Game 4, then winning Game 5, 4-3. The Indians then gained revenge for '96 by upending the Orioles in six games in the ALCS, winning Game 6 1-0 as the Orioles wasted ten hits.

But the World Series against the Florida Marlins, the National League wild-card team that had somehow upset the favored Braves in the playoffs, proved to be the keenest disappointment. Thome had two homers in the Fall Classic as the Indians forced Game 7 at Joe Robbie Stadium on October 26, 1997. In one of the more notable last-ditch rallies in World Series history, the Marlins rallied with one out in the ninth off Mesa after the Indians had nursed a 2-1 lead going into the inning. Edgar Renteria's two-out, RBI single in the eleventh eventually won the Series for the one-year wonder Marlins.

"In 1997, it was more of a crushing blow to us," Thome said. "We had it won. To be two outs away in the seventh game of the World Series, you can't get any closer, unless you're one out away."

Thome tried his best to get the Indians back to the World Series in 1998. After disposing of the Red Sox in the Division Series, Cleveland was again matched against New York. Thome slugged two homers in Game 3 as the Indians took a two-games-to-one lead. However, the Yankees came back to win the next two. The Yankees grabbed an early 6-0 lead in Game 6, but Thome's grand slam in the fifth was the big blow in a five-run Indians inning that temporarily made it close. The Yankees eventually won 9-5, and the

Indians seemed to have already taken their best shot with their powerful lineup.

In 1999, the Indians bowed to the Red Sox three-games-to-two in the Division Series, while two years later the Mariners similarly disposed of Cleveland in the first round. The increasing struggles to keep the Indians contender going was symbolized in the 2000 season, when the White Sox left Cleveland in their rear-view mirror with a June-July spree. The Indians had to stage a furious September rally just to get within hailing distance of a wild-card berth, falling short in the end.

By 2002, a rebuilt Indians roster under new GM Mark Shapiro would play very unevenly. Dreams of another World Series seemed far off in the future. But Thome would live his professional life without many reservations.

"We can't live and regret things that have happened," he said as Indians stars departed. "We have to look at the positive things, to look at now."

Looking at the present enabled Thome to adjust to an increasing mainstay role after Albert Belle's departure following the 1996 season. He found himself batting third, fourth, and fifth in the lineup.

To be sure, he had plenty of protection with the likes of Manny Ramirez, Juan Gonzalez, Matt Williams, Roberto Alomar, David Justice, and Ellis Burks batting in front and in back of him. But now he was the Indians' big left-handed bat, and he had to display more consistency in his game.

No Indian will soon touch Thome's career power numbers. Early on in his forty-nine-homer, 124-RBI season in 2001, he became the franchise's all-time home-run leader with his 243rd, surpassing Belle. Later in the season, he also surpassed Hall of Famer Tris Speaker as the Indians' all-time walks leader.

"He is the Big Kahuna, we all call him that," Burks said in 2002. "He's now out of the shadows. He's accepted that well. He's performing at a peak where a lot of guys can't touch."

Thome long ago earned the respect of opponents.

"With his makeup, he rises to the occasion," then–Athletics manager Art Howe said. "He's team-oriented, a class act."

"He's a lot smarter than people think," former Royals manager Tony Muser said. "He's a thinking man's power hitter."

Pitchers had to now devise a careful game plan to work Thome.

"Keep him off-balance," said Red Sox pitcher Frank Castillo. "Pitch him in and try to get him out with the changeup. Get him out on his front foot. He's not missing the mistake pitches anymore. He's taking advantage of everyone."

But even old hitting guru Manuel believes there's another level to which Thome can aspire.

"If he cuts down on his strikeouts, he can still improve a lot," he said. "I can see him within the next two or three years having a bigger year."

◆ ◆ ◆

Part of the mythology of the Super Slugger is his ability to "call" his shots while dedicating home runs to some sick or underprivileged kid, who then is miraculously uplifted by the timely blast. It's simply a corny piece of Americana.

A lot of that mythmaking centered around Babe Ruth, greatest of 'em all, helped along with compliant sportswriters and less-than-mediocre movies. But sometimes, in real life, there's a grain of truth to these supposedly tall tales.

With Jim Thome, it was intertwined with reality and sadness, hitting close to home with his beloved family, triumph and tragedy mixed in during his most productive summer up to that point in his career.

Emotionally, much of what Thome accomplished is thanks to older brother Randy, the resident Cardinals fan in the family. Randy's son Brandon, sixteen in 2002, naturally is one of his uncle's biggest fans while playing baseball, basketball and football at his father's and uncle's alma mater, Limestone High School. But never more so than when Brandon's life changed forever on June 19, 2001.

Lounging around the Peoria pool of friends Ryan and Aaron Lucas, Brandon, then a sophomore, dove into four feet of water at the shallow end. He never figured he'd hit his head on the bottom, but he did. Brandon was paralyzed and unconscious. He was underwater for more than a minute before his friends pulled him out and revived him.

Diagnosed with a C-5 spinal cord injury, Brandon at first could not move his arms and legs. After initial treatment in Peoria, he was moved to the Rehabilitation Institute of Chicago to start on a program trying to get movement back in his limbs. He made a little progress, actually playing catch with his father a month after the injury. But he was still paralyzed from the chest down.

Jim Thome slugged a trio of two-run homers in a 14-2 rout of the Cardinals in an interleague game on July 6. The next morning, Jim spoke via phone with his nephew.

"He told me to hit him another one," the slugger said. Sure enough, Thome blasted the first pitch he saw in the tenth inning from reliever Dave Veres for his twenty-sixth homer to beat the Cardinals 7-6.

"I guess I'm going to have to keep calling him regularly," Thome said after the game.

Visiting Brandon turned out even better for both. When the Indians made their first visit to Chicago after Brandon's injury on July 18 and 19, Jim Thome and Indians reliever Bob Wickman visited the teenager at the Rehabilitation Institute. Brandon then attended the game, unsure if his uncle would come through again. The kid was getting a little ambitious, asking this time for two homers.

Never underestimate Jim Thome, apparently. He launched a homer to center off the White Sox's Sean Lowe in the third inning. In his last at-bat, Thome came through with a blast halfway up Comiskey Park's right-field bleachers off reliever Bob Howry.

"When I asked him for two before the game, he just laughed and said, 'I'll see what I can do,'" Brandon Thome told the *Chicago Tribune*'s Scott Merkin. "When the count got to 2-and-0, I told my grandfather he was going to hit it out. I just had the feeling.

"My first reaction was to stand up because I always jump up and throw my arms up when he hits a home run. But I knew I was going nowhere. I was just so excited he had done it."

"That deal with Jim hitting homers was great for his spirits," Randy Thome said. "It's something he'll never forget."

The home run heroics had to suffice for drama in Brandon's recovery, which leveled off as another year passed.

"He's about the same now," Randy Thome said. "He's still paralyzed from the chest down. He's in therapy in Peoria. He can't wait to go and loves his therapists. The therapy is just to keep him strong, and maintain his strength and mobility. He can write. He has good bicep strength, but lacks feelings in his fingers."

Brandon Thome is welcome front row and center anytime around his uncle.

"He's a guy who liked the outdoors, likes baseball, and I told my brother whenever he can he should come and watch baseball," Jim Thome said. "The important thing for him now is to be around people. Mentally he's done a tremendous job. He's done more than anyone thought he could do."

Thome wishes he could do more for his nephew than just dedicate homers to him, hoping body, bat and ball connect in just the right sequence to produce that special long ball sound and feel at the right time. Frustratingly, he realizes all too well the limits of humanity.

"Here you are, this pro athlete, you're given a lot of gifts, and you ask why can't you give this back [the ability to walk] to him?" he asked. "Sometimes it just doesn't work out.

"You wake up today and wake up tomorrow, it can all change. With a cure, with [the advance of] technology, I would hope we can get a cure for kids with spinal-cord injuries. I contribute to the [former umpire] Steve Palermo project, do a lot with him. It's a neat deal. But when it hits home like with Brandon, it makes it more special when you do it."

♦ ♦ ♦

Don't think for a moment that Jim Thome's accomplishments, loyalty and giving nature weren't noticed by Indians fans. His personality drew them close to their hearts in a way the stony silent Albert Belle, Manny Ramirez and Eddie Murray couldn't.

No wonder 40,672 Jacobs Field fans chanted "Thome, Thome" on the night of August 16, 2001, when he celebrated the Indians' picking up his 2002 contract option by slugging two homers in a 6-1 victory over the Twins.

"I've enjoyed my time here," Thome said. "The Indians organization has given me everything. They've given me the chance to go to two World Series, to go to three or four All-Star games. They've given me the chance to make a lot of money by signing me to two long-term deals."

As a person, Thome was the same bred-in-Peoria boy as he was when he broke in with Cleveland a decade before. Every offseason, he'd repair to his hunting lodge an hour's drive southwest of Peoria in western Illinois along with friends and teammates. The only change was in his homerun production, both in numbers and distance.

"The man doesn't change," Thome said. "Your lifestyle might change, but the man doesn't change. That comes from my mom and dad. I was fortunate to live in the Midwest, to have good values. Little things rubbed off on me. My dad showed us kids you have to do hard work to achieve stuff."

In 2002, Thome and pitcher Charles Nagy were the only two Indians that were part of the original John Hart–Dan O'Dowd home-grown rebuilding process still on the Cleveland roster. The fans, who have long memories, regarded Thome as special because of this status.

Chris Freeman is assistant sports editor of the *Times of Northwest Indiana,* but the 400-mile distance to home is greatly shortened when he thinks of his Indians. He still mutters about Joe Carter's mid-1980s shortcomings under his breath, the sting of all those ninety- or even hundred-loss seasons that provided the fodder for *Major League* still lodged in his soul. So Thome's emergence as a fan-friendly super slugger will forever be appreciated.

The words thus came easily when Freeman penned his ode to Thome:

Three players have exemplified the new age of the Cleveland Indi-ans. And it's not Albert Belle, Kenny Lofton, or Carlos Baerga. It's Charles Nagy, Sandy Alomar, Jr., and Jim Thome.

Alomar Jr. came over with Baerga in the Joe Carter deal, but Nagy and Thome were the first major products of the fruitful Indians farm system. Nagy was the anchor of the pitching staff of the future while Thome was the hitter who fans got to watch come up through Class AA Canton-Akron—just an hour's drive from Cleveland—all the way to the majors.

He was supposed to be a gap-power hitter, a guy who'd hit over .300 with 20 homers a year at third base, but fans oohed and aahed over those huge forearms and mighty swing. He was a country boy, but a quiet, hard worker whom blue-collar Cleveland fans immediately iden-tified with.

When the Indians' first hopes for success were dashed in 1993 by the horrific boating accident that killed Steve Olin and Tim Crews, they got through it by pulling for guys like Thome. When the strike cut away their best season in years in 1994, bitter and disgruntled fans kept hop-ing Thome, Nagy, Alomar, and the rest of the kiddie corps could brighten their day. And when Belle, Lofton and Baerga led their domi-nant 1995 campaign, Thome quietly held his own batting sixth or sev-enth in the lineup.

By the time 1997 rolled around, Thome was at the center of every-thing. Fans cried for a move to first base after seeing his shaky defense at third, and Thome politely obliged. We never saw him work on his game, but by the time Opening Day came around, it was obvious he had done his homework. Manny Ramirez was the star in the lineup by now, but Thome was still there, the fans' hero—never the best, never the flashiest, but always one of them.

Cleveland fans may not have the tradition of New Englanders, the biting scrutiny of New Yorkers or the fervent passion of the Rocky Mountain faithful. What they have are blue-collar aspects you'd expect—faith, trust, loyalty, love. Mark Price may never have been the greatest, but he will be in Cleveland. Bernie Kosar never got his team to the Super Bowl like John Elway, but he'll never buy a beer for himself in Cleveland. And while Jim Thome moved on like all the other top Cleveland players, he will forever be revered by Indians fans. He'll always be one of them.

Such admiration registers with Thome every day of his big league career. He doesn't take his good fortune for granted, nor will he ever throw the cheers and good words written about him back at the fans and media in the manner of Dave Kingman.

"Never, ever ten years ago would I have thought I'd accomplish some of the things that I've accomplished," Thome said. "I think sometimes as players, you get eight, nine, ten years into the big leagues and you lose track of what you've accomplished, and the fact this is a great life. Whether you go good or whether you go back, you should always cherish the fact this is always a great life.

"We're blessed, to me personally, to sit out here and talk to you about our lives, how good it is."

No wonder Thome isn't eager to set a time limit on his career. He had his struggles in establishing himself as a first-rate power hitter. Now, in the style of Eternal Pitcher Mike Morgan, he'll make them tear the uniform off him before he leaves baseball. If Thome can hack it at age forty, he'll still don his high stirrups, rub some Ben Gay on the aches and pains, and go on out there.

"You play until they run you out," he said. "Whatever way you can help the club, until they say you gotta go home. I would love to [play until forty]. It's getting back to my mom and dad. Now I can give them a lot of joy and happiness in what I do. It's really a blessing to have parents like that."

The kid brother didn't do anything out of the ordinary in a sports-crazed Peoria family. He just got paid for his pleasure, and he was able to hit the ball a lot further than his kinfolk.

In the end, he played for the same quality as the others—love of the game.

"Absolutely," Jim Thome said.

Time to go. Time for a Super Slugger to go out there, rev up the swing and aim for targets outside the ballpark, to do Dave Kingman one better, again and again and again.

5

∽◦∽

THE ETERNAL PITCHER

The Arizona Diamondbacks pitchers all lined up like ducks in a row, waiting to expend some kinetic energy in spring training drills on their sun-splashed Tucson diamond one late-February morning in 2002. But one of the group, dressed in the midnight purple workout jersey, was already moving his muscles, flitting from one pitcher to another, gesturing, gossiping, being true to himself.

He was the "Mo Man," known in official records and biographies as Mike Morgan, but very much his nickname in speech, action and passion. Of course Morgan would talk to all. Of course Morgan would keep on moving and couldn't stand still. He'd been doing exactly the same thing for twenty-three years and eleven previous teams (including the same one on two different occasions). And that was the key reason why long after most of his age cohorts are pitching coaches, broadcasters, hanging around golf courses or selling insurance, Morgan had virtually an assured job in the World Champion Diamondbacks bullpen at age forty-two.

Like the shark, Morgan has to keep moving for his very existence. His jaw muscles, though, work even faster. He talks a mile a minute to his family, teammates, business associates, and inquisitive media. It's "MoSpeak," a language all its own, but a language that has a place in baseball.

"Even a court reporter might have trouble keeping up with Mike," said Diamondbacks general manager Joe Garagiola, Jr., who knows him better than most, having been his longtime agent from early in his big league career.

"When I'm not around him, that's the only time I can get a word in edgewise. He doesn't keep anything in," said wife Kassie Morgan, who has been with her husband throughout his entertaining, generation-long journey through baseball.

The run-on thoughts, slang and constant animation are just a natural part of Mike Morgan.

"I have no idea where I got that from," he said of his 78 rpm pace.

Morgan's old cell-phone voice-mail message informed the caller that he is "out rippin' some lip . . . hold on."

Could his Diamondbacks teammates of the time decipher "MoSpeak?"

"Occasionally," said reliever Bret Prinz. "It's a lot of fun talking to him. You could talk to him about anything. He's a great person having played the game for twenty-three years, to sit down and joke with a rookie like me [in 2001]. He's here to have a good time, play the game and enjoy the people around him."

That Morgan does with relish. You can't have gone where he's gone, experienced his life, played as long as he has and endured all the frustrations of playing with twelve teams—the most ever in modern-day baseball— without being a people person. Even if sometimes a universal translator is needed for communication with the Mo Man.

"Give me one friend, I'll get along with him," Morgan said, slowing down just a tad.

Every team seems to need a Morgan type, not one of the main talent, but a fellow who is combination baseball sage, court jester, and cheerleader.

"He enjoys the game, goes about the game the way you need to go about it," said Randy Johnson, Morgan's near-verbal opposite on the Diamond-backs. "He's very upbeat, a very positive person, and you want to be around people like that."

"He's an amazing guy," Diamondbacks owner Jerry Colangelo said after one season with Morgan. "He's the heart and soul of our locker room. He's just perpetual in everything he is. He's like Father Time. He hasn't lost one bit of enthusiasm. Mike's like a kid in a candy store in enthusiasm."

The Mo Man's reputation and the concept of MoSpeak precede him.

"Sandy Johnson [assistant Diamondbacks GM] got a call from a friend with the Rangers when we signed Mike," Garagiola said. "Sandy was told you're going to have an experience that everyone in baseball should have, to get to know Mike Morgan. This was one of the all-time, all-time greats to be around. You're in for a treat."

Maybe not a treat, but certainly an earful. Morgan and the game are inseparable, from the day in 1978 he was a too-green eighteen-year-old rookie, less than a week out of Valley High School in Las Vegas, starting a Sunday game in Oakland against the powerful Baltimore Orioles.

He moved on, in order, to the Yankees, Blue Jays, Mariners, Orioles, Dodgers, the Cubs, the Cardinals, the Reds, the Twins, the Cubs again (for a month), the Rangers and finally the Diamondbacks. He got a then-handsome $50,000 bonus to sign, went back to bus rides and scant meal money after he pitched in the majors out of high school, earned megabucks contracts in mid-career and was happy to pitch for $750,000 on a one-year deal in 2002.

All the while, Morgan's pitched through the administrations of five presidents along with endless losing seasons for himself and his employers. He could pitch until he's sixty, and he couldn't crack the .500 mark after he came into the 2002 season with a 140-185 record.

Morgan also kept plowing ahead through personal tragedy, including two pregnancies for Kassie that ended badly either during the season or at the start of spring training, adding to the normal stress of competition. But at the same time, Morgan always finds joy in the game and the blessings of two daughters, born later in the long journey, who gave him the green light to continue pitching.

"I'm the 'White Satchel,'" Morgan said in MoSpeak, his age and his travels being as close to the ageless Satchel Paige as millennium-era baseball will permit.

Maybe there was going to be a lucky number thirteen team in his future after the Diamondbacks cut him following the 2002 season.

But as his forty-third birthday beckoned at the end of the season, Morgan was not looking at his swan song. He can't. He's got to keep moving. It's his credo that has kept him going since Jimmy Carter and disco ruled. Always, Morgan hears the voice of his beloved father, who sired him at a young age, but also died much too young at fifty-nine. Tile-setter Henry Morgan's ultimate blue-collar philosophy is seared into his kid's soul.

"He told me to make them tear the uniform off of you," Morgan said. "The first time he said that to me was when I was eight. Once I wanted to quit, and I told him I'm going to come and lay tile with him. He said go find a job somewhere else.

"Quitters never win, and winners never quit."

Put a flannel uniform on Morgan, trim his tousled hair so that the breeze can be felt on the neck and sides of his head, and he'd have been perfect in all the bygone eras, when pitchers would take their old soupbone everywhere until they ran out of teams. Always, Eternal Pitchers such as the George Brunets, the Dick Littlefields, the Moe Drabowskys, worked the circuit going on fifteen to twenty years, always finding another job even as their skills diminished. The arm, in fact the whole body, could have been aching, the player could have felt homesick and rootless, but as long as there was baseball, they kept going. You can't stop until they tear the uniform off of you. And then you go kicking and screaming.

"The highest compliment I can pay a player is to say you could have played in any era," Garagiola said. "The '57 Cardinals, the '44 Dodgers, the '32 Cubs, put on your flannel uniform, sit down and you'd be at home. We have a number of guys like that on our team. It's no coincidence, not happenstance that we have people like that. It's a big reason why were so successful [in 2001].

"Mike Morgan is certainly one of those guys."

◆ ◆ ◆

To think that a pro athlete matched Mike Morgan in number of teams for which he played is astounding. But that's exactly what happened when guard Chucky Brown signed with the NBA's Sacramento Kings late in the 2001–02 season. Brown had previously played with Cleveland, the Los Angeles Lakers, New Jersey, Dallas, Houston, Phoenix, Milwaukee, Atlanta, Charlotte, San Antonio, and Golden State.

Still, Morgan has to be the spiritual champ, having faced 11,716 batters over twenty-one big-league seasons going into 2002. He beat out two pitchers, Bob Miller and Ken Brett, and have-bat, will-travel Tommy Davis, who each played with ten teams.

"I will make anybody's team in baseball," Morgan told Scott Tyler of *Diamondbacks Magazine* in 2000, just after he arrived in Arizona. "I don't care who it is, if you give me the baseball and give me the opportunity, I will do it."

Dick Littlefield gives Morgan a bit of a run for his money. The lefty squeezed the most travels into the shortest time, playing for nine teams in nine seasons in the 1950s. Littlefield started with the Red Sox in 1950, moved to the White Sox in 1951, split 1952 between the Tigers and St. Louis Browns and continued with the Browns in 1953. Then he split 1954 with the Orioles (the re-christened Browns) and Pirates, continued with the Pirates in 1955, played for three teams (the Pirates, Cardinals and Giants) in 1956, moved on to the Cubs in 1957 and finished with the Braves in 1958.

George Brunet and Chuck McElroy pair with Brett and Littlefield as the epitome of the "well-traveled lefty." Brunet hurled for nine teams from the 1956 Kansas City Athletics to the 1971 St. Louis Cardinals. McElroy started with the 1989 Phillies and last pitched for his ninth team, the Padres, late in 2001. He was about to match Brett, Miller and Davis in total big-league employers, but was released by the Astros midway through spring training 2002.

With the exception of McElroy, these well-traveled folks shared a common bond: pitching mostly prior to the free agent era, when all but the brightest stars had to scramble for a decent payday. And if you were labeled a "journeyman" pitcher, well, that was an apt tag. You had to travel to where the work was, hoping to out-pitch the competition in spring training or that a well-timed injury at mid-season would create an opening in spring training. Two-time batting champion Davis was a little different. He was a Dodger mainstay for half a decade before injuries slowed him. But Davis hit well enough to always find work as a complementary lineup presence, and played long enough to latch onto designated-hitter roles in the early and mid-1970s.

Morgan didn't have to chase the jobs for the income. He landed good, lifetime-security contracts by mid-career after he developed into a reliable starting pitcher. He and wife Kassie had few commitments, not owning a home for years while they split offseasons with their two sets of parents. The couple delayed trying to have children until he was in his mid-thirties and the supposed end of his career was in sight. With money salted away, a near-rural lifestyle established in Park City, Utah, and some business interests on the side, Morgan didn't have to keep seeking the next opportunity, moving to the next city, and setting a record for employers that won't soon be broken.

His reason for continuing is so simple, it's beyond old-school.

"Competing," he said. "It's a kids' game."

"He loves to pitch, he loves to compete," said first baseman Mark Grace, a Morgan buddy from their 1992–95 days with the Cubs. "Another guy like him is Terry Mulholland. They're going to keep pitching until everybody says you can't pitch anymore. There's always plenty of people who say you can't do things. That feeds Mike Morgan's motivation.

"I'll give you a good analogy. Pitching, to Mike Morgan, is like his heroin. He's addicted to pitching. It's what makes him happy. It's what Mike Morgan does and it's what he's about. He's so full of energy. It's not something that becomes a grind to him."

Morgan's fate was to be the Eternal Pitcher, on the eternal journey. Who's to say he wouldn't have had the same amount of satisfaction had he been a big-shot ace pitcher like teammates Randy Johnson and Curt Schilling? But, it should be pointed out, for all their talent and power Johnson and Schilling also have had to pack their bags, each pitching for four teams.

"Have arm, will travel," Morgan said. "I love the game. Sure, it would have been nice to be 250-150 and on my way to the Hall of Fame, to stay in one or two places my whole career.

"But my first dream was to play major league baseball. My second was to pitch in the World Series. I did both. If I was in one place, I wouldn't have had this journey. It was the way it was meant to be. It was the cards I was dealt with at birth, to sign with Oakland [and pitch in the majors at eighteen]. I wouldn't trade anything in the world for it. I wouldn't trade my career for anything.

"This whole, long journey—it's been a long and winding road with all the ups and downs—has built my character. I've learned that patience is a virtue. I respect the game. I live for today, then worry about tomorrow."

Morgan got lucky early on finding his partner in the wanderings through baseball. Demoted to Ogden, Utah, he met a teenage Kassie Kenny, certified Air Force brat, the eighth of a brood of nine children of Col. Patrick H. Kenny. Pops was a longtime veteran who graduated to test-pilot status after having served all over the world and gone "through so many sonic booms," Kassie said.

One of Kassie's brothers was an Ogden team ballboy. He invited several of the players, including Morgan, over to the colonel's house for dinner. Kassie cooked for the squad.

"The way to his heart was through his stomach," she recalled. "They loved my barbecue chicken."

Kassie Morgan was born in Japan, moved to Tehran, and came back with the team-sized group of Kennys to domestic postings in Utah, Newburgh, New York, and Albuquerque.

"I didn't know any different," she said. "It wasn't until I got into baseball where I wanted stability. But two or three times a year I can pack with the best of them, like a puzzle.

"But I look at it as it's good to be wanted. My dream come true was to have a home in Arizona in the offseason. We have that now. We were young, having fun, and had no children. We never owned a home. We'd spend two weeks in Utah [in her parents' six-bedroom home] and two weeks in Vegas [with Morgan's parents]. There, we stayed in his itty-bitty twin bed.

"It never became an issue. I couldn't take this away from him. It was difficult once—in the Dominican Republic in winter ball in 1983. It was a culture shock. I was stuck in the Dominican at Christmas. I broke down once, being away from my family then."

Sticking closer to the ground compared to his active-duty days, Col. Kenny gladly served as the Morgans' "base commander" while his son-in-law was dispatched on duty to the far-flung baseball universe.

"They used me as a permanent address," Kenny said. "I had big stacks of mail for them.

"I wish they could have settled down, sort of like they're doing today [in Arizona]. But Mike had to accept them [jobs]. I'm sure he wanted to do what I did. I always tried to steer to better assignments, better planes. I guess when you're younger, like what I did, you can get used to a transient life."

The Morgans soldiered on until he landed on his feet as an effective starter with the Dodgers and Cubs. By then, the couple figured it was safe to start a family, the logic being that Morgan would retire before their first child was in kindergarten to ensure stability of residence.

But then the first of two tragic outcomes to planned pregnancies took place in July, 1994, testing the couple's willingness to continue the baseball lifestyle. Kassie had to terminate the pregnancy in the second trimester when the fetus was diagnosed with spina bifida. A month later, the debilitating baseball strike began.

"Maybe the strike did help us out," Kassie speculated. "Maybe we could accept this and move on."

The sorrow of a failed pregnancy would revisit the family, compounded by Kassie's own life briefly hanging in the balance, at a time when the Diamondbacks' 2001 World Series win should have had a permanent afterglow on the now-settled couple. About a week before Morgan was to report to 2002 spring training in Tucson, there was celebration in their Chandler, Arizona, home over another pregnancy, Kassie's fourth.

But just as the couple planned to travel for a weekend at red-rock-ribbed Sedona, a two-hour drive north of the Phoenix area, Kassie began to feel a sharp abdominal pain. The intensity increased until Kassie, whose pain threshold was high, told her husband it seemed like a "twenty on a ten scale." Morgan did not initially call paramedics, but later wished he had. Soon he rushed Kassie to a local hospital.

"They were looking at five things, whether it might be a gallbladder or an appendix," Morgan said. "It turned out to be the worst case."

Kassie Morgan was diagnosed as suffering from an ectopic preganancy, in which the embryo was developing in a fallopian tube. She was bleeding internally. Morgan said his wife had two liters of blood (out of five in the circulatory system) in her midsection. The couple had the closest call they ever experienced. Emergency surgery saved Kassie Morgan's life.

"Kass, at thirty-nine, has led a good life," Morgan said.

The pitcher got permission to report to Diamondbacks camp late. When he showed up after Kassie was released from the hospital, he'd go through his morning workouts in Tucson, jump into his truck, race up Interstate 10 at speeds up to 100 mph and make it home to Chandler in about an hour. He'd look after Kassie and their two daughters, spend part of the evening with them, then reverse course to Tucson to a hotel room to get enough sleep before the early-morning call to the practice fields. Morgan continued the commute for about a week until Kassie felt stronger.

Their two children, both delivered via Caesarean section in the years after Kassie's failed first pregnancy, have been the couple's blessings and a major motivation for Morgan to continue pitching.

"The bottom line, my children are healthy," Morgan said. "My dad raised me to be a man, my mother's a role model. I consider myself a father, a husband and a teammate."

Mattison Taylor Morgan was born June 16, 1995, in Utah. That same day, Morgan was told by then–Cubs general manager Ed Lynch that he was being traded to the Cardinals for infielder Todd Zeile.

"That was a hard one," Kassie said. "The new baby gave him something to work for."

Mikhail Kendall Morgan was born with a little better timing, just before spring training on February 16, 1997.

"Those two are like partners in crime," Kassie said. "The kids love the baseball lifestyle."

After the kids got a mini-tour of baseball together following their dad to Cincinnati, Minnesota, back to Chicago briefly, Texas, and finally to Arizona, they got a taste of the postseason. Kassie schlepped her daughters to the 2001 playoffs in St. Louis and Atlanta in the nervous times of post–September 11 travel. "Matty asked if the plane will crash," Kassie said. The daughter of a man who would fearlessly scramble his jet to defend against an enemy attempted to carry on in the family tradition. "I was trying not to show fear to the girls," she said. "I travel with a rosary."

When Mattison and Mikhail began recognizing their father's cool profession, they informally gave him the go-ahead to continue his journey. But then Morgan was hit by a kind of aftershock to Kassie's brush with death while in spring training with the Diamondbacks.

"There was a tough one on the telephone," he said of a talk with Mattison. "She was not happy. She told a neighbor she was upset because her daddy was going to be on a road trip and she would not see him. It kind of blew me away. That's one of the reasons why Kass and I waited to have a family."

Once the games got going, Morgan was confident his kids would love the ballpark atmosphere again. Yet Mattison's plea and his wife's harrowing pregnancies have affected Morgan. He may have an emotional and verbal gear stuck in fast forward, but he does stop to take stock, gather himself, and let some of that stolid exterior crack a bit. This will be a solo shot, out of sight and earshot of all others.

"I have my down times," Morgan said. "That's the way my father raised me. I can be down in my truck going home, down in the hotel room. But to the public, my family, I try not to cry. My dad didn't cry in front of us, but behind closed doors, to quote Charlie Rich, it was different. He sobbed every now and then when no one else could see. You've got to act a little bit, and try to do that in front of your wife and kids."

But fate and physiology have not given Morgan too much reason for private tears. He could get pounded around in middle relief, he's in the record books for giving up Mark McGwire's record-tying sixty-first homer in 1998, he's got one of the poorest winning percentages of any active pitcher. The bottom line was the motivation-busting arm injury never came knocking at his door through all the decades, enabling him to keep on chuckin.'

"I have a rubber arm," Morgan said. "I never ice it after the game. I'm very proud of my longevity."

"As his career has gone along, he's become a very versatile pitcher," Joe Garagiola, Jr., said. "He can start, pitch long relief, pitch three days out of four. From a pitching standpoint, he's a very useful pitcher to have on the staff.

"He's sort of the anti-specialist."

Or as Terry Mulholland once called it, "utility pitcher." And if utility infielders who can pick up a grounder keep moving from team to team, why not their mound brethren?

Perhaps Morgan is starting a new trend. Or keeping alive a very old one. Either way, he will keep going until he's old enough to be most teammates' father.

"It was such a tough time for the Mo Man down the ladder, up the ladder, like a yo-yo," he said. "The struggles at the early times made me better at the late times. I had a million-dollar arm with a ten-cent head. I learned.

"It wasn't an easy road. Stops, bus rides, planes, winter ball, 'B' games in spring training where you get up at six. 'Invited to camp, invited to camp.' It was perseverance, not letting the game get the best of me."

"I had character I had to develop. I got it from my dad. He emphasized 'team, team, team.' I have a passion, more of it now than when I was younger. I took it for granted then. Not anymore.

"I'm very thankful to have spent one day in the major leagues."

◆ ◆ ◆

Morgan's long, strange journey began thanks to the combination salary skin-flint and P. T. Barnum promotional philosophies of then–Oakland Athletics owner Charlie Finley, whose franchise entered into a serious state of decay as free agency began to envelop the baseball landscape in the late 1970s.

He had come from the ultimate blue-collar background. Father Henry Morgan had migrated west from Kentucky to Visalia, California, to find work in the late 1950s. "He dropped out of high school as a sophomore and got my mom pregnant with me when she was sixteen. He was seventeen," the younger Morgan said.

Mike Morgan was born in Tulare, California. Henry Morgan then set out with his teenage bride and their baby in another search for work in Las Vegas. "I rode in the car in a five-gallon bucket with sponges around me," Morgan said.

From day one, he was very serious about playing baseball, almost to the exclusion of everything else. "I told my second-grade teacher I wanted to be a ballplayer," he said, remembering how he had to repeat that level of school.

All the while, Henry Morgan tried to teach his son some values to which he adheres today.

"He taught me never to drink or smoke," Morgan said. "I never tried a cigarette. My dad would give you the shirt off his back. We were buddies [because of the close age difference]."

Helping fulfill the baseball dreams of his father, Morgan eventually passed enough classes to get to Valley High School in Las Vegas, later the alma mater of Greg Maddux. In his senior year in 1978, he had a 7-1 record, 0.68 ERA and 111 strikeouts in just 72 innings.

By '78, battered by rising salaries, Finley had totally eviscerated his front office and scouting staff. He relied heavily on the pooled reports of the Major League Scouting Bureau and the same word-of-mouth network that had landed talent for him in the past.

Morgan recalls working in the landscaping business when he wasn't pitching. Toiling in a Vegas gated community, he mowed the lawn of a "Dr. Friedman." Through that connection, Finley heard about the hot high school pitcher. Henry Morgan soon got a call that his son was earmarked as Finley's number one pick for '78. The scouting report on Morgan stated he had an extraordinary major league fastball and a high school curve. "I need coaching on my curve, and also on how to hold runners on base," the teenager said at the time.

The elder Morgan acted as his son's agent. All parties agreed as part of the negotiations that Mike Morgan would start out his career in the majors.

"Forty-man roster, in the big leagues, we got a deal," Morgan said of his $50,000 signing bonus, which included a guaranteed big league minimum salary of $21,000 even if he was eventually sent to the minors. The kid pitcher would use part of the bonus to buy himself a BMW along with carpeting and drapes for Henry and Nellie Morgan, his mother.

Mike Morgan graduated from Valley High on Monday night, June 5, 1978. The next day, Finley drafted him fourth in the country, after Bob Horner (Braves), Lloyd Moseby (Blue Jays), and Hubie Brooks (Mets). Picked after Morgan were such players as Kirk Gibson (twelfth, Tigers), Tom Brunansky (fourteenth, Angels), and Rex Hudler (eighteenth, Yankees). Mel Hall was taken in the second round by the Cubs.

Finley desperately needed a gate attraction for his bargain-basement team. The Athletics were an early-season surprise, staring out 32-24 in first place with the likes of Miguel Dilone, Mitchell Page, Wayne Gross, and Jeff Newman in the lineup. Never a strong draw in their first decade in Oakland, the crowds were underwhelming even by A's standards. They drew just 3,323 fans for a Friday night, June 9, game against powerful Baltimore. Just 11,422 showed up the next day with Jim Palmer pitching for the Orioles.

Finley thus slated Morgan for a Sunday afternoon, June 11, start to boost the gate, despite his own reservations. "There is a danger of him getting his head knocked off," he said at the time. But he was merely recycling one of his old ideas. Finley had signed high schoolers Lew Krausse in 1961 and Catfish Hunter in 1965, sending them directly to the big leagues without minor league seasoning.

Morgan was wowed by the treatment Finley accorded him arriving in the Bay Area. He was a kid fallen into the cookie jar.

"Here I am riding in a limo after riding in the back of a pickup truck," Morgan said. "I'm in a limo at the airport with M. C. Hammer [then known by his real name, Stanley Burrell, Finley's teenage gofer who was actually named as a club vice president] and Bobby Hofman. I'm wined and dined in San Francisco and sitting in Finley's box."

The pressure built on Morgan as the first pitch neared. The night before, he fielded a phone call in his hotel room. "They said, 'You better win, we laid $100 on you,'" Morgan said at the time. "They also said they'd hit me for some of my bonus money when I got back to town if I didn't do it for them." He recalled being "nervous at the ballpark" with a host of high school teammates looking on in the Oakland Coliseum.

In the actual game, Morgan did not embarrass himself, drawing a big ovation from the crowd of 17,157 who arrived to check out the hoopla. The Orioles scored on him in the first as he walked leadoff man Larry Harlow, gave up a single to Billy Smith, then Harlow scored on two infield grounders. He gave up an unearned run in the third, then Lee May slugged his twelfth homer of the season in the eighth. Morgan allowed ten hits and five walks,

Mike Morgan pitched for the Oakland A's right out of high school, going 0-3 before being sent back down to the minors.
Nellie Morgan

but did not strike out a batter. The winnable game went for naught as opposing pitcher Scott McGregor pitched a six-hit shutout.

"He did a good job," McGregor said after the game. "But I don't agree with what the A's are doing. It's just too tough to come right out of high school and pitch in the majors."

McGregor's logic was obvious. After two more forgettable starts (0-3 record overall with a 7.30 ERA), Morgan was optioned to Triple-A Vancouver on June 23 for the rest of the season. He would resurface for a truly horrible A's team in 1979, going 2-10 with a 5.94 ERA. He would not don the green and gold uniform ever again.

"I was rushed," Morgan said in another century, in an understatement.

He was fortunate, indeed, that his Oakland experience did not totally derail his career. Not only was he thrust into the majors long before he was ready, but Morgan hardly learned much in the stripped-down A's farm system of the time. He might have been better off going to junior college, then signing with another organization a year or two later.

"Unfortunately for Mike, at eighteen he probably was not the most mature eighteen-year-old around," said Joe Garagiola, Jr. "Couple that with the fact you could have not found a worse player development system in those days. It would have been tough anyway for high school pitchers to make the jump to the big leagues. Then Mike went to the minors, a system that, in terms of player development and support, was totally inadequate. It was a double-whammy. That minor league system would have been tough for the most mature young player, much less for someone who still had some growing up to do."

Former Cubs general manager Larry Himes also believed Morgan was hurt badly by his premature promotion by Finley. Himes would grant Morgan his best-ever contract, a four-year deal with Chicago in late 1991 that was "one year and several million dollars beyond" what the Dodgers had offered, according to Garagiola, who negotiated the deal.

"He absolutely wasn't ready [in 1978]," Himes, now an Orioles scout, said. "When I saw him pitch in high school, he was one of the top pitchers in the United States. But to take him out of high school and bring him directly to the major leagues with Oakland was absolutely terrible for his career. It set him back, as far as his maturity and consistency, three to four years, maybe more than that."

Morgan recognizes that Finley almost ruined his career.

"I thought, If I could go back to '78, '79, '80, wipe that off my bubble gum card, and use all those years for rookie ball, it would have made my career different," he said.

Morgan said a lot of optimistic things after his ballyhooed first start. "I wouldn't mind going for the Cy Young one of these years, being a twenty-game winner," he said. He would never achieve such goals.

But he was perfectly prescient about one other vow.

"I've got a lot of baseball left," Morgan said. Sometimes you do get what you ask for.

♦ ♦ ♦

The Oakland experience was mostly wasted time for Morgan. But it did provide an unexpected benefit—a generation-long relationship with Garagiola, who as his agent would help shepherd him through a lot of choppy waters, and now is a kind of patron as Diamondbacks GM.

Garagiola met Morgan through his agenting work for Athletics reliever Dave Heaverlo, one of the first shaven-headed athletes in the majors. Heaverlo also was the A's player rep.

Braves slugger Bob Horner, drafted number one ahead of Morgan in 1978, had filed a grievance, protesting Atlanta's plans to cut his salary in spite of the player union's contention that his signing bonus was part of his salary.

"One day in talking to Heaverlo, I told him you've got a guy on the team in the same position as Horner—Morgan," Garagiola said. "Dave said why don't you explain it directly to Morgan, that he didn't have an agent. Dave introduced me to Morgan, who said he didn't fully understand what I was saying, but would I like to be his agent.

"That was the beginning of one of the more special relationships I've had in my life."

Garagiola would not represent any player who had as eccentric a career as Morgan's. The then-agent would not duel long with the A's. Only two and one-half years after his ballyhooed drafting by Charlie Finley, Morgan was sent packing to the Yankees in a November 3, 1980, deal for infielders Fred Stanley and Brian Doyle. He now was in the personnel meat grinder that George Steinbrenner passed off as stability for the Yankees in the early 1980s. A year at Double-A Nasvhille in 1981 was followed by a mostly full-time stint in the Yankees rotation. Morgan was 7-11 with a 4.37 ERA, a record that made the Bronx Bombers management of the day restless. The Yankees packaged Morgan with two other notables—first baseman Fred McGriff and outfielder Dave Collins—to the Blue Jays in exchange for pitcher Dale Murray and outfielder Tom Dodd on December 9, 1982.

McGriff's career was soon on the ascendancy, but Morgan found himself in limbo with Toronto. He was taught a lesson in humility after developing a larger-than-normal ego. He was 0-3 with a 5.16 ERA in sixteen games as he was shifted to relief, before enduring one of his very few bouts with arm trouble, a nearly two-month disabled list stint due to tendinitis in his right shoulder. Morgan was outrighted to Triple-A Syracuse, where he was 13-11 in twenty-eight starts, for the entire 1984 season.

"That was a wake-up call," Morgan said. "I thought I was bigger than the game and the two best people in our business, Bobby Cox [then–Blue Jays manager] and Pat Gillick [then the Jays' GM] told me I was not that big. At the time I did not believe them, but when I look back at that time, they were right."

But the Blue Jays honchos didn't believe in Morgan's future enough to keep him. He was made available in the Rule 5 minor league draft on December 4, 1984. The Mariners organization selected him. He made the parent club's starting rotation out of camp, but suffered a severely pulled right groin muscle in his second start on April 16, missing the rest of the year.

"All that time I spent on the disabled list during those years might add up to three, four years in the big leagues," Morgan said. "It ended up saving on my body. It's why my arm and body are the way it is. I was able to train, train, train on the disabled list."

Morgan came back to pitch full-time in the Mariners rotation, but he labored in obscurity with Seattle, a poor team and the majors' most remote franchise. Perhaps playing in the Pacific time zone out of sight from the mainstream of the game was best for his reputation—he went 11-17 and 12-17 in 1986 and 1987, giving up 488 hits in 423⅓ innings overall.

The offseason trade market beckoned for Morgan again after 1987. He was dealt to the Orioles for pitcher Ken Dixon. He went from one prodigious loser to another. He was swept up in the O's record-breaking 0-21 start in 1988. Morgan went 1-6 with a 5.43 ERA splitting his time between the rotation and bullpen. But the injury bug bit again. He lost almost three months due to right calf and foot problems.

His confidence wavering again, Morgan got a break when he was traded to the Dodgers for outfielder Mike Devereaux in spring training 1989.

"Going into that season, he was a long shot to make the Dodgers' staff," Garagiola recalled. "He had pitched for Phil Regan in winter ball, and had a tremendous record. That put a very positive image in Regan's mind and he let the Dodgers management know about it. That allowed him to come to Vero Beach in great shape. He had a lights-out spring training. Mike was dazzling."

Morgan pitched better than ever in '89, although it was not reflected in his won-lost record. He was 6-11 with a 2.74 ERA in 19 starts (8-11, 2.53 ERA overall). The Dodgers averaged just 1.45 runs in his 19 starts.

"He had the worst pitcher's luck imaginable," Garagiola said. "He always seemed to be out there when the Dodgers forgot their bats."

Morgan was taking losses, but making gains in his pitching mechanics at the same time. Dodgers pitching coach Ron Perranoski made one adjustment after taking a look at Morgan's motion and legwork. He shifted the pitcher's feet from the right to the left side of the rubber, perhaps again proving baseball is a game of inches.

"He got me once on the mound," Morgan said. "I had always thrown from the right side of the rubber, going back to Little League. 'Perry' had me move to the far left side of the rubber. Now I had more control of pitches through the strike zone."

Morgan still had awful luck in the won-lost column with an 11-15 record in 1990, but he tied for the National League lead with four shutouts. Finally, his fortunes turned in 1991. Despite more tough luck as the 2-0 complete-game loser when the Expos' Dennis Martinez spun a perfect game on July 28 at Dodger Stadium, he enjoyed his first big league winning record with a 14-10 mark and 2.78 ERA. Morgan gave up only 197 hits in 236⅓ innings.

The three years of effective pitching enabled Garagiola to negotiate Morgan's aforementioned best-ever deal, a four-year contract with the Cubs, for 1992. Attracted by the presence of fellow Valley High School product Greg Maddux, Morgan did not disappoint. While Maddux won his first Cy Young Award with a 20-11 record and 2.18 ERA, Morgan was a capable side-kick with a 16-8 mark and 2.55 ERA. That ERA figure ranks fourth best for one season among all Cubs starting pitchers since World War II after Dick Ellsworth's 2.11 in 1963, Maddux's '92 mark, and Bill Hands' 2.49 in 1969. Morgan also earned National League Pitcher of the Month honors for May with a 5-0 record and 2.32 ERA. A mediocre Cubs lineup doomed Maddux's chances to win 25 games and Morgan's to achieve his only 20-win season. Still, he seemed to find a home in Wrigley Field with frequent pitcher-friendly winds and high grass.

But one thing Morgan was not was a staff ace. The Cubs badly bungled Maddux's negotiations for a new five-year, $25 million contract before the '92 season, and could not recoup any ground in subsequent talks. Maddux fled as a free agent to the Braves, putting pressure on Morgan to be the Cubs staff's number one pitcher. Soon, Morgan confided he would not have signed with the Cubs had he known Maddux was going to leave.

Morgan's effectiveness and health abruptly declined over the next two seasons in Chicago. In fact, he would start a string of seven straight seasons in which he spent time on the disabled list. Despite a better lineup in 1993, Morgan was 10-15 with a 4.03 ERA without the safety net of Maddux lead-ing the rotation. He was hobbled by a sprained right knee at midseason. Then, in 1994, the season degenerated into chaos. Morgan reversed the clock to his 1980s nightmares with a 2-10 record and 6.69 ERA. He had three stints on the disabled list with an elbow inflammation, migraine headaches and a lower back strain before the season mercifully ended due to the strike.

When baseball resumed nearly a month late in 1995, Morgan lost addi-tional time due to shoulder inflammation. Only four starts after he was acti-vated, he was traded to the Cardinals for Todd Zeile. Morgan was 5-6 in 17 starts the remainder of the season for a mediocre Cardinals team.

He did not last long under new manager Tony La Russa in 1996. Getting off on the wrong foot with La Russa with a sore right shoulder in the spring, he did not pitch until nearly midseason, going 4-8 with a 5.24 ERA in 18 starts. Finally, La Russa and Cards general manager Walt Jocketty decided to cut the cord. The meeting at which Morgan was handed his walking papers is still seared in his memory, and he carries the note La Russa wrote as a reminder in his Nike bag.

"It was a slap in the face," Morgan recalled. "Tony said in a roundabout way that my career was over. I came to the park to work and see what was going on. They called me in. Tony looked at the wall, they didn't want to give you eye contact. Walt [Jocketty] was doing the talking. I hit the road. Being released, though, that doesn't mean your life was over."

Not with the Eternal Pitcher. Morgan picked himself up and signed with the Reds on September 3, 1996. He was 2-3 with a 2.30 ERA in five starts, getting a chance to gain some revenge by pitching against the pennant-hunting Cards, but losing 2-0 to Todd Stottlemyre. Morgan then continued in the Reds rotation in 1997, going 9-12 in 30 starts. The season was marred by another disabled list stint, this time a strained rib cage.

With the Reds always counting their pennies, Morgan was on the move once again after 1997, signing as a free agent with the Twins. Two more disabled list visits, this time another rib-cage shutdown and a strained abdominal muscle, punctuated his eighteen-game Minnesota tenure in which he was 4-2. His time in the Northland went by seemingly in a blur. The Cubs, desperate for starters due to then-rookie Kerry Wood's sore elbow in the final month of the '98 season, got Morgan back via a deal for a player-to-be-named later on August 25.

Morgan had to employ his stalwart-pitcher persona to survive his cameo return to Chicago. He was tagged for Mark McGwire's sixty-first homer on Labor Day in St. Louis, then was left in to soak up a seven-run Brewers third inning in his next start, the better to save a tired Cubs bullpen. But Morgan got one benefit out of the quickie trip to Chicago: his first-ever postseason appearance, pitching one and one-third scoreless innings in relief over two games as the Braves swept the Cubs in the NL Division Series.

But the Cubs had no use for Morgan afterward. Once again, he became a free agent, this time signing with the Rangers. Morgan went 13-10, but had a hefty 6.24 ERA while giving up 184 hits in 140 innings. After yet another turn on the disabled list (right shin bruise), he faded badly in the second half with just one victory in the final two months.

Was he running out of both teams and time by this point? Not with former agent Garagiola holding forth as GM and another former boss from his

Orioles days, Roland Hemond, also on hand as a senior executive with the Diamondbacks. Once again, Morgan would re-invent himself as a pitcher while defying the ravages of time, injuries and baseball politics.

◆ ◆ ◆

It's not easy to get Mike Morgan to say three bad words about all the cities in which he's played and the organizations that have always given him a chance to pitch.

The following is a transcribed (getting writer's cramp taking dictation of MoSpeak) rating of each city and team, in chronological order:

Oakland (1978–79): "I was eighteen, and I liked everything about it. It had been a dynasty before. This is a great opportunity, and the Bay Area was great for a kid out of high school. The downfall of the whole deal was that I was rushed. But it was a great place to start a career."

New York Yankees (1982): "Going to the Yankees, there was all this great tradition. Can I say anything else? It's the greatest sports franchise of all time. It was the only place I could get around without problems. Any other place, I'd get carded. There were no bad moments. I remember all the window-washers coming wanting money while you were driving. Kassie was homesick, but she was only nineteen."

Toronto Blue Jays (1983): "A great place to visit, a fun place to live. My stop was short. Bobby Cox and Pat Gillick handled it professionally. Great players, great organization. Years later, they offered me a good deal, but I signed instead with the Cubs. I would have had two [World Series] rings."

Seattle Mariners (1985–87): "Land, trees, water, hunting and fishing. I'd fly-fish for steelheads before I'd got to the ballpark. Great seafood restaurants. Seattle was a great stop for the Mo Man. They fired Chuck Cottier, one of my favorites. Phil Regan [pitching coach], I loved to death. The downfall was the owner [George Argyros] never backed the team, and moved people out when they wanted to make money. They had Mark Langston, Mike Moore, Jim Presley, Alvin Davis—good family men."

Baltimore Orioles (1988): "The ugliest time until 1994. They fired Cal Ripken, Sr., and Frank Robinson is in the job and can't get out of his office with a bad back. Sure, we lost, it was terrible, but it still was a great time. I met Cal Ripken, Jr., and Eddie Murray. We had a Super Bowl party at Ripken's house. I bought a place nearby and it was good hunting and fishing. I liked ol' Memorial Stadium—that was tradition."

Los Angeles Dodgers (1989–91): "Where it all turned around for the Mo Man. Ron Perranoski was the pitching coach and moved me over to the far left of the rubber. I'm around Orel Hershiser, Don Drysdale, Sandy Koufax.

I'm throwing at the strings in Vero Beach. It's a wake-up call for me. Hershiser taught me the 'comebacker' pitch in '89, and showed me to point the fingers on the seams toward the target. Tommy Lasorda was loud and flamboyant. There was traffic and smog. It took an hour and a half to get there to Dodger Stadium, twenty minutes to get home. But there was nothing negative about the place."

Chicago Cubs (1992–95; 1998): "My numbers at Wrigley Field were probably the best in my career [21-15, 2.75 ERA]. Even when the wind was blowing out, my ball moved more. A great mound and high grass. I shut out the Pirates over eight innings with the wind blowing out fifty mph. Day games, 1:20, 2:20, you have a light breakfast and get to the park. It was great to be around the fans, they were so close to the action. And I walked to work on Waveland Avenue. Great food in Chicago. I don't know why that team couldn't win a division title. That was my favorite place to pitch other than Arizona. If they could have won the World Series there, it would have been the perfect life."

St. Louis Cardinals (1995–96): "The fans, all dressed in red, the Clydesdales, I like that kind of living. They were country people, good wholesome people. Everybody knows everybody, everybody calls you a friend. But I got released by Tony La Russa."

Cincinnati Reds (1996–97): "The Reds called me after my release in St. Louis and asked me to pitch. I went over there and pitched against the Cards in a pennant race. [Todd] Stottlemyre beat me 2-0. I pitched good in 1997. I remember the catfish and black-eyed peas."

Minnesota Twins (1998): "I enjoyed playing the game for Tom Kelly. He made you play the game right, threw batting practice, and hit fungoes. It was the land of 10,000 lakes and good fishing. I didn't get to all 10,000, but I got to a few. But there was a black cloud over the Metrodome, where you had to go to work. Both teams had to play there. You couldn't see the ball when it goes up and when it comes down."

Texas Rangers (1999): "One of my favorite states. Just good people, cowboys and blue collars. Good food, hunting and fishing. It could have been nice if it had a big ol' fan over our heads. I hit a wall in August. They said he's old, he's had it. I was sent to the bullpen. I met some great people. We won the division, and I loved to go to the ballpark."

Meanwhile, Kassie Morgan was almost as effusive in her praise of the stops she made with her husband in his post-Oakland days. She learned to adapt, having been an Air Force brat and traveled the world.

"We are a team," she said of her and her husband. "Let's make the best of it."

Kassie had some capsule ratings, too:

"The Dodgers were the number one organization because of the O'Malleys," she said. "Chicago was a fun city, but I had more fun in New York. The wives took me under their wing. We had barbecues at people's houses, where we saw Ken Griffey, Jr., and Goose Gossage's kids. We lived in the same complex as the [Dave] Righettis.

"I loved Seattle, loved Baltimore, and there were good people in Minnesota. Texas, there was nothing better than Southern hospitality. Cincinnati? One of the cabdrivers there called it 'Cincinnasty.'"

Now the couple is thrilled to call the Phoenix area home. But Morgan still has an occasional case of the wanderlust. He'll sometimes make the all-day drive to hometown Las Vegas to visit his favorite barber.

◆ ◆ ◆

Mike Morgan's ego was long-buried by the time he reported to Diamondbacks camp in the spring of 2000. Owner Jerry Colangelo wanted to win now, so he gave Joe Garagiola, Jr., the green light to sign a host of veterans, even if they came with a hefty payday due.

"He can start, [long] relieve, short relieve, come back the next day, and he's always volunteering to get the ball," Roland Hemond, then a D-Backs senior executive, said. "He's been a grinder, a competitor and a great teammate whenever he's on the ballclub.

"Players admire his spunk and his savvy. He improves out there. He invents pitches to get a hitter out."

Sure enough, Morgan fit in well with the veteran mix, appearing in sixty games—all but four in relief—in 2000. When he made his Arizona debut on April 5, 2000, he became only the twenty-fifth big leaguer (nine pitchers) to appear in four decades. Showing his willingness to do anything as a pitcher, he earned saves in each of his first three appearances.

Morgan won over Bob Brenly, who took over as manager in 2001.

"Whatever role we put him in, he never blinks an eye," Brenly said. "He never complains. You want me to start today and relieve tomorrow, fine.

"The most important attribute Morgan has—other than the obvious great physical condition, great arm and great head on his shoulders—is he knows what it means to be part of a team. In this day and age, sometimes that gets lost a little bit. A guy comes to the majors with a little hoopla, sometimes he sets himself a little apart from the other twenty-four guys. Mike has never and will never do that. I don't think there's a selfish bone in his body. That's what makes him so valuable for a team."

Brenly backed up his praise with action when the Diamondbacks made their run at the 2001 postseason. The ageless right-hander had lost even more time to injury. He was out most of the first three months with a strained right arch and did not return until July 22. But Brenly used Morgan in critical set-up roles down the stretch. From August 10 to September 26 he gave up just one earned run in sixteen and two-thirds innings. He got two critical eleventh-inning outs in a September 29 tie game against the Dodgers, setting the stage for Luis Gonzalez's game-winning homer in the bottom of the inning.

Morgan was called on three times in the Division Series against the Cardinals, allowing one run overall. He worked twice in the National League Championship Series against the Braves with a shakier yield of three runs.

Finally, his time had come after twenty-three years when Brenly used him in Games 1, 3, and 5 of the World Series against the Yankees. In the latter appearance, Morgan retired all seven men he faced after entering with the scored tied 2-2 in the ninth. He was ready to pitch in extra innings in the climactic Game 7, but Gonzalez's soft single to left settled matters. The sight

In his fourth decade in the majors, Mike Morgan finally brought home a World Series ring with the Arizona Diamondbacks in 2001. *Arizona Diamondbacks*

of Mike and Kassie Morgan and their daughters hugging and giving prayerful thanks on the mound at Bank One Ballpark won't soon be forgotten.

Viewers of the Fox Sports Network got a healthy dose of "MoSpeak" when Steve Lyons and Kevin Kennedy corraled the entire Morgan family for an on-field interview amid the postgame celebration.

"I came in and told the boys I'm going to outlast 'em," Morgan said at maximum warp. "I'm still a starter by heart. It was tied, and if I had to come in, I'm going to outlast whoever they had. My dad raised me to just go one pitch at a time, one hitter, outlast people. That's our family gig, outlast."

Then he put his own journey into proper perspective.

"Ernie Banks and the guys I met in Chicago, I've been on every team that would like to have one of those things," he told Lyons and Kennedy. "It's overwhelming to win in this fashion. I've had a lot of journeys. It's special, believe it, it's very special."

Kassie Morgan got a few words in edgewise as her two daughters hugged close. Then came more "MoSpeak," but Lyons got the word from his director he had to move on. They cut off the Mo Man in his greatest moment of glory.

No sweat. A dream had been achieved, and there might be a few more to come.

True to form, Mike Morgan did not go around flashing his World Series ring when he received it in a pregame ceremony at Bank One Ballpark on April 2, 2002.

"I don't even wear my wedding ring," he said. "I take it off, put it on. I had one lost, another one stolen. I don't want to go through three World Series rings. I'll set it up on the mantel, with a picture of my wife and two kids saying a prayer on the mound. If the kids want to wear it, I'll let them wear it."

But Morgan does not have to be adorned with special jewelry to really symbolize a career-long quest for the best.

"It speaks to Mike Morgan's character that despite all those hurdles to climb, he's had a wonderful career in the big leagues," Joe Garagiola, Jr., said. "And he has now added to his resume the line, 'World Champion.'"

◆ ◆ ◆

Mike Morgan's fiftieth birthday is October 8, 2009.

He's thinking of giving you odds that he might be pitching in the postseason on that day.

"Can I play until I'm fifty? I think I can do it," he said. "I've been throwing the palmball in the bullpen for two years, but I haven't used it in a game. I told the guys when the heater gets below 86 and a quarter [mph], I'm going to bring out the palmball and it will get me over the hump until 2010. I've tried everything else in the book, from the split to the fosh. I've tried to tinker around with the knuckleball, but I haven't been able to get the concept."

The concept that all around Morgan get is that he's irrepressible. Don't bet against him. If he says he'll go to fifty, who can deny him?

"I don't know why not," Brenly said. "His stuff has changed over the years. There was a time he was a very hard thrower early in the big leagues. He learned he needs to pitch differently to get people out. Some people can't make that change. We've seen him make adjustments from outing to outing. One time, sinkers and ground balls. Next time he'll throw sliders. He always has a game plan. If 'A' doesn't work, he'll go to 'B.' If 'B' doesn't work, he'll go to 'C.'

"And he's not afraid. He has a genuine love of baseball. I don't see any reason to think he couldn't pitch until age fifty."

"If I get the pink slip and I know I can't get 'em out, I'll stay in it," Morgan said. "I'm sure it's going to happen eventually."

At that time, Garagiola may just point the freshly-retired Morgan to a part of the spring training complex in Tucson and tell him, "Be yourself."

"The ideal is he could come to spring training for a month because I don't think he will want to commit himself to a full-time position," Garagiola said. "Give him a group of the young kids, a fungo and a bag of balls, take them over to the back field and the Mo Man will talk to them about what it takes to play in the big leagues."

"I'll just feed the [pitching] machine and work up a sweat," Morgan said.

The young pitchers will work up a sweat and get out of breath if their instructor gets up to speed verbally and tells them of all the places he's been, the men who were his teammates, his wins and even more losses. The story will be so fantastic they scarcely will believe him.

But believe it they must, because the Eternal Pitcher had always believed in himself.

6

⚬⚬⚬⚬⚬

THE UTILITYMAN-
TURNED-MANAGER

Junedale Field offered a healthy open space in what appeared to be a halfway-decent Glen Park residential neighborhood on the southern edge of Gary, Indiana. But on this sultry, near ninety-degree Monday afternoon during the All-Star break in 2001, not a kid was to be seen throwing or batting a baseball around, not until the first arrivals in an organized youth clinic started trickling in.

A sign at the park fieldhouse wall proclaimed cooperation between U.S. Steel, once Northwest Indiana's dominant employer, and the city of Gary to build a bigger and better field. But there was little evidence of recent work, a symbol of the area's steel industry decline in recent decades. The few structures appeared rusty and unused. Grass grew on the infield, while the field itself could have used a lawnmower.

Thirty years previously, Junedale Field was the mecca of youth baseball all over Gary, the prime field on which championship teams proved themselves. The park was finely manicured then, better than the inner-city fields further north. Young players truly had arrived when they got to play a qualifier at Junedale for the Indiana state Little League championship, as Lloyd McClendon's Gary team had done back in 1971. McClendon had tossed a shutout and slammed a homer for the game's only run against East Glen Park, part of an amazing stretch of heroics that led his team to the championship game of the Little League World Series in Williamsport, Pennsylvania.

"Believe me, it wasn't like this," McClendon said as he scanned the mangy conditions of the diamond. "We qualified for the state championship here. Competition in the city was pretty tough. Certainly to get to this ballpark and play in the semi-state, you had to be pretty talented.

"It's really sad, because there's some opportunity to have these type of facilities, and it doesn't take a lot of work to get them in shape."

McClendon would return to Junedale on this afternoon, but this time as a mentor to another generation of ballplayers, albeit smaller in numbers than in the first Nixon Administration. His MAAC (McClendon Athletes Against Crime) Foundation, operating in its tenth year in northwest Indiana, was holding one of two baseball camps at the park. And on this day, he returned as one of the biggest sports names to come out of Gary. McClendon was taking a break from his job as rookie manager of the Pittsburgh Pirates, and was lucky enough to spend six days at home in nearby Merrillville. The Pirates had just played a three-game series in Chicago with the White Sox, but McClendon is so committed to his annual clinics that he'd have shown up even if he had to fly in late the night before from a road trip.

"We really enjoy it, because of the fulfillment I get," McClendon said, mopping his brow as he pulled up in his car after the twenty-five-some players had arrived. "The only drawback is it's so hot. It's never been quite this hot. This morning's clinic [two miles south in Merrillville] took a lot out of us. But you get some ice tea and get recharged."

With a dual message of keeping kids off the streets and away from drugs, and teaching some baseball fundamentals, the MAAC Foundation invited high school and Senior League players from Gary and Merrillville. McClendon, in the midst of myriad frustrations in a Pirates season gone bad, hadn't lost his zest for teaching. He appeared at the front of a train of players demonstrating leadoffs from second base, then attended to other fundamentals as the heat of the afternoon wore on.

"My mom and dad always told me if you forget where you come from, you really don't know where you're going in life, and I always try to remember that," McClendon said. "Coming back and doing these things is selfish; it keeps my feet on the ground, and [helps] keep my reality.

"It makes you appreciate everything that's been given to you and what you've been afforded in life."

McClendon had started his youth organization when he was a utility player on the Pirates, continuing it and building its reach as he retired, went into minor league coaching, was promoted to the Pirates staff as hitting coach, and fulfilled a dream when he was named manager for the 2001 season. Now he had a higher profile, which could only help in his efforts to help turn around a community that fell into decline when the mills began shedding jobs at the start of the 1980s.

"I think it's my responsibility [to turn around the community] in a lot of ways," McClendon said. "I'm in a position where I can knock on some doors and get some attention. Anything to do with baseball, I plan to reach out, particularly at a facility like this.

"I'm realistic. I don't care what profession you're in or what you do, you're not going to reach 100 percent of any group that you try to reach out to. Certainly if you can save one life or turn one life around, it's all been worth it.

"Put the kids on an even playing field. Get them off the street, away from drugs and into other interests. As a city, we have a responsibility to do that."

McClendon wasn't alone working with the kids and talking up the straight-and-narrow path with them. He enlisted former big leaguer Joe Gates, a fellow Gary native, and Benny Dorsey, his coach at Gary's Roosevelt High, to help out as clinic instructors and advisors. Local police officers pitched in to help.

"Lloyd saw a problem and went to the chiefs of police in Gary and Merrillville," said Joe Romeo, coordinator of the Merrillville portion of the camp, a Merrillville police officer and a 1971 graduate of Lew Wallace High School in Gary. "He said, 'I'm here to help. How can I help?'

"Lloyd's been great with the kids," Romeo added. "We can't say enough good things about Lloyd. This camp's not just about baseball, but also about life and working together, setting up skills and goals. We have a message here: We're here to help, don't be afraid of the police."

McClendon ensured that the good advice and baseball counsel did not end when the kids dispersed into the heat of the day from Junedale Field.

He would return to Roosevelt High on December 8, 2001, to hold another clinic indoors in the school gym. He hoped to win a few converts back to baseball, once the predominant youth sport in a Gary that not only produced himself, but also Ron Kittle, LaTroy Hawkins, and Wallace Johnson. Kenny Lofton hailed from neighboring East Chicago.

The sight of that empty Junedale Field, save for his clinic, distressed him.

"We are as much to blame as anyone else," McClendon said of baseball's decline among urban youths. "We haven't done the things to market baseball in the inner city, particularly with the younger kids. We're losing them. Look around, it saddens me. We have such a great facility here, and we're not taking advantage of it. It was immaculate [decades before]. These fields are empty. School's out. This is a summer day. Where are the kids? Why aren't they out here playing baseball? [In 1971] the park would be packed.

"Major League Baseball has a lot to do with it. Basketball's done a tremendous job in marketing the sport. Football, too. For some reason, we're always twenty years behind.

"Basketball rose up before Michael Jordan. They had great marketing, far exceeding baseball's. You've got to do that if you want to get the kids."

Drawing kids into baseball certainly was one objective of the MAAC clinics. McClendon tries to practice what he preaches.

"We've got to get in there and get the kids to have fun," he said. "We need qualified coaches, with more educational courses for them. If you lose, so what? It's not the end of the world.

"Baseball's the most difficult sport of all the sports. There's so many things you have to grasp. In basketball, you can shoot or play great defense. You have to play both sides in baseball and do everything."

That's what McClendon did starting out, but he was able to thrive in an entirely different environment. He grew up in a Gary that would be scarcely recognizable today. In the good ol' days, baseball dreams were commonplace—and sometimes turned to reality.

"Baseball in this community was everything," he said. "It brought everyone together. When you wanted to find kids in the neighborhood, you knew where to find 'em—on the ballfield.

"I remember the days when Ernie Banks came over, talked to us and talked about how great the game of baseball was."

McClendon agreed. He played a little football and sometimes got his clocked cleaned. Baseball was his game, his goal. The greatest player in Gary in his era, he was good enough to get drafted into the pros, good enough to make it as a platoon left fielder for a rare first place Cubs team, good enough to stick around as a utilityman for some contending Pirates clubs. Not good enough for stardom, McClendon did more watching than playing, enabling him to soak up the little nuances about his beloved sport.

By the time he reached his late thirties, McClendon had managerial aspirations. Watching Ernie Banks as a kid, along with Jim Hickman's clutch hitting and Willie Smith's dramatic pinch-hitting, he had a soft spot in his heart for his childhood heroes. One day early in his tenure as Pirates hitting coach, he uttered the magic words: he wanted one day to manage the Cubs.

Mentally, he was getting ready. McClendon had witnessed Don Zimmer's lucky hunches and Jim Leyland's chess-piece maneuvers, often from vantage points a few feet away from them in the dugout. These managers had trod the same path, Zimmer as a sometimes starter, Leyland as career minor leaguer, trials by fire that led them onto the managerial path. They weren't that much different than Sparky Anderson, for one year a light-hitting Phillies second baseman, or Tony La Russa, with scattered bench appearances for the Athletics, Braves and Cubs. Likewise with scores of managers who were familiar with the bench long before they ran their first team.

Few of those supporting-cast guys, if they even got that far, ever forgot their modest roots. McClendon similarly was well-grounded. To be sure, he'd always come back to northwest Indiana, be it at the All-Star break for the MAAC clinics or an off-season of snow-shoveling at his home when he could have easily moved near the Pirates' spring training base of Bradenton, Florida. His blue-collar bearings eventually would be transferred to a group of twenty-five players who didn't win, but held their heads high even while stumbling and falling. The Little League hero-turned-utilityman-turned-manager wouldn't let them slough off, just as he had never shifted to a lower mental gear.

♦ ♦ ♦

The baseball world of Gary in the mid- and late-1960s would scarcely be recognizable today due to the emptiness of poorly-maintained fields. Kids swarmed all over the rough but playable fields in the inner neighborhoods of the steel capital. They could easily get teams together, with more than enough coaches for direction. The sense of community was stronger. Enough men had decent-paying jobs in the mills to provide stability. Two-parent families were more common than at the end of the century.

McClendon credited his parents, Grant and Hattie McClendon, with guiding him in life.

"They were so instrumental in our lives, not just in sports, but in education, how to treat people, how to be decent human beings. People look for athletes to be role models. Maybe to an extent we are. But it all starts at home. If we get parental involvement, it would be a lot better."

But the amount of person-to-person involvement would be foreign to the hard-pressed Gary residents of almost two generations later.

"There are so many things that are different," McClendon recalled in 1997. "It was such a community pride and involvement, with parental participation. Coaches were proud to be coaches. There was such a camaraderie. It was a great thing.

"We must have had fifteen teams in our league. There was a waiting list to become coaches and try to get on the teams. All of this in our community. Baseball was so thriving then.

"Part of the problem is so many kids now having babies, they never really have a chance to become kids themselves. That's why we don't have the parental participation I had when I was growing up."

McClendon's childhood heroics can only be summoned up in memories. Few landmarks remain from his "Legendary Lloyd" days. His old Little League field has been swallowed up by the urban blight afflicting inner-city

Gary. Only a new minor league ballpark for the Northern League Railcats gives a hint of revival amid its once-thriving downtown chock full of empty stores, its grand, domed county and federal courthouses near the USX steel plant entrance huge monuments to a postwar era when Gary really mattered.

"Gary was in better shape because the steel mills were in full function and everybody was making good money," said Benny Dorsey, McClendon's coach at Gary Roosevelt High in the mid-1970s, who retired in 2002. "Then everything went down. Jobs went down. People had to take care of their needs first. You can't do that being out there playing ball."

In the long-ago halcyon time for the steel town, McClendon started down the path of any eager young ballplayer.

"I was eight years old," he said. "I remember my first uniform. I didn't have gym shoes. I wore street shoes for my first picture. I played for the Anderson Little League Giants, minor league. Later I played for the major league team."

By then, McClendon discovered he was more talented than his teammates. "At an early age, I didn't know the fundamentals," he said. "I was just a very talented kid."

McClendon was the focal point as star pitcher, catcher and hitter for the Anderson team, which began dispatching all opponents in the spring and summer of 1971.

Manager Jesse Lawson directed a team comprised of Darren and Ben Jones, Larry Reynolds, Ron Henderson, Gerald Steele, Carl Weatherspoon, Vincent and Ralph Basemore, Keith Tillman, Marcus Hubbard, Harold White, Damen Ware, and Kenneth Hayes.

"First thing we had to do was win our district," McClendon said. "Then we went to semi-state, state and regionals. It involved about twenty games for us.

"We had some tough battles along the way. But the good thing about us is we were out having fun. There was no pressure. We didn't even know there was a Little League World Series. If parents and coaches can learn anything today, it's not to put any pressure on them at all."

On August 19, 1971, McClendon homered to lead Anderson to a 3-1 victory over the Nationals of Ottumwa, Iowa, in the regional semi-finals in Harvey, Illinois. Two days later, McClendon belted another homer in a 7-0 victory over Alpena, Michigan, in the regional title game. Better yet, he hurled a no-hitter, striking out sixteen in six innings. Overpowering pitching was old hat by now to McClendon, who had fanned all eighteen batters when Anderson won the Indiana state title. Having just completed sixth grade, the young star was thrilled to be mentioned in the major newspapers, even if his name would be temporarily misspelled as "McLendon" in game stories on Anderson's march to Williamsport, Pennsylvania.

After qualifying for the Little League World Series with the victory over Alpena, the kids brought swarms of Gary rooters with them as a cheering section.

"We flew," McClendon said. "It was an exciting time. For most of us, it was our first time on a plane. The great thing was the entire community shut down and everybody went with us. We had busloads there. We had a home-field advantage until we ran into Taiwan in the championship game. We almost pulled it off in extra innings."

Most of the cheers were soon directed at McClendon, who put on an unbelievable performance that gave him the nickname, "Legendary Lloyd."

In the first round on August 25, 1971, Gary overwhelmed Lexington, Kentucky, 7-2 as McClendon struck out twelve and allowed just three hits. He slugged a towering homer over the center field fence with two on in the first. Then he led off the third with a blast over the left field fence.

McClendon thrilled the Gary fans with an encore the next day. He smashed two more homers while Reynolds hurled a three-hitter, striking out fifteen, in Gary's 7-0 win over Madrid, Spain, comprised of sons of service-men at Torrejon Air Force Base.

In the first inning, he lined Mike Pribonie's first pitch over the center field wall with a man on base. Then McClendon led off the third with a homer over the right field fence.

"It was almost like a fairy tale, fantasy land, like it wasn't real," McClendon said. "Every time I swung the bat, the ball was really going far and long and out of the ballpark. The fences were 230 to center, pretty big for Little League.

"After the fourth home run, I couldn't believe what was happening."

Midnight for Gary's fairy tale struck in the championship game on Saturday, August 28, 1971. Working on the mound again, McClendon slugged an unbelievable fifth homer in the first inning. But he was almost the entire offense as Taiwan pitcher Hsu Chin-Mu allowed two hits in the first inning, then none the rest of the way as the game went into extra innings.

Taiwan finally unknotted a 3-3 tie with nine runs in the ninth inning off a tired McClendon with six hits, four walks, and numerous passed balls and wild pitches. The inner-city kids' dream was dashed, but they came away witnessing an unforgettable series by McClendon. In addition to his then-record five homers, he walked in his other five trips to the plate.

McClendon returned to Gary a hero, but without an inflated ego—and

Lloyd McClendon meets with Vice President Spiro Agnew after leading his team to the runner-up spot in the 1971 Little League World Series. *Little League Baseball*

with absolutely no clue what awaited him exactly three decades into the future.

"Despite the fact he had all those records in Little League and all that fame, he was a well-grounded individual," said Dorsey. "He had a good support system from his family. That made him an excellent person to coach. He was very level-headed and mature for his age."

Dorsey ended McClendon's pitching days, putting him behind the plate full-time at Roosevelt High. Catching was a perfect position to develop his leadership skills.

"He took over the team, and was in charge of the team from day one. Lloyd was focused. He really had his sights set on being a major league ballplayer. Due to the fact his father was a good supporter made Lloyd dedicated to be the best he could be at the time.

"He possessed all the qualities I like to see in these guys now. He was on time, a hard worker, dedicated and determined to fulfill those goals. If he didn't make it as a major leaguer, in some area of his life he'd become a success.

"He very much was old-school. He believed in getting dirty. Your mom and dad could wash that uniform later. Not only did he dream, but he worked at it. Dreaming is not enough. You've got to put in your time and work."

McClendon never developed into a "holler-guy" player, coach or manager. That was merely a style carried over from his high-school days.

"Lloyd has always had a quiet demeanor, but don't be fooled by the way he talks," Dorsey said. "In high school, he led by example. If you messed up, he would quietly tell you where to go, how to do it. And if you didn't do it, he'd crack you."

After achieving All-State status at Roosevelt, McClendon went on to play baseball at nearby Valparaiso University. Finally, pro baseball beckoned in 1980 when he was drafted in the eighth round by the New York Mets. But the high profile he achieved as a youth baseball sensation would escape him for the next two decades—a period of time and myriad of experiences that gave him the necessary preparation for his twenty-first century calling at Pittsburgh's PNC Park.

◆ ◆ ◆

McClendon's first six minor league seasons were fair-to-middling, the only distinguishing characteristic being his status as one of the players the Cincinnati Reds obtained when the New York Mets orchestrated a short homecoming for all-time ace Tom Seaver after the 1982 season.

The move to the Reds eventually turned out to be a small break as his advancement through the minors was slow, with McClendon not reaching Triple-A until age twenty-five. Playing at altitude at Mile High Stadium for Triple-A Denver in 1985–86, McClendon earned notice by leading the American Association in homers with twenty-four in '86. The following season, he earned his first trip to the majors at the start of the season in Cincinnati. With trips down to Triple-A Nashville also on his agenda the following two seasons, McClendon served as the Reds' backup catcher while making himself even more valuable playing other positions. He began to log cameo appearances at first base, third base and in the outfield.

McClendon learned while in the Reds organization. He cited Reds coaches Ted Kluszewski and Tony Perez, and then-manager Pete Rose as positive influences on him as he struggled to gain a foothold in the majors.

McClendon got another break on December 8, 1988, when he was traded to his childhood favorite, the Cubs, for outfielder Rolando Roomes. Although he started the following season at Triple-A Iowa, he didn't stay long. Injuries to all three starting Cubs outfielders prompted McClendon's callup on May 15, 1989. In his first at-bat that day, McClendon slugged a three-run homer off the Braves' Derek Lilliquist to power a 4-0 Cubs victory.

His handyman status and clutch hitting earned him a spot in manager Don Zimmer's player rotation. McClendon soon became the platoon left fielder against right-handed pitchers, alternating with Dwight Smith. He also saw first base service, filling in for an injured Mark Grace in June. McClendon homered in three straight games against the Mets in one June series.

Now he could simply race up forty miles to Wrigley Field via the Indiana Tollway and Lake Shore Drive from his Merrillville home. McClendon finished with 12 homers, 40 RBIs and a .286 average in 92 games, batting .339 against left-handed pitching. Approaching age thirty, he knew he belonged in the majors, and he was home.

But his comfort zone lasted shorter than he expected. After winning the National League East in 1989, the Cubs, beset by injuries and player slumps, stumbled out of the gate the following season. The magic of '89 was truly gone. McClendon batted just .159 in forty-nine games before a contending Pirates club obtained him in a waiver trade on September 9, 1990.

Buccos manager Jim Leyland appreciated the handyman's presence. McClendon became his jack-of-all-trades fill-in over the next four seasons, helping the Pirates win back-to-back NL East titles in 1991 and 1992. His first full Pirates season was his best with a .288 average and seven homers in 85 games.

McClendon continued to try to improve even though he knew he'd never play full-time with Pittsburgh.

"He was limited to some extent to start with," longtime Pirates coach Bill Virdon, the outfield coach under Leyland, said of McClendon's skills in the outfield. "But he really worked at it, and as he went along he matured and got better. He enjoyed the work. He really thrived on someone pushing him a little bit. We enjoyed our times together. The thing he's recognized over the years is it takes work to be successful."

That work would not be limited to shagging flies or taking extra batting practice. All the while, McClendon wasted little time while he sat on the bench, waiting for the call to pinch-hit, come in late in the game in a double switch or make the occasional start. An idea began stirring in his head, and he began boning up on the research necessary to make it come to fruition years in the future.

"When I played in Chicago, I started thinking about it," McClendon said of managing. "It solidified at Pittsburgh, seeing Jim [Leyland] and how he worked. Watching Jim and his staff, it gave me a pretty good inclination that was what I wanted.

"Obviously, I tried to strive to learn as much as I could. I was fortunate to have played for Leyland and Zimmer. I was able to sit next to some pretty good people in the game. I certainly asked questions about why a move was made, what was the purpose? More than anything, I wasn't afraid to ask questions. I became a student of the game, so to speak."

McClendon also noticed the personalities of Zimmer and Leyland, and filed that away in his head.

"Both are fiery, feisty guys," he said. "One thing that impressed me the most is they were fearless about winning and losing. They were never afraid to lose a game."

McClendon not only learned while on the bench, but also during his earlier career behind the plate.

"Him being a catcher helps out," Pirates catcher Jason Kendall said. "I know that just from doing it. You have to look at situations—double switches, matchups, what the guy hit the last time. You're the only one who sees the whole field, like a quarterback."

While still a player, McClendon began displaying the leadership image necessary for a manager.

"Jimmy [Leyland] liked Lloyd in the clubhouse," said longtime Pirates coach Tommy Sandt. "I don't think Jimmy took anyone under his wing, but the smart guys listened and watched and learned. Mac was one of those guys. He paid attention to what was going on. He studied the game. I knew he had aspirations."

In both Chicago and Pittsburgh, McClendon became close with fellow benchwarmer Dave Clark, now one of his Pirates coaches. McClendon already was in his teaching and counseling mode.

"He was one of the main guys who taught me how to pinch hit," Clark said. "He accepted that role and gave me the insights. It's tough when you don't play. But he accepted that role with grace."

McClendon accepted the end of his career with grace. After his release from the Pirates during the strike in 1994, he signed for one more shot at the majors with Cleveland. He played only thirty-seven games with the Indians' Triple-A team in Buffalo in 1995, but never got called up to Jacobs Field.

But he already had made an impression on Pirates general manager Cam Bonifay. McClendon was hired as the Pirates' minor league hitting instructor in 1996. The apprenticeship in the bushes was short. He joined the Pirates as hitting coach in 1997. McClendon's goal was squarely in his sights.

◆ ◆ ◆

McClendon was too busy as Pirates hitting coach under manager Gene Lamont to campaign or politic for a manager's job. As hard of a worker as

While he was never a star, Lloyd McClendon's time in a Pirates uniform nonetheless helped impress management. After retiring, he signed on with the Pirates as their minor-league hitting instructor. *Pittsburgh Pirates*

he was as a player, he'd immerse himself in videotapes or pore over charts in an effort to help the often under-productive Pirates hitters.

Neither Lamont or McClendon had much to work with. New owner Kevin McClatchy kept tight reins on the player payroll while he tried to get a new stadium project under way. The Pirates never reached .500 during the 1997–2000 period, and twice won only sixty-nine games in a season.

The latter downturn, in 2000, greased the skids for Lamont's departure, a scenario that was debated around the team the entire season. McClendon began being mentioned as a potential successor, but was leery of being connected with any kind of public campaigning for the job.

But McClendon's longtime Pirates association, youth (forty-one at the time of his appointment on October 23, 2000), dedication and status as a qualified minority candidate gave him the edge.

His experience as hitting coach enabled him to relate to his hitters immediately as his first season got underway. The holdover Pirates responded to him from day one.

"Number one, he's a very knowledgeable baseball person," catcher Jason Kendall said. "He's as good as they get. Number two, he respects the game. Number three, some coaches I've had in the past lose perspective about how hard the game really is. He knows that, the mental aspect. He's going to be one of the good managers that ever was in the game."

"He's in your corner," outfielder Brian Giles said. "He treats everyone the same, no matter who you are. Anytime you have a guy who's fighting for you, no matter how bad things get, you get the respect of your players. The good thing about Lloyd is he hasn't forgotten how tough this game is. He remembers what it was like to struggle, and he's carried that over as a manager."

As if he needed any reminders of struggling, the Pirates fell into the National League Central cellar, skidding twenty games under .500 by June as injuries and slumps took their toll. The mounting stress caused him to blow up in the most comic act by a manager during the 2001 season.

In a June 26 game at PNC Park, umpire Rick Reed called Kendall out on a close play. Upset and ejected from the game for protesting the call, McClendon grabbed the first-base bag off its moorings and carried it off the field. The Pirates were obviously inspired. They eked out a 7-6, twelve-inning victory over the Brewers that night.

The next day, the base was put on display in the clubhouse along with a photo of the enraged McClendon pulling off the heist.

His actions got the full endorsement of those who knew him the best.

"That shows how much he cares," Kendall said. "I was the one who hit the ball. Everyone on this team knows Lloyd McClendon has got our back. He's going to be there to protect his players. It was one for the highlight reel."

"We loved it," first baseman Kevin Young said. "We know he's going to fight for us. If you look at our record, you would think this team has no fire and that's not right. We play hard, and it's because of Mac."

Even one of his baseball mentors backed McClendon.

"I was proud of him," said Benny Dorsey, his old high-school coach. "He usually doesn't show his anger publicly. But this time, this was two bad calls. The last call, something snapped. What he did, the results were positive. I would have done that. I might have taken first *and* second."

McClendon had second thoughts about his actions in hindsight.

"If I had to do it all over, I probably wouldn't do it," he said. "But, since he [Reed] had already tossed me, I thought I might as well take it with me. I was mad."

All he wanted was some respect for the Pirates.

"I've been nice to these guys all year, and I know all about the new relationship we're supposed to have with the umpires, but my club has been taken advantage of all year," McClendon said. "You can sense they [the umpires] relax against my club. . . . It seems like they make calls nonchalant. It's like it doesn't matter with us if they get the call right or wrong.

"If you can guarantee me we'll win tonight, I'll steal second base."

As the season dragged on, McClendon's challenges mounted. But he would not vary from his basic personality as a manager. He would be more instinctive than mechanical.

"I try to research, I try to plan," he said. "If I'm afraid to lose, I'll never win. I'm not afraid to take a chance.

"More than anything, if I'm going to be me and be the best I can be, then I have to listen to my heart. If I do that, I'll always move in the right direction. Certainly if I feel something, I'm not afraid of going with my instincts.

"I try to be well-rounded. I believe in the computer and what it can spit out. But to be a good manager, I have to have a pulse on my team, what they're capable of doing and what they're not capable of. A computer print-out can't tell you that—how big are their hearts, how big is their drive and determination?

"The most important part of managing is understanding, communicating. When they step between the lines, your job is pretty much done. I don't want the credit when they win or the blame when they lose."

As a rookie manager, McClendon benefited from the presence of Bill Virdon as bench coach. After tutoring McClendon on outfield play earlier in the 1990s, Virdon now would bring his manager's experience as an extra set of eyes and sounding board.

"He certainly was a tremendous influence," McClendon said. "Bill kept me calm, kept my feet on the ground. His demeanor and what he brought to the table put me in a more relaxed state of mind, on how I approached the game. I don't know where I would have been from the mental point if it hadn't been for him. He was a tremendous force in my stability. It was hard to put in words what he meant."

"I don't know if you're ever completely confident about everything you do," Virdon said of managing. "Things don't always work out, even though it may be the right thing to do. That makes you question it sometimes. It's a tough business. It's an instinct thing, about knowing your players, about knowing what they do best. I think Lloyd's excellent at that. He's a people person. He has a knack of knowing how to treat people, knowing how to get the best out of them."

To be sure, McClendon needed some help in navigating through the turbulence of his managerial debut. Obviously, the advice was heeded, building upon an already strong personality in the clubhouse.

Everything else was bad timing for Pittsburgh in 2001, but not the presence of McClendon.

"Mac's kept this thing together all season," Brian Giles said during one of the low moments. "If it wasn't for Mac, this thing could have fallen apart a long time ago."

Statistically, 2001 fell apart early on. Emotionally, the Pirates were Lloyd McClendon's team, an extension of his personality. They would not die easily.

♦ ♦ ♦

On a quiet Sunday morning, October 7, 2001, with the season finale at Wrigley Field just a couple of hours away, McClendon had his feet up on the desk of the tiny visiting manager's office. He looked none the worse for the wear for enduring a 61-100 season up to that point.

McClendon could tally up some staggering numbers, almost all negative. A total of seventeen Pirates players officially spent time on the disabled list during the season. Two players were disabled twice. A total of 1,275 games were missed. That forced McClendon to use a total of 132 different lineups in the 162 games, compared to 122 employed by predecessor Gene Lamont in 2000. The Opening Day lineup was used just three times, and the Pirates lost all three games.

"You lose your number one, two and three starters," McClendon recounted. "The number four starter goes down in his first game. The right-handed setup man goes down. The best utility player in the game goes down. The center fielder who hit .315 goes down."

"It was a lousy, rotten season."

The short roster took its toll. The Pirates went 16-34-2 in series during the 2001 season. They were swept thirteen times. In two different months, May and August, the Pirates went 8-20. Pittsburgh finished last in the National League in batting. Only Colorado, with its numbers inflated by mile-high Coors Field, had worse pitching statistically. The gloves had holes; the Pirates finished fourteenth out of sixteen teams in fielding.

But after all of that, McClendon wasn't complaining. They would not be a hangdog team on his watch.

"Those kids in the locker room never gave up," he said. "I'll have a good offseason.

"It's tough to have a season like we had, but I'll sleep good this winter because I know I got everything I could out of every one of my players. They gave me everything they had.

"I'm proud of this club. Not once this year did they come into the locker room and say, 'OK, what's going to happen today for us to lose?' They came out every day expecting to win a ballgame. That's the first step to becoming a winner, to shut off the losses, come back the next day and compete. I think they've done that.

"You deal with it. It's tough. I really believe that sometimes when you lose, you actually win, if you're doing things the right way. It can be a tremendous foundation for things to come. It was tough, but I saw positive things here. We were doing things the right way."

All the trying times could not change McClendon as a person.

"I am who I am," he said. "I don't try to equate myself with anyone else. I live my life by trying to be responsible. I think I've been very responsible to this organization. I've given them everything I've had every day. I've tried to prepare myself to win every day. I've tried to get these players prepared to win every day. From that end we were a little short. We couldn't overcome the injuries this year.

"I really believe that my players will take on my personality and the way I go about things. If I'm in a state of panic, that's not good. But if they see me full of confidence and in a very calm manner and ready to go about my business, they'll do the right thing."

So how does he shake off a typically tough loss?

"Two or three shots of vodka," he laughed. "I come back every day recharged, re-energized and ready to go. I have to. I believe your players take on your personality. If you're beaten, distraught, and show no confidence, that's what your players are going to show.

"If you're going to be a good leader, coach, manager, there has to be a scenario where there are going to be injuries, there are going to be adversities, along the way. There will be thunderbolts. But I didn't have a plan for seventeen guys on the disabled list. Someone put it at 2,000 innings on the disabled list."

Playing in spanking-new PNC Park took away some of the obvious pain.

"Best ballpark in all America," McClendon said. "The foundation is there on the field, too. We just need to get people healthy. We'll take our chances. Just give me a full deck, and I'll play my poker."

Before the first pitch of the next season, McClendon would get his chance to meet two conflicts head-on. His adversaries hadn't taken the measure of the steadfastness that had first formed on the Gary sandlots, and later coalesced into a finished personality on benches in Cincinnati, Chicago, and Pittsburgh.

◆ ◆ ◆

Healthier bodies, but not attitudes, greeted McClendon when he reassembled the Pirates for spring training 2002 in Bradenton, Florida.

The seemingly solid esprit de corps which kept the Pirates from an emotional meltdown through the trying 2001 campaign was breaking down. By March 22, outfielder Derek Bell said he was going on "Operation Shutdown" when McClendon told him he had to compete with Armando Rios and Craig Wilson for the starting right-field job. Bell's historical track record as a run producer did not cut it with McClendon; he had been among the platoons of training-room folks, not playing after July 3 due to a strained hamstring. Bell's final 2001 numbers were .173 with five homers and 13 RBIs. That did not sit well with a lot of Pirates people since Bell had been tendered a $9.75 million, two-year contract.

Next on the gripe brigade was journeyman right-hander Pat Rapp, who said he was upset about his camp workload after signing a minor league contract shortly before spring training. Rapp had come into spring training among eleven candidates vying for five spots in the starting rotation.

"I thought I was coming here to get a chance, that they weren't completely happy with their starting pitchers because they were either always hurt or too young," Rapp said. "I don't know what to think now. I have no idea what is going on or what is going to happen."

The complaints did not get the reaction from McClendon the players intended.

"Usually, people who make excuses are losers," he said. "We lost 100 games last year but we never made excuses. We took our beatings like a man. We're not going to start making excuses around here now."

Realizing he had teed off the wrong person, Bell tried to backtrack. But he still came out as requiring a happy home elsewhere.

"I don't know if I can go back to Pittsburgh because I don't have any friends there now," he said. "Everyone there is mad at me. I won't have any fans at home, and I won't have any on the road. I'm going to be a lonely man."

"Everything has kind of gotten out blown out of proportion," he said. "I didn't mean what I said to come out the way it did."

The proverbial horse had gotten out of the barn. McClendon's old-school standards had been violated. The penalty was not negotiable. Neither Bell nor Rapp went north with the Pirates.

"They [controversies] were diffused," a relaxed McClendon said on April 2, 2002, in that same cozy visiting manager's office at Wrigley Field. But in the same breath, the manager put it all in perspective.

"Eventually my ass will be leaving, too," he said with a wicked laugh. "That's a fact."

McClendon said during his rookie season as manager he would handle problems with players quickly and decisively. Now he practiced what he preached.

"You're going to have conflicts and controversies, that's just the way life is," he said. "Usually it's of a personal nature, not a team nature. Certainly the conflicts we had in spring training were of a personal nature. Guys felt they were personally left out or not being treated fairly.

"You're dealing with a lot of different personalities, different backgrounds. I tell the players all the time, 'This is not all about hugs and kisses' and 'I love you, you love me.' Hard times will arise, we'll meet them head-on and we'll deal with them.

"I don't try to be a tough guy. It's more important for the players to respect me. I don't want the image of being a tough guy. My philosophy is that I don't want to embarrass players, and I don't want them to embarrass me. The best way to deal with problems and confrontations is to meet them head-on. When you do that, you usually deal with the truth and meet it head-on, but usually you don't have a problem anymore. Players may not like what you say, but they certainly understand and respect what you have to say."

The Pirates continued playing hard coming out of the gate in 2002. Eventually a big league–low team batting average, symbolic of a bad offense, dropped them under .500 as the weather warmed. But the team still showed perceptible improvement, and new acquisitions Kip Wells and Josh Fogg paid dividends in the rotation after coming over in a trade for starter Todd Ritchie.

"I would agree our kids are playing just as hard as they did last year," McClendon said. "We're just getting better results. I'm a firm believer that all the trials and tribulations we went through would make us a better club. You would hope some of the young kids would grow up.

"One thing I tell the players, we don't go by limitations. We took our knocks last year, dealt with them and are better because of them."

McClendon believed he was a better manager due to all the trials and tribulations he experienced.

"Certainly I'm better because of all the things we went through, no question about it," he said. "I'm probably a lot more patient and understanding of situations. The fact is, I'm only as good as the players. If they perform well, then I'll look good. If they don't get it done, then it looks like I stink."

But fouling up the Pittsburgh baseball landscape is always the furthest thing on McClendon's mind. He sold himself to his players even before he became manager. He sold management on his ability to run a team.

Now he has to sell the outside world that his organization is on the upswing, and that he won't get the gate when his three-year contract expires at the end of 2003. Of course, he'll give you the pitch, because optimism that there's a better world around the corner has been his companion ever since he batted and pitched Gary into the Little League World Series.

"The light is there at the end of the tunnel," he said. "The entire organization, from Kevin McClatchy on down, a lot of good things have happened. Certainly the management style is more dynamic and energetic.

"It may be baby steps, but they are there."

7

THE CONSCIENCE OF A TEAM

Jose Valentin lockers in a corner of the home clubhouse in Comiskey Park (now U.S. Cellular Field), next to the entrance to the spacious trainer's area that White Sox players sometimes have used as a lounge, far away from the media's prying eyes.

It would be so very easy for Valentin to simply take two steps to supposed safety. But the personable infielder minds it not one bit when he gets visitors by his cubicle who want to engage in conversation.

More amazing than Valentin's usual hospitality is his ease in maneuvering through English. That was his second language after growing up in Manati, Puerto Rico, yet he employs English better and with more confidence than a lot of natives. And what he says often has greater meaning and potential impact than anything uttered by most major leaguers.

As a player who loves competing, who will play through injuries, who has standards to which he'd like teammates to adhere, Valentin doesn't mind speaking his mind, positively or negatively.

He was overjoyed when he was liberated from a sinking Milwaukee Brewers ship after the 1999 season in a crafty trade pulled off by then–White Sox general manager Ron Schueler. Rejuvenated, he had his best-ever season to help spark the Sox to a surprise American League Central title in 2000. Chicago won ninety-five games, tied for second-highest in team history since 1964. Valentin's switch-hitting talents, including surprising power for a five-foot-ten, 185-pounder, to go along with his speed, hustle and aggressiveness, prompted White Sox manager Jerry Manuel to call him the "heartbeat" of the team.

In the offseason of 2000–01, Valentin passed up a more lucrative offer to bolt to the Baltimore Orioles, opting to stay with teammates he liked and a supposed budding winning atmosphere he had never previously enjoyed in a decade's big league service. And he never complained when Schueler's successor, Ken Williams, picked up slick-fielding Royce Clayton to take his place at shortstop, making Valentin a kind of super utilityman, slated for center field one day, third base the next, some second base, in addition to giving Clayton an occasional break at his old position. The Sox were merely getting stronger by picking up Clayton, so Valentin was eager to serve in any role. He would be the good team player he always insisted he was, a persona seconded by his teammates.

But as the 2001 season got underway, the new Sox dynasty was stillborn. Injuries and pitching ineffectiveness slammed them down. Frank Thomas was lost for the season due to a torn right triceps. David Wells, the big offseason pitching acquisition, performed below expectations leading up to a season-ending back injury.

A 2-7 homestand dropped the Sox's final April record to 8-15. Within a week, the Sox were 8-19.

After a brief surge, the Sox slid downhill fast again. They lost the first seven games of a road trip to fall to 14-28. After that unlucky seventh in a row, a 10-3 stinker in Toronto on May 21, Valentin could no longer hold his tongue. He let loose with both barrels at his teammates.

"If guys are out there just playing for their stats, then they better not get caught," he said. "That's a bad situation, and you better believe I'll let them know about it.

"I don't want to play with anyone like that. I'm getting paid a lot of money, and I want to earn it. No one should be here who wants to steal money. That's the kind of thing that splits a team apart."

Valentin did not believe any of his teammates had similarly stepped up as leaders.

"Hopefully [others will step up], but I don't see it. If I saw that effort, then we would be playing better baseball. I'm seeing too many people who don't care about what happens."

Through his production on the field, his attitude on and off the diamond, and his heartfelt comments, Valentin had earned the status as conscience of his team. And in doing so, he had followed in the footsteps of the greatest player to come from his home island—a man whose memory is overpowering three decades after his tragic death. Valentin would never duplicate the on-field career of Roberto Clemente, but he surely could follow his lead as the center of perspective in the clubhouse. That role would go unquestioned, even if his teammates didn't always respond to his prompts.

"No one has come up to me and said, 'Hey, you shouldn't have said that stuff,'" Valentin said. "Some guys have realized that it was probably true. A lot of guys didn't take it personally, but knew I was right. I didn't care if we won or lost. I just wanted us to play hard. No one was. I was frustrated. I was asking for help."

One other player who can be blunt on occasion backed Valentin.

"Jose's one of those guys we all respect," then–White Sox closer Keith Foulke said in 2001. "He goes out there and busts his tail every day. He's one of the few guys who can say that on this team, where everyone takes note and says, 'Can I be doing a little more to help this team out?'"

"He backs what he says. He's not an arrogant player, just a good player. He does the things you ask of him, and does the things you wouldn't expect of him. It's not what's good for Jose, it's what's good for the team."

Valentin also made an impact on younger White Sox players, such as budding left-handed ace Mark Buehrle.

"He's the vocal guy on this team when J. B. [James Baldwin] left," Buehrle said. "There would be big shoes to fill, and he stepped in. Because he's one of the leaders, everyone will look up to him and listen to him. He's going to do whatever's best for the team. If they're out there not hustling, it's in the best interests of the team."

Management types endorsed Valentin's outspoken stance.

"Anybody can kind of say what they want, but you really have to lead by example, and he does," Manuel said.

Schueler got even more than he bargained for when he dealt pitchers Jaime Navarro and John Snyder to Milwaukee for Valentin and pitcher Cal Eldred.

"He's a class person," Schueler said. "Very popular with most of his teammates. He plays hard every day. He's pointed some fingers and you need a guy to do that every now and then."

Months after his statement of purpose in Toronto, Valentin could coolly analyze why he spoke up.

"After the year we had [in 2000], no way that we play that kind of baseball," he said. "We had a lot better team than we showed. We had a lot of players go down with injury, but that's no excuse. When I make that comment, I didn't make it to point fingers. I was asking for help.

"It was frustration, that I've been through so many times like that in Milwaukee. I don't want to go back there, especially after the year we had [in 2000]. I would feel that I found a team where I start winning, start having fun, [having] happiness. The way we played, it was the same way I feel in Milwaukee. A lot of people say it's early, early. But you can't think like that.

Four games you lose early in the year, those games you need to qualify for a playoff spot."

Like Clemente, a player does not have to possess a mainland birth certificate to show the way to his teammates. Baseball has its own language that transcends borders and cultures. There's no discrimination when it comes to leadership.

"I think I should be able to handle that role," Valentin said. "Once you've played the game a lot, if you say something, say something for the good, not the bad. This is a family, a team sport. I just show that I care for those guys, do it the right way. Being a team leader is not an easy job, it's tough. You have to deal with twenty-four more guys. This is not about baby-sitting, this is about playing the game."

Maybe Valentin's tongue-lashing wasn't the true motivating factor in the end. But the Sox picked themselves up despite their injuries, played competitive baseball and reached the .500 mark at 36-36 by June 24, 2001. Improvement was more gradual from that point forward, with the Sox never really climbing back into the AL Central race. The season's high point was reached on September 30, when they were 82-74 after a 5-2 win over the Royals. But they had no more finishing kick with a final 83-79 mark.

Valentin was not fooled by the end result.

"You know what the best thing about this season is? It's over," he said on the season's final day.

He would not be snowed by what passed for effort by the Sox in the future. The speech in Toronto would not be the last time he'd take his teammates to task.

♦ ♦ ♦

Valentin's vocal style comes from the heart, as Manuel accurately analyzed. He embodies the best qualities that a manager covets in a player.

"He comes with a different level of intensity than most players," Manuel said. "He's fun to watch. In 2000, he was probably our best baserunner, whether it was a steal, a ball in the dirt or reading a ball off the bat. When you see a guy with good baserunning skills, you also feel good about his instincts for the game. He's shown all those qualities as well as leadership."

Valentin had no problems pegging what makes him tick.

"Desire is first," he said. "When you have desire, it makes you play the game hard. You hustle, you do whatever it takes to win. I don't just play the game for fun, I play to win. I betcha there's a lot of players who do the same thing. This game isn't about competing, it's about winning. [In 2000] I was close to it [World Series]. Just going to the playoffs is not enough.

"I always play the game with desire. You hustle, get dirty, play the game hard. It's going to make you feel good. Come here, play nine innings, and you can't be where you're not getting dirty. It's going to take teamwork—what's my role today?"

Although Valentin finally broke through as a significant run producer in 2000–2001, he realized that statistics alone were not going to win games. He'd have to hustle and push himself to his limits in every game.

"That's how you're going to get credit," he said. "You like to win. When you play the game hard, the way it's supposed to be, you're always gong to feel good about yourself, you're always going to hear people talk about you the right way. When you play the game the way it's supposed to be played, there's always somebody going to be looking to you and going to start following you. It's a role model. I like to be an example to my teammates. If I play hard, the team will play the same way."

What if Valentin fails despite his trademark aggressiveness?

"I'm not going to be afraid to play the game, because when you're afraid, you fail," he said. "There's always a chance when you make a mistake, there's always a chance you can make over it. Whatever comes around, goes around. When you play aggressive and try, you're always going to see some result."

If an injury is a byproduct of his playing style, then Valentin is ready to accept the risks.

"If you play the game hard, sooner or later you'll get hurt," he said. "But that's not going to take away from me, the way I like to play the game."

Pain often has been his close companion, and he keeps overcoming the hurts.

"I pretty much ignore it," he said. "You know you're already hurt, so why think about it? Just go out and do your job, nice and easy. I've got to suck it up and do it. I won't let anyone take an at-bat away from me. I never was afraid, that's the reason why my career has been this long. I've been playing this game [ten years], why change?

"If you're going to get hurt, you're going to get hurt no matter what."

It all adds up in his head. Valentin understands the cause-and-effect process better than most players. You hustle and stay aggressive, you succeed. You succeed, you win. You win, you get your payday.

The man is practical if nothing else.

"Fans like to see wins, but they also like to see some people who deserve the money," Valentin said. "People get a lot of money, but they're not doing what they're supposed to do. People don't like that. If you play the game the way it's supposed to be, you'll always get more. The offers will be there.

If you want the money, if you think your value is $1 million, $2 million, play like it. Play like you want to get there. Don't talk about it and then not do it."

"I never thought I'd be the guy I'd be right now. But I think I earned it and worked hard enough to be where I am. That's why I have the money."

He figured he had enough by staying with the White Sox after the 2000 season instead of taking a more lucrative offer from the often free-spending Orioles.

"That says a lot about us as teammates, that he would take less money to stay here," Keith Foulke said. "We were as happy as hell when we heard he signed back."

Orioles outfielder Chris Singleton was still with the Sox when Valentin opted to stay put. He also was buoyed by his decision at the time.

"You can't just go for the money," Singleton said. "He's played the game for awhile. It wasn't as if the contract was going to make or break him. There's no use to be penny-pinching and squeeze everything for the last dime. You can't really put the dollar figure on the comfort level."

Settled into a comfortable financial stature for himself and his family as his thirties progress, Valentin can now begin planning his own legacy in the game.

"I don't want to be one of the greatest players who ever played this game," he said. "I want to be a good player who plays this game for as many years as I can. I wanted to play twenty years.

"I want to do something for the team. I want to be the guy to win. You'll hear more people say that we won this game because Jose made this play or because of the way Jose plays."

♦ ♦ ♦

Puerto Rico in the 1980s was still considered the baseball mecca of the Caribbean.

Not every team had begun to mine the mother lode of talent in the Dominican Republic. Puerto Ricans were not yet subject to the June amateur draft. Scouts combed the island looking for talent, building up relationships with families to get that edge on signing a player. Between the legacy of Roberto Clemente and other great Puerto Rican players, and the strong presence of big leaguers playing winter ball on the island, local kids could easily dream about a baseball future.

Jose Valentin was no different.

"My feeling about the game started with my dad [Jose]," he said. "He played for many years with a semi-pro national team. They traveled all

Jose Valentin bucked the trend and re-signed with the White Sox in 2000 for less money than other teams were offering, gaining his teammates' admiration. *Ron Vesely/Chicago White Sox*

around the world. The way they talked, my dad was a good catcher. He played the game hard, always. Later he was a player-manager in semi-pro ball. We'd watch a game on TV, and he'd 'manage' that game, letting me know about situations.

"He taught me how to play the game the way it's supposed to be played. He taught me how to swing a bat, how to catch a ball. It was his idea to

125

switch-hit. I started at fourteen. The reason he waited was he wanted to see me grow, to see how much I liked the game. Kids right now start the game at six, seven, eight, and a lot of parents push their kids to play the game when they don't want to play the game.

"My dad didn't push me, but he taught me. He waited to see what position I really wanted to play. It was shortstop because of my size and my arm. He hit me some grounders and more grounders. I wasn't shy. Cal Ripken, Jr., was one of my role models. We could only see one game a week [on TV], but I used to see Ripken play winter ball. I also remember Tony Gwynn and Don Mattingly in Puerto Rico."

Valentin would encounter another talented big leaguer at his own level—future Yankees center fielder Bernie Williams, who he faced in Little League in Manati and nearby towns.

"I remember he used to live two towns from mine," Williams said. "They used to bring him and his brother to play us. Jose was a pitcher and I used to hate facing him. He used to strike me out all the time. He had a good curveball. He was a guy who stood out from the crowd, even that young."

But in the end, neither player ended up with an advantage over the other. Both were talented youngsters.

"He was a tall guy, one of the biggest guys, and I was a little guy—I still am a little guy," Valentin said. "He's a superstar in the big leagues, but he was already a big star in Little League. Bernie's same guy as he was now.

"I had to throw a curve. In those years, he was almost five feet tall. You don't want to make a mistake to a guy like that."

Still another youth league opponent was Juan Gonzalez. "To see those guys playing at the same type of level, as superstars, is nice," Valentin said. "That was our dream. We always were thinking and talking, 'We want to be like this, we want to be in the big leagues, we want to do this and this.' And here we are, doing the same thing we were talking about."

Valentin was good enough to start attracting attention in high school. His shortstopping talents would soon take him far.

"When I was sixteen, a bunch of scouts were following me, heard my name all over the place," he said. "A bunch of scouts were calling my house, asking my age and what were my grades? It was kind of exciting. My dream by then was playing in the major leagues."

Eventually, Valentin signed for $22,000 with the Padres on his seventeenth birthday on October 12, 1986. He laughs at the modest price compared to latter-day paychecks. Sandy Alomar, Sr., manager of the famed Santruce Crabbers and then third-base coach with the Padres, was instrumental in his signing.

"Every time I see him, I just shake his hand," Valentin said. "Not only was he a friend, but he was a teacher."

Alomar had been put in charge of Puerto Rican scouting for the Padres after the departure of noted scout Luis Rosa from the organization. He went to see Valentin play.

"I liked his moves, everything he did in the field. I told them [the Padres] he would be a good sign for us. He would help us. We felt like he'd become a good player."

In that era, the Padres had the one of the best talent pipelines of any team in Puerto Rico. In addition to Valentin, they signed Sandy Alomar, Sr.'s sons, Sandy, Jr., and Roberto, along with Benito Santiago, Carlos Baerga, Ricky Bones, and Luis Lopez. But in ensuing years, that advantage was lost when Puerto Ricans became subject to the amateur draft.

"Teams are going to Venezuela and the Dominican [exempt from the draft] because it's cheaper for them," Alomar said.

Upon graduation from high school in 1987, Valentin immediately broke into pro ball at Class A Spokane. He did not perform particularly well, making sixty errors in his second season at Charleston and forty-six errors the following year in Riverside, batting just .194 at the same time. In 1990, a dislocated left shoulder wiped out most of his season at Wichita.

The Padres eventually let Valentin go in a trade after the 1991 season due to a need for a big league third baseman (they got Gary Sheffield). A long line of home-grown shortstops starting with Ozzie Smith, then Ozzie Guillen, and now Valentin was exiting the organization.

"The Padres said they didn't want to get rid of me, but Milwaukee asked for my services," he recalled.

Valentin would be a September call-up by Milwaukee in 1992 and 1993. Soon he'd get his chance to play regularly.

"Bill Spiers, the shortstop, had back surgery," he said. "It was a team on which I was going to have a chance.

"Halfway through the [1994] season, injuries came up and I got my opportunity to play. When that happened, I never looked back. The Brewers were my first team that gave me a chance and they taught me a lot."

The low-budget Brewers tolerated Valentin's modest averages (.239 in 1994 and .219 in 1995) along with his erratic fielding. But he showed flashes of power with 11 homers each season. In 1996, he enjoyed a huge offensive year as a shortstop with 24 homers and 95 RBIs.

Valentin was further buoyed by his first multi-year contract, a three-year deal with an option he signed in 1996. He'll also be indebted forever to then–Brewers manager Phil Garner.

"He was the guy who put me in there to play," he said. "The player I am now, I have to give credit to him. Without him, I probably wouldn't be here now. He was the first manager to put me in the lineup on a regular basis."

Valentin kept his forward momentum going even as the Brewers wallowed in mediocrity. He had forty-three homers from 1997 to 1999 while losing time to injuries. He kept hustling even as each season was lost by the All-Star break.

"That's the way it is," he said. "If a lot of players take that same approach, a lot of good success will happen. It's not a reason why you have to give up. You have to battle, battle and battle. There will be a day when you'll break out, have a big year, and that's when the big contract will come."

Valentin had to break out of Milwaukee to enjoy his big year.

◆ ◆ ◆

Then–White Sox general manager Ron Schueler rid himself of a first-class headache when he got the Brewers to take troublesome starter Jaime Navarro off his hands in a January 12, 2000, trade. Throwing in young right-hander John Snyder, who had shown some promise as a starter, Schueler landed Valentin as his regular shortstop to replace struggling youngster Mike Caruso. Also making the short trip down I-94 was starter Cal Eldred, whose early 1990s successes had been derailed by a host of arm problems.

"After Cal and Jose came over here, they kind of talked about Milwaukee, how they were happy to be here," Keith Foulke said. "Those two individuals did so much for us."

Valentin ended up a true sparkplug for the Sox. He gave the team instant offense near the top of the lineup with 25 homers, 92 RBIs, and 107 runs scored. He hit for the cycle, only the fifth player in Sox history to accomplish that feat, on April 27, 2000.

"It's surprised a lot of people," Valentin said of his power. "This is the way I use my lower body, where my strength comes from. You need to use your legs. Pitchers see how short you are, how skinny you are, and figure 'He won't do any damage.' And then you get your pitches, you make them pay."

To prove 2000 was no fluke, Valentin slugged twenty-eight homers the following season. But one old-time backer hoped he'd shorten up his swing somewhat.

"I just wish he played more of the little man's game, line drive to left, line drive to center, use his speed more," Sandy Alomar, Sr., then a Cubs coach, said. "He's a smart guy. But sometimes he tries to overswing and go for the fences, when I think he should go for the base hits."

But his firmly-established extra-base style seemed to work for Valentin. He ranked next to Frank Thomas as the team's best clutch hitter as the Sox raced to a commanding first-place lead in June and July, 2000. Opponents began to respect Valentin.

"He can get some things goings offensively," former Little League foe Bernie Williams said. "He has a very good arm in the infield. He's pretty fast, too. To me, he's one of those guys who you cannot take lightly, because he can hurt you at any time.

"He plays hard. He's a fundamentally sound player."

Although a switch-hitter, Valentin was most devastating from the left side. All but one of his 2000 homers came left-handed. But from almost day one of his youth baseball career, he was made to understand the value of switch hitting.

"I've always been a natural left-handed hitter," Valentin said. "My dad told me I'd have a good chance to be an everyday player, even if I don't make it to the professional level."

"It was hard to learn. It's difficult the way I started. You're going to face a lot of right-handed pitchers [and not get a chance to bat right-handed all that much]. I didn't face many left-handers, either in Little League or American Legion back in Puerto Rico. It's easier for guys who are natural right-handed hitters to become a left-handed hitter. For me it was a different story. I just worked on it every day. In batting practice, I hit a lot from the right side."

While his hitting pleased White Sox management, his fielding led to questions about what to do with him. Valentin had thrown the ball all over the place in the low minors, and he never got rid of his fielding bugaboos in the majors. His thirty-seven errors with the Brewers in 1996 led all big league shortstops. Many times they were errors of commission, the result of his trademark aggressiveness.

"That's the reason why I'm getting to a lot of balls not too many shortstops got to," explains Valentin. "Those guys don't have the range I did. The balls in the hole, they go for a base hit with some, but I tried to make the play."

When he first obtained Valentin, Schueler was willing to gamble that his fielding would improve.

"I had talked extensively to Eddie Brinkman, who I consider one of the best evaluators as far as looking at shortstops," the former GM said. "We knew he had great range to get to balls, but then he'd throw them away. We thought that with a lot of work in spring training, he'd get better."

Statistically, Valentin did not improve in 2000. His thirty-six errors resulted in a .950 fielding percentage, lowest among AL shortstops. But the Sox were 17-11 when he committed an error. Only sixteen of the errors led to runs. He helped turn 117 double plays, third among big league shortstops after Alex Rodriguez and Neifi Perez.

"He made errors, but I don't know how many of the errors hurt the team," Sox pitcher Mark Buehrle said. "He got to balls that a lot of guys didn't get to."

Nevertheless, new Sox GM Ken Williams felt the team needed a defensive upgrade, obtaining Royce Clayton to play shortstop for 2001. Valentin would now wander from position to position to keep his bat in the lineup.

Eventually, management decreed Valentin should stay at one position—third base. He opened the 2002 season there. But two months in, he was shifted back to shortstop, pushing Clayton aside. Valentin was happy to return to familiar territory.

If Valentin has to get on the move once again, possibly shuttling among different positions, he'll apply his old team-player philosophy. His bottom line is staying in the lineup.

"I'll play anywhere," he said. "Jose Oquendo did it for many years. He made a great career as a utilityman. He played every position like he played there every day. I'd be more than happy to do it. I'm capable to play all the positions. Not great, but I'm smart enough to play every position."

◆ ◆ ◆

Competing against a weakened Indians franchise and a Twins club that shouldn't have been more than their equal, the White Sox logically should have had a clear shot at repeating the glory of 2000 two seasons later.

But the Chicago springs have not been kind to the Sox. That attracted Jose Valentin's attention once again.

During spring training 2002, he had repeated his admonition for his teammates to give 100 percent. Otherwise, he'd jump them verbally.

He only had to wait two months into the season. On the night of May 31, 2002, the White Sox stunk it up in a 7-0 loss to the Indians in Cleveland, hard on the heels of a heartbreaking three-game sweep at the hands of the Yankees at Comiskey Park. Jerry Manuel called a forty-five-minute post-game meeting to address the issue of team intensity.

Valentin could have just as well called his own meeting and got more attention. He said unless he witnessed "more fire" by his teammates during the Indians series, he'd call them out.

"We're still missing that one piece," Valentin said. "And it's not hitting or the pitching. It's about everyone coming to the park every day and wanting to play.

"When you get beat, you want to feel like you played all nine innings and played them as hard as you can. When you have the team to do it and you're not, it's bad. I'm not saying we have guys on this team that show up for the uniform and just go out there for nine innings, but I haven't seen the fire.

"The 2000 team couldn't wait to get to the park because we knew we could beat everybody. We're just a few games back right now, and it's right there. We can't let it get away."

But the Sox kept on losing, getting swept for the second consecutive three-game series in Cleveland. In an 8-4 loss on June 1, Valentin's error opened the floodgates for an eight-run Indians fifth as starter Todd Ritchie could not stem the tide. All the runs were unearned.

"It's true that I made a mistake and it cost the perfect game or whatever for him, but after that, the house came down on us," Valentin said of Ritchie, who had retired thirteen consecutive batters going into the inning.

"[Ritchie] has to make his pitches, and he didn't make it after that. I don't know if they tried to blame it on me or whatever. But we were winning 3-0, and I made that mistake. But if you make your pitches, probably it's still the same situation.

"I've been trying to explain everything. I wish I could explain what was going on out there. But it's just been going on too long."

Not too much longer in the future, Valentin would like to stop lecturing big leaguers as teammates. He believes he has much to contribute helping run a team.

"After I retire, I'd like to be a coach," he said. "A few years or so [down the road], maybe the first Puerto Rican manager. Let's see what happens. But one of my goals is to be a coach in the minor leagues, big leagues or college. Will I ride buses again? Good question. But wherever, I'd like to teach young players how to play the game. I just want to help people."

Valentin already has plenty of experience on his resume in that field. In his adopted language, he's able to say things that silence too many of his teammates, because they'd have to look in the mirror as a result.

8

THE FIREBALLER

It wasn't just the cloudless seventy-degree late afternoon in Mesa, Arizona, that made for the glow on Kerry Wood's face as he arrived, accompanied, at a local café in March 2002.

Life is good when you start with becalmed Southwest spring weather, the best in the country, and go from there. Sitting down for an al fresco talk alongside the Chicago Cubs' young, but now-experienced flamethrower was his fiancée, Sarah Pates. The couple gave off that special aura of love and devotion always shown when two people start out life together.

The presence of Pates, probably the one person Wood could classify as his "soulmate," was one reason for the calm, confident, mature manner that marked a different Wood than the twenty-year-old kid who stunned all of baseball with his whiff-whiz performance back in 1998. If he was a slightly reticent, unassuming kid then, now with Pates as the better half of himself, Wood seemed supremely sure of every word he said, every bit of emotion expressed as the conversation got underway.

But there was more, a lot more, than just the assuredness that the pretty, personable Pates provided him. That had to be the realization that he possesses a special athletic gift that is bestowed on few others. Not even a date with the surgeon, three years previously, had been able to snatch that gift away for more than two years.

Wood is one of those pitchers who could throw the proverbial baseball through a car wash without it getting wet. Adding a tricky slider (some called it a combination slider-curve, or "slurve") that resembled Ray Milland's chemically-induced wood-repelling pitch in *It Happens Every Spring*, Wood became the most unhittable pitcher in the majors as a rookie. A whole lineup of Astros went back to the bench muttering to themselves after Wood, still only twenty on May 6, 1998, became the only pitcher to strike out his age. Even Wood is astounded when he looks at tape of that famed game, possibly the best-ever pitched in modern baseball.

"Now that I'm not throwing the other slider, and I see footage of what that slider was doing in '98, I say, 'Huh, how did I do that?'" he said. "I kind of get caught up when I see the old stuff."

A due bill came from throwing that other-worldly slider. Wood's career crashed when the tendon in his elbow steadily frayed to the point of break-down, the stresses of that magical pitch taking part of the toll. "Tommy John" transplant surgery ensued near the start of the 1999 season, and Wood was shelved for the rest of the year. But with only the 2000 campaign serving as a sometimes-shaky transition back to his old form, Wood got all of his old velocity back. If he could throw up to 100 mph in 1998, then topping the radar guns at 97 to 99 mph in 2001 was not a bad comeback at all.

Wood's gift was so powerful, his basic inner drive so strong, that it couldn't be yanked away permanently. The ability to approach, if not exceed, triple-digits on the radar gun is not far from being singular in base-ball. Those who have the natural ability, combined with a special drive, to deliver the "heater," the "Number 1," the "giddyup," any number of nick-names for a blazing, strikeout-spree fastball, roll off your tongue with the greatest of ease.

Walter "Big Train" Johnson. Bob Feller. Sandy Koufax. Nolan Ryan. Jim Maloney. Roger Clemens. "Sudden Sam" McDowell. Randy Johnson. And now Kerry Wood.

It's a talent that can't be taught or developed. It's bestowed on the fortu-nate few by the raw powers of nature. Fireballers appear on major league rosters as if they're dropped from the sky. Teams fortunate enough to land one thank their lucky stars. Curses and fear dominate opponents. Who can ever forget John Kruk's comic surrender to Randy Johnson, The Big Unit, in an All-Star Game?

"I couldn't tell you," Wood said when asked from what source he received his power. "I was born with it. It was given to me."

And the feeling of throwing so hard, so free and easy? "It's like playing catch," Wood said, echoing the exact words of another fireballer, Todd Wor-rell, who nudged the 100 mph mark as a Cardinals closer in the late 1980s before the surgeon beckoned.

Hitting coaches and weight trainers can get a slap-slash hitter to upper-cut and start belting twenty-five homers; Jim Frey never realized that when he foolishly traded .300-hitter Rafael Palmeiro from the Cubs to the Texas Rangers in 1988. A slightly-above-average-speed baserunner can became an adept base thief by studious research on pitchers' moves, and leadoff and first-step techniques from first base.

But no training or conditioning method exists to make a purveyor of an 85 mph fastball into a monster-man who can chuck it at 97 or 98 mph. Perhaps a diligent pitcher, via physical maturation or whatever, can add 2 or 3 mph onto his fastball. Yet he stays within his classification of pitcher. No one humps up from sinker-slider specialist to fireballer. Never.

Supreme confidence also is part of the package. The flamethrower expects nothing less than the best for himself. Some say little of such a goal. Others are unabashed about their place in the baseball universe. Wood's transformation in 2002 puts him in the latter group. He has swagger, he has panache. Sarah Pates said her man has "got the John Wayne presence about him." He's noticed, he's respected, he's feared. Wood only wants to back up the reputation with appropriate numbers. He believes with good health that he could be the best pitcher in baseball.

"I wouldn't be in this game if I didn't think I could be the best," he said. "I think I can always get better. I think anyone can always get better. I believe I will be. I think I have that mentality when I step out there."

Those who have shared a clubhouse and bullpen with him as teammates don't disagree.

"He has the ability to step up and be one of the greats of the game," former Cubs pitcher Kevin Tapani, who retired after the 2001 season, said. "For the first ten years of the twenty-first century, he could be the guy as far as pitchers go, and lead the pack of young talent coming up."

Wood could get to that exalted status simply because of confidence. The fact he throws so hard while augmenting his "Number 1" with knee-buckling breaking stuff does not seem out of the ordinary to Wood.

"I know what I'm capable of doing," he said. "That's what I expect of myself. It doesn't seem out of the ordinary to me because that's what I've always done."

If he does reach that goal and throws the no-hitter he believes he has a chance to record at some point, he'll cement a special linkage that he already possesses with other fireballers. He wears the uniform number 34, same as Ryan, who already has counseled him and categorized him. Wood shares agents—brothers Alan and Randy Hendricks of Houston—with Clemens. When he fanned twenty Astros, he smashed the Wrigley Field game strikeout record of eighteen set in 1962 by Koufax, a pitcher with whom he was favorably compared by Billy Williams and Ron Santo on that May day.

The flamethrowers' club is so small, so elite, that the grand masters of the past take special care to counsel those who will carry on for them. Kerry

Wood will not lack for advice as he tries to become the preeminent member of the club in the early twenty-first century.

♦ ♦ ♦

Possessed of his special talent, Wood had only one logical person to idolize growing up in suburban Dallas: Ryan. The all-time strikeout artist's pitching mechanics were used by Garry Wood when he began working with his son on the mound, at about the same time when Ryan came to town to pitch for the Rangers. The emotional connection became stronger when Wood and his father attended Ryan's seventh and final career no-hitter at Arlington Stadium in 1991.

Fellow Texan Clemens also drew Wood's attention, but Ryan was first and foremost.

"Nolan for me was bigger, just from being around so long," he said. "He was accessible, I'd see him [pitching] more often."

But a decade later, on July 21, 2001, here was Nolan Ryan watching Wood's between-starts bullpen session in Houston. And in the following offseason, there was Ryan again, running into Wood at the Players Choice awards banquet.

That budding master of confidence was nearly overwhelmed on both occasions.

"It was intimidating at first," Wood said of the bullpen session. "Here's a guy I watched growing up, a Hall of Fame legend, who has records that will never be approached."

Sarah Pates recalled her fiance's continued nervousness at the awards banquet. "He said, 'What am I going to talk to Nolan Ryan about?'" she said. Apparently it was one thing to listen to some homespun advice in a bullpen; it was another to talk to a living legend conversationally, out of uniform, on an equal footing.

The Ryan-Wood connection seemed logical to others in the game.

"I remember when I first saw him, I thought he looked like Nolan Ryan," said Hall of Fame pitcher Robin Roberts. "He throws a curveball like Nolan did. When they get that curve over, it's very hard to hit. He's fun to watch. I hope his health holds up."

Still living on his Alice, Texas, ranch, not far from Houston, Ryan connected with Wood initially in a telephone conversation in May 2001 through his relationship with Don Baylor and then–Cubs pitching coach Oscar Acosta. Wood had lost three starts in a row, including a horrific outing in Busch Stadium in which the pesky Fernando Viña slammed a triple off an eye-high pitch. Wood then reeled off six wins in a row.

Next came the Cubs' first trip into Houston that season. Ryan was invited to sit in on the workout after talking to the entire pitching staff.

"I told him to just do his normal routine," Ryan said to the *Chicago Sun-Times* after the workout. "I was going to observe, and if I see something I may make a recommendation. But I don't like to interfere with people's program and change things during the course of a season and a pennant race. That's a fine line."

Ryan was asked to compare Wood with Randy Johnson.

"I see the same potential," he said. "Randy and Kerry both have a tendency to overthrow. That's something that most people who grow up being power pitchers, that's the way they develop. They have a tendency to fall back on doing that, and I was the same way.

"When you get to his level, a lot of it is the mental approach. Getting them to see it and recognize it. The one thing I have seen [with Wood] watching on TV was that he gets his fastball up. We talked about getting his fastball down and trying to be more consistent with his delivery."

Months later, Ryan was asked if Wood was a throwback to him. He threw a curve in response.

"He reminds me more of a Roger Clemens because he's further along at this stage of his career," he said. "Roger was very much similar to him. If I do a comparison, he's one to compare him with."

Ryan also picked up the signals that Wood was poised to make a great leap forward in his professional life.

"He's getting close to putting it all together," he said. "It's real important that he continues his development. He has the potential of reaching the status of a [Curt] Schilling, a Clemens, and a [Randy] Johnson. He just needs to work on his changeup some and get ahead of hitters a little more."

Ryan wondered why so few teammates came up to him for advice during his career. The Cubs pitchers did not exactly pepper him with questions after his talk in Houston. Johnson took advantage of his magnanimous personality back in 1992 when he was struggling with the Mariners; the two conferred in the Kingdome bullpen despite the fact Ryan was an opponent pitching for Texas. Might Wood follow The Big Unit's lead and take on Ryan as his occasional guru?

"I think he's accessible if I've got something I can't figure out," Wood said. "I think I have that at my disposal at this point. I think he's been willing to talk to me if I need to. I think I can give him a call. By no means is he obligated, but it shows what kind of man he is to get this done. He's a great source."

Wood must get over the final shreds of idol-fright when approaching

Ryan. The two are so logical to share the wisdom of the ages, like Yoda and a new Jedi Knight in *Star Wars*.

"I enjoy working with people who want to improve and are willing to make that commitment," Ryan said. "Long-range, it depends on what people's needs are. [Working with Wood long-term] depends on who he looks at and who he respects. It depends on what kind of attitude he has."

♦ ♦ ♦

Ryan did not have a chance to get to know Wood that well. The pitcher does possess the right attitude. He desires another gift—the art of mound craftsmanship.

Dreaming of the day he can harness all his power to his satisfaction, he observes carefully a non-fireballer who seemingly wills his pitches to the exact desired destination. Every time Greg Maddux pitches a televised game, Wood tunes in, taking mental notes about how The Master sets up hitters, trying to figure out a way to apply that other kind of gift for himself.

The observation process had gone both ways. Maddux had intently watched Wood, and gave his stamp of approval.

"It's as good as anybody's I've seen," Maddux said in May 2000. "It's the whole package when combined. Someone might have a better fastball than Wood, someone might have a better curve. But when you put the two together, it's the best. He's got a pretty good slider, too."

Perhaps Wood is starting to learning how to observe the opponents in Maddux-like style. No small detail escapes The Master.

"I watch Maddux ten times as much as anyone else because he's on TV all the time," Wood said. "That's his gift [the backdoor fastball that cuts over the inside part of the plate to left-handed hitters]. Everyone has a different gift. I've learned about setting up hitters, little things. You've still got to set up hitters, whether you throw 95 or 90 mph.

"I basically just watch it so I can laugh, because I can't believe how much his ball moves. It's ridiculous. It just disappears on hitters. I'd take any one of his five pitches."

A Wood-Maddux meeting finally took place at the Players Choice soiree in the 2001–02 offseason. But the pair did not get a chance to talk turkey. "Just chit-chat," Wood said. "I heard he's an interesting guy, if I could get him to be serious."

Wood is serious about developing better control, but he could never conceive of being razor-sharp like Maddux. He always has piled up high pitch counts with walks and full counts back to his high school days, in the tradition of a young fireballer feeling his way to success.

"I would love to [go long stretches without a walk]," he said. "I'm going to walk my share of guys. But I'm never going to go seventy innings without a walk. It would be nice to have."

Wood would gladly sacrifice some of his trademark strikeouts to save on his arm.

"I don't like throwing that many pitches," he said. "I don't like guys fouling balls off so much and I end up walking them on twelve pitches."

Walks and high pitch counts prevented Wood from consistently going beyond the seventh inning early in his career. In his first full pro season at Class A Daytona in 1996, he walked seventy in 114⅓ innings. At Class AA Orlando in the first half of the 1997 season, he walked seventy-nine in 94 innings, then averaged almost a walk an inning with fifty-two in 57⅔ innings after being promoted at midseason to Triple-A Iowa.

The majors have hardly been any different. In his Rookie of the Year season in 1998, Wood walked eighty-five in 166⅔ innings. Coming back from elbow surgery in 2000, he walked eighty-seven in 137 innings. An overall fine season in 2001, despite a month off in August due to shoulder tendinitis, featured ninety-two walks in 174⅓ innings. Especially in 1998, Wood would reach and exceed the 100-pitch mark by the sixth inning, and would have to be pulled from the game to save his arm.

Managers and pitching coaches have been trying for 150 years to determine the sources of pitchers' wildness. Wood's own theory about himself stresses the little things that Maddux will notice in a heartbeat.

"I think a lot of it was mechanics and the ability to repeat the same delivery every time," he said. "Just being able to repeat the same delivery and mechanics, be able to adjust to fix it and go from there.

"I think I'm starting to get there [knowing where his pitches are going]. I've never been a control guy. I've been effectively wild, close enough in the zone where I'd have success."

Oddly enough, Maddux himself saw the logic in Wood being a little off the plate. Remember, The Master was never really into his walkless record in midsummer 2001.

"It's not that bad of a thing to be a little wild," he said. "Kerry's got a chance with his stuff to get away with mistakes."

Former Cubs pitcher Kevin Tapani believes the more Wood pitches, the better his control will be.

"The lack of control seems to do more with the amount he throws," Tapani said. "In the twenty-strikeout game, it was pinpoint. You watch a tape of it, and you don't see the catcher's glove move. It was like Maddux.

"He's obviously going to walk more people than someone like me did, because he throws 8 mph harder and he's got that arm speed. They'd put the ball in play more against me, but against him they'll swing and miss or foul the ball off. So he's just going to throw more pitches."

Wood also emulates Maddux in his desire to be a factor at bat. Maddux is serious about hitting and bunting, once leading the National League in hits for pitchers. Wood isn't quite up to that standard. But with his six-foot-five, 225-pound frame, he does possess more power than Maddux.

"I feel like I'm a ballplayer," Wood said. "I don't want to be classified as a pitcher. I played shortstop, I played third, I caught [in high school]. I played every position except the outfield. I love hitting. When I come up, hopefully I'll be bunting. But I'm not afraid to swing. Pitcher or no pitcher, you should at least make contact and put it into play. It's embarrassing when I go up there and look like a clown, like I've never swung the bat before."

Wood slugged two homers in his rookie season in 1998. He was so modest about one clout he refused to take a curtain call afterwards; Sammy Sosa had to doff his cap to delight the crowd in Wood's stead. Then in his first start after returning from elbow surgery on May 2, 2000, against the Houston Astros, he slugged a two-run homer off Jose Lima.

"You're always surprised when you hit it out," Wood said.

The ultimate in intestinal fortitude is yet another Maddux trait coveted by Wood. "We call it having balls," he said. "Not being intimidated in any situation. If the bases are loaded and there's nobody out, it's having the balls to throw a 1-and-0 fastball. He's [Maddux] got balls.

"You can have the biggest guy in the world, six-foot-seven, 260 pounds, solid as a rock and looks mean, but if he's throwing 2-and-1 changeups or 3-and-0 changeups with the bases loaded, he doesn't have balls. It's getting the ball and saying, 'Maybe you have the advantage, you're going to beat me with my best stuff. I'm not going to get beat myself by giving in to you.'"

Channeling one's fiery emotions properly is also on the agenda for Wood. Again, he can look to Maddux as a model. Maddux can swear a blue streak on the mound after a setback. He's a workout for lip readers watching on TV. But when it comes time moments later to work both the hitter and umpire, Maddux is an iceman on the mound, cool and composed.

Wood still could blow up like a volcano in 2001. Sarah Pates and her mother watched in near-horror as Wood came too close for comfort to an umpire after he felt a call was missed.

"I'll never forget his face, it was July 15 [2001] in Pittsburgh," Pates said. "It was a call on a curve. The umpire warned him. Oscar [Acosta] was holding him off. He was this far [holding her fingers apart] from the umpire's face. My mother said, 'Oh my God, that's not him.'"

Wood knows he has to keep the lid on as best as possible when the call doesn't go his way. Eventually, as he puts his time in and makes umpires' lives easier with more strikes and faster-paced games, he'll get the benefit of the doubt—á la Maddux and Braves teammate Tom Glavine.

"I can handle errors, I can handle giving up a bomb, I can handle not getting out of an inning because of an error," Wood said. "That's part of the game. The part of the game I need to work on is getting frustrated at umpires when they miss calls. You let that affect you, you're taking that much away from your next pitch, the next at-bat.

"Those guys [Maddux and Glavine] took their lumps getting to this point. I was told by an umpire that it's time for me to take some. He made a bad call, I was mad, he told me he took his lumps, I need to take mine. With umpires, we get into it, but we say 'hi' the next day like nothing's happened. If you're there long enough, umpires learn your mannerism, style, attitude. You'll be fine as long as you're not coming off as being an asshole all the time, yelling at them."

Wood also will learn through maturity that a hitter trying to bunt on him is no insult. One published report in the spring of 2002 related stories of Wood allegedly throwing at hitters who had attempted to lay one down on him. If that was the case, his control hadn't been in Maddux's league to punish hitters. If Maddux plunks a batter, it's a pretty good bet there was a purpose behind the pain.

The effort to combine the best of both worlds—Nolan Ryan's power and Greg Maddux's moxie—will continue for years to come for Kerry Wood. If he's successful, he'd be in nirvana. A Wood who could throw 99 mph while expertly working the hitters? It wouldn't be fair. At that point, he'd be pitching in a higher league than the majors. He would then walk with Sandy Koufax, perhaps the best of all time.

◆ ◆ ◆

Wood may have been born with lightning in his arm, but even the great flamethrowers had long grooming processes, with plenty of fits and starts. Ryan, who struggled with his control throughout his twenties, would be the first to admit that.

Wood's first playing field was the family's back yard in Irving, Texas. In classic fashion, he and his brother built up their arms playing catch with their father, Garry, every day after work. There would be no fascination with first-generation video games in this early 1980s scene.

"We didn't have all that stuff like that back then," Wood said. "We weren't spoiled with a lot of video games. We spent most of our time outside, playing with the other kids. My dad would come home from work, and we'd drag him out to the backyard to play catch for an hour or two."

But Garry Wood was no six o'clock coach. He'd coach his sons in Little League. And he saw a pint-sized kid with giant desire, but no indication he'd eventually become a physical tower of power on the mound.

"Kerry was five and he was playing on the seven- and eight-year-olds team," the elder Wood said. "He'd always been a good skills player, but he was always small growing up."

Wood didn't even pitch much at the start.

"I remember being a middle infielder, not much of a pitcher. I played third, short and first, and caught a little bit. I was fast, had a good arm, and could hit the ball and put it in play. I could play pretty much everywhere, except the outfield.

"I always had a pretty good arm. Occasionally, I'd come in to pitch a little bit. I didn't really get serious about pitching until I was a sophomore in high school."

The big breakthrough came when Wood began growing as a sophomore at MacArthur High School in Irving.

"He grew a lot and threw harder and harder," said Garry Wood, who taught his son the curveball grip at about the same time. Wood began "messing around" with the curve, which remained the only other offering in his repertoire until his second year in pro baseball.

The first scout who noticed Wood, after his sophomore year, apparently was the late Pat Rigby, a local scout for the Texas Rangers. Other scouts then gathered to watch Arlington High School and its ballyhooed outfielder, Ben Grieve, play MacArthur. They saw Wood warming up and approaching 90 mph.

Garry Wood moved his family to Grand Prairie, another Dallas suburb, before Kerry's senior year in 1994. Playing summer ball that season, then–area Cubs scout Bill Capps first noticed Wood. "I saw a tall kid with a loose arm. He was a good-looking kid," Capps said in 1998. Capps, who died in 2001, filed reports back to the front office in Chicago, same as he had for Roger Clemens and Johnny Bench, both of whom he recommended—futilely—that the Cubs draft.

Coaching Wood at Grand Prairie was Mike McGilvray. By now, Wood was a rawboned six-foot-four, 185 pounds, "with the potential to fill out," the coach said. Wood began working out with weights and in the swimming pool at McGilvray's behest.

"We used those little boards you held out in front of you so you could kick and strengthen your legs, and we did exercises for the shoulder in the water," McGilvray said. "You can't pull a muscle in the pool. It's a great conditioner and helps with flexibility."

Scouts began to track both Wood and Grand Prairie left-hander Kevin Walker. "At our first scrimmage [of 1995], we had thirty-five to forty scouts," McGilvray said. "Soon it was an every-week deal with scouts calling me, asking when Kerry would pitch. The big thing in his senior year was to keep him focused on the season, to get him to have fun, to get him to relax, knowing that there would be thirty-five guys with [radar] guns watching him."

Wood did not disappoint. He kept gaining velocity, up to 94 mph, as his senior year progressed. By the time of the draft, he had amassed a 12-0 record, 0.77 ERA, and 139 strikeouts in 72⅓ innings. Meanwhile, scouts administered vision and psychological tests to the pitching prodigy. Capps reported back to Wrigley Field that Wood was a potential number one pick. Cubs cross-checkers arrived to watch Wood.

The 1995 draft finally arrived on June 1. Darin Erstad of the University of Nebraska was the consensus number one pick, selected by the Angels. Next up was high school catcher Ben Davis of Malvern, Pennsylvania, picked by the Padres. Then the Mariners tapped into some baseball bloodlines with outfielder Jose Cruz, Jr., of Rice University.

Al Goldis, the Cubs scouting director in '95, later claimed he sweated out Wood's availability. He loved drafting pitchers, anyway. The first ten picks of what later turned out to be a disastrous Cubs draft in 1994 were all pitchers. When Wood's name came up on the board, Goldis naturally pulled the trigger. Goldis would soon be drummed out of the Cubs organization, disenchanted and discredited, but Cubs president and general manager Andy MacPhail always took pains to praise him for doing his due diligence in picking Wood.

"I think we got the best pitcher in the draft," Goldis said immediately after the announcement of the number one pick. "Every outing was better, better, better.

"I haven't seen a guy throw like this in ten years. If Dwight Gooden was in this draft, I would have taken Wood over him. We felt, 'Let's take a kid with a higher ceiling.' You can take a safer player who will get to the big leagues faster, but they won't be as good as the one who takes a little longer."

A group of reporters gathered in Wrigley Field's Stadium Club to talk to Wood via a teleconference. "How's it goin' y'all?" Wood chimed in with a homespun Texas greeting over the squawk box. He was appropriately humble when talking about his talent.

But within a few days, the Cubs got an authentic scare with an ominous report out of the Dallas area about Wood. It seems Grand Prairie was involved in a playoff doubleheader. Wood pitched both games, throwing 175 pitches. Speculation started up that Wood had hurt himself, and that his family was angry at McGilvray for endangering the golden goose.

"It was my idea to pitch in both games," Wood said on July 29, 1995, when he made his first appearance at Wrigley Field after being signed for a $1,265,000 bonus. "I pitched seven innings in the first game, and two innings in the second game. I feel fine."

Subtly, though, the stress of channeling that lightning through his right arm was starting to build up in Wood's elbow. Although McGilvray claimed that his star "had the best mechanics of any high school pitcher I ever saw," Wood in fact would periodically drift off-course in his delivery. He'd throw across his body, a precursor for arm problems. Wood was not a stickler for rigorous conditioning, carrying a few extra pounds while getting by on pure talent. Perhaps recognizing the possibility of disaster if he wasn't placed under glass, the Cubs handled Wood with kid gloves. As it was, Wood spent three weeks on the disabled list in May and June 1996 with right elbow soreness during his first full season at Class A Daytona of the competitive Florida State League.

But when he took the mound, the warning signs blew away as Wood wowed the front office and fans with his potential. He was 10-2 with a 2.91 ERA with 136 strikeouts in 114⅓ innings at Daytona. His arrival at Wrigley Field seemed sooner rather than later.

The following spring, outside the Cubs' minor league locker room at Fitch Park in Mesa, Wood sat down to talk about his seemingly limitless future. Yes, he was confident his day would come. But with the publicity building over his strikeout feats and the Cubs in dire need of a savior, surely the hoopla and hype would be crushing when he finally arrived in Chicago?

"I'll be able to handle it," said Wood, still only nineteen at the time.

But even wet-behind-the-ears fireballers couldn't be prepared for the whirlwind of 1998.

◆ ◆ ◆

Kerry Wood first faced major league hitters in a spring training game at the Maryvale ballpark against the Milwaukee Brewers. Strikeout victim John Jaha barely saw Wood's pitches. There was surprisingly little hoopla. Only two reporters visited Wood to ask about the milestone afterward in the visitor's clubhouse.

He would never be so alone again in his baseball rounds.

An almost unanimous consensus of players and media in spring training proclaimed Wood, at twenty, ready for the Cubs rotation. But the management duo of team president Andy MacPhail and general manager Ed Lynch was known for its caution and deliberate nature at the time. Wood was optioned to Triple-A Iowa at the end of spring training. The by-product of the demotion, of course, was that Wood's eventual free agency year would be delayed by not putting in a full season in Chicago.

Wood couldn't be kept down for long. After one start for Iowa, he was called up to start on April 12 in Montreal. Although Wood took the loss in a 4-1 decision, he struck out seven in four and two-thirds innings, including Mark Grudzielanek, the first batter he faced.

But in his next start, on April 18 at Wrigley Field in his home debut, Wood lived up to his billing, beating the Dodgers 8-1. For good measure, Wood collected his first major league hit off Hideo Nomo in an eight-run Cubs first inning.

Cubs fans began gathering "K" signs in the left field bleachers as Wood settled into the rotation. But they almost ran out of poster board on the rainy, dank Wednesday afternoon of May 6 with the Houston Astros, a top Cubs tormentor throughout the 1990s, in town.

Wood might have approached his first pitch with dread, and not because of the Killer Bs—Jeff Bagwell, Craig Biggio, and Derek Bell—along with a future teammate, Moises Alou, waiting to take their cuts. He was positively putrid warming up.

Almost four years later, sitting at the café in Mesa, Wood still marveled about the contrast once he crossed the white lines.

"It was the worst bullpen [warm-up] I had all year," he recalled. "I don't think I threw one strike. I was horrible. I was bouncing them, threw them over the catcher. All my pitches."

So what happened?

"I was concentrating, especially after my bullpen was so bad," he said. "I went to the dugout, stopped everything, sorted everything out and got everything under control."

He experienced the same vibes, but not the results, in ensuing starts.

"I look at it, and I say I need to get that feel," Wood said. "I've had that feel since then. I haven't struck out twenty, but I've had the feeling like I'm playing catch. I felt like I was in a tunnel, that all I could see was the catcher and the hitter. I saw Sandy Martinez and the hitter. Strike one, strike two and then strike three. It [concentration] just came as I started the innings."

Martinez simply squatted behind the plate as the other end of baseball's greatest mound virtuoso act in memory. Wood began employing his special slider-curve that he had began using in the minor leagues.

"I love the slider," Wood would say. "I'll throw it anytime. It helps the curve. The last five feet, it dives toward the left-handed batter's box. It's a pitch that looks like a fastball coming in. It's a pitch I throw when I need a ground ball with a man on base."

Wood got a lot more than grounders when he broke off the slurve. The predominantly right-handed Astros lineup, always susceptible to a good breaking pitch, began eating out of his hand.

He fanned Biggio, Bell, and Bagwell [looking] in the first. Then Jack Howell and Moises Alou whiffed to start the second. Left fielder Dave Clark finally made contact, flying to center to end the second.

Wood had to be sharp, since mound opponent Shane Reynolds also had a strikeout pitch going. Reynolds fanned Brant Brown, Mickey Morandini, and Sammy Sosa in order in the first. Reynolds was nicked for a run on Mark Grace's double and Henry Rodriguez's sacrifice fly in the second. But other than another run on a Jose Hernandez grounder in the eighth, Reynolds pitched a game worthy of a victory most days. He would go on to strike out ten Cubs.

How the Cubs did at-bat gradually faded into the background as Wood starting flirting with history. He really would have gone to the front of all pitching gems had third baseman Kevin Orie dived for a slow grounder by Astros shortstop Ricky Gutierrez leading off the second. The ball dribbled under his glove. Official scorer Don Friske ruled it a hit.

"I figured maybe I had a chance to get it, but it died," Orie said afterward. "It came off the bat quick, but it's always a tough road when this grass slows balls up.

"So I ended up trying to stretch for it and it stayed outside. I was thinking of diving and then not diving. Diving's not my style, but maybe if I dived, I could have got up and made the play."

Unshaken, Wood then fanned Brad Ausmus. Reynolds sacrificed Gutierrez to second, but then Biggio grounded out to end the third.

Wood plowed ahead, the slider dancing all over the plate when he wasn't throwing a high-90s mph heater. Bell flied to right in the fourth, then Bagwell and Howell were called out on strikes. That was the same fate in the fifth for Alou, Clark, and Gutierrez as Wood reached ten strikeouts.

Meanwhile, light rain that had plagued the game began intensifying. Grace began lobbying the umpiring crew to keep the contest going. The politicking apparently worked; no action toward preparing for a delay was ever noticed.

Ausmus grounded out to start the six, then Reynolds was called out for number twelve. Wood then hit Biggio, baseball's top target, but Bell popped to first to end the sixth.

Then Wood really went to work in the manner of all the great fireballers, who knew how to finish with a flourish. Bagwell, Howell, and Alou went down swinging in the seventh. When Clark did likewise leading off the eighth, Wood now had the all-time single-game Cubs record of sixteen, supplanting Dick Drott in 1957, Burt Hooton in 1971, and Rick Sutcliffe in 1984. Gutierrez (swinging) and Ausmus (looking) made it eighteen to finish the eighth.

Amid a Wrigley Field pressbox abuzz with activity and tension with the developing story, Cubs media relations stalwart Chuck Wasserstrom turned around to a baseball history buff to inquire as to when and where the rookie record for strikeouts in a game that Wood had just tied took place. Bill Gullickson at Montreal against the then–last place Cubs near the end of the 1980 season (September 10) was the response. Also tied was the Wrigley Field record of eighteen set by Sandy Koufax against another weak Cubs squad on April 24, 1962.

But Wood would soon take his team off the hook for those log entries of baseball ignominy.

Wood now had gone long past the informal pitch-count limit that management had prescribed for him, but Cubs manager Jim Riggleman had no choice. His prized pitcher was hurling a game for the ages.

The rookie went back out in the ninth as the 120-pitch count was surpassed. Bill Spiers, pinch-hitting for Reynolds, fanned for number nineteen, his seventh straight strikeout to tie a team record set by Jamie Moyer, of all people. Also reached with nineteen were the all-time strikeout highs for Wood idol Nolan Ryan, Randy Johnson, Steve Carlton, Tom Seaver, and David Cone. Only one more remained to equal Roger Clemens's nine-inning record, set in 1986 and 1996.

The plucky Biggio made contact, but grounded out to shortstop. Now, he couldn't surpass Clemens, but still had a shot at twenty. Bell was the last man up.

Wood ran the count to 1-and-2. Bell was helpless, missing the tricky offering for number twenty.

Wood was mobbed by his teammates. Bulletins rang out through broadcast networks and wire services. History had been duly recorded, and awe was the predominant mood for everyone in the clubhouses afterward except for one key participant.

Kerry Wood.

Young fireballer Kerry Wood was compared to Ryan, Clemens, and Koufax, especially after his 20-strikeout masterpiece against the Houston Astros in 1998, when he never registered under 95 mph on his fastball. *Stephen Green/Chicago Cubs*

"I didn't care if it was a five-hitter," Wood said when asked about the scoring call on the Gutierrez dribbler. "We won."

Oh, but who has ever won like that? A twenty-strikeout game that seemed better than most no-hitters. Hey, Cubs lefty Ken Holtzman somehow pitched a Wrigley Field no-hitter without a strikeout—twenty-seven batted balls for outs—on August 19, 1969. Exactly four years to the day previously, the Reds' Jim Maloney pitched a ten-inning no-hitter in the same ballpark—with a record ten walks.

Immediately, Cubs bench coach Billy Williams and radio color analyst Ron Santo were sought out for the magic comparison to Koufax, whose combination of high 90s mph fastball and "12 to 6" curveball have not really been surpassed. Koufax had pitched the last of his four no-hitters, this time a perfect game, against the Cubs on September 9, 1965. Williams and Santo, then two of the best hitters in baseball, were helpless against Koufax, who struck out fourteen, including the last six in a row, that night in Dodger Stadium.

Was Wood's performance a direct reminder of Koufax, up to the lefty's Valhalla standards?

Both Williams and Santo replied in the affirmative.

"The only thing comparable to this was Sandy Koufax's perfect game," Hall of Famer Williams said. "This game compares with Koufax's best."

Astros manager Larry Dierker also had been witness to Koufax's artistry as a young Houston pitcher in the mid-1960s. He also set the rookie apart from his peers.

"You can clearly distinguish what he is throwing from what everyone else it the league throws," Dierker said.

One Astros radar gun reading had Wood at an even 100 mph at his tops. He hit 99 mph several times. The fastball was not clocked below 95 mph all afternoon. The curveball was 72 mph, while the all-powerful slider-curve was between 82 and 84 mph.

"It's really hard to believe he's only twenty years old," White Sox scout Dave Yoakum said after the game. "He's a full-grown man out there. And he throws one pitch 99, then comes back and throws the next one that's a curveball and starts in your face and breaks into the strike zone."

In the excited Cubs clubhouse afterward, Wood tried to downplay his feat. Later, he turned down offers of late-night show appearances. But he would not be successful in returning to an ordinary routine. His life would change for the better—and the worse—over the next year.

♦ ♦ ♦

Wood's first workouts after the twenty-strikeout game attracted far more attention that the average pitcher's. Cub pitchers Steve Trachsel, Mark Clark, Terry Adams, Bob Patterson, and Marc Pisciotta stood by, watching, as Wood went through his paces with pitching coach Phil Regan.

Whatever he did worked. In his next start on May 11, he set the modern record for strikeouts in consecutive games by fanning thirteen Diamondbacks at Bank One Ballpark. He struck out pinch hitter Yamil Benitez to end the seventh inning to run his total to thirty-three, beating a record shared by—who else—Nolan Ryan, along with Randy Johnson, Luis Tiant and Dwight Gooden.

Sammy Sosa had not yet recorded his record-breaking twenty-homer month in June, 1998. The home-run race with Mark McGwire was still a couple of months into the future. Along with McGwire's hot start, Kerry Wood became baseball's top conversation piece.

Just turning twenty-one, Wood at first struggled to handle all the distractions.

"For me coming up in that situation with all the attention I was getting there early on, there were just so many things going on I was forgetting all kinds of stuff," he said. "I came to the field one day and left the stove on at the apartment. I was pitching that day. I'm sending for fire trucks while I'm on the mound. I had to go have somebody call the apartment."

Wood, obviously, was overjoyed as Sosa gradually took over center stage by midsummer.

"He was a poster boy and he handled it well," Wood said near season's end. "He's definitely taking a lot of the tension and pressure off me, which definitely couldn't hurt."

Sometimes Wood and Sosa would combine for an on-field spectacular. Sosa slugged seven of his sixty-six homers in Wood's starts. Sosa even took a curtain call on behalf of a reticent Wood on August 31 after the pitcher slugged a two-run homer off the Reds' Brett Tomko.

"They didn't come to see me take curtain calls," Wood said.

He was right. The fans stirred in their seats, waiting for strikeouts. He'd go on to fan sixteen Reds in an August 26 game in Cincinnati. He recorded two other thirteen-strikeout performances and four other outings with ten or more whiffs. Wood even bested The Master. On July 21 in Atlanta, he fanned eleven Braves in seven and two-thirds innings in outdueling Greg Maddux, 3-0. He would go on to total 233 strikeouts in 169^2/$_3$ innings, a league-leading 12.6 per nine innings. Opponents batted just .196 against him.

Wood sometimes would save his best for last. Cubs pitching assistant Rick Kranitz manned the team's radar gun during games. On several occasions, Kranitz reported that Wood's top speed of the game, 100 mph, was on his last pitch before being pulled. Wood knew his time was about to be up as manager Jim Riggleman fidgeted in the dugout, and had just enough gas in the tank to finish with a flourish.

But trouble started to brew as August began. Wood was said to be experiencing what was euphemistically called a "tired arm." Word began to circulate that he was suffering elbow problems. The sixteen-strikeout game [over eight innings] in Cincinnati and the August 31 start at Wrigley Field preceded the stunning announcement that Wood had sprained the ulnar collateral ligament in his elbow. He was disabled for the entire month of September while the Cubs' wild-card playoff hopes nearly took a fatal tumble.

Against a torrent of opposition concerned about his elbow, the Cubs brought Wood back to pitch Game 3 of the Division Series against the Braves at Wrigley Field on October 3. This time, Maddux was a bit better as Wood departed after five innings, trailing 1-0. The Braves went on to win 6-2, sweeping the Cubs in the series. With his 13-6 record and strikeout feats, Wood went on to beat out Rockies first baseman Todd Helton for NL Rookie of the Year honors.

He would have to rest on those laurels for another year. The elbow remained a concern for Wood and the Cubs throughout the offseason of 1998–99, and the team was cautious in re-starting him in spring training. He did not take the mound until March 13. Wood was even wilder than usual, lasting just one and one-third innings against the Angels. There was good reason for the disastrous outing. The ulnar collateral ligament had torn. Wood underwent "Tommy John" surgery, performed by noted surgeon James Andrews, on April 8. He would not throw off a mound again until December 20, 1999.

While he waited for nature and a rehab program to mend the elbow, Wood remained optimistic about his future. His logic? The old ligament had been weak. Now he had a brand new, no-mileage one transplanted in its place. Wood was not afraid of any drop in velocity when he eventually returned to the mound. In fact, he replied in the affirmative when asked if he'd take 95 mph with control as a top speed in a comeback.

"From day one, after the surgery, I didn't have a second thought in my mind that I couldn't make it back," he said.

Wood eventually would bump it above 95 mph, but it would come after plenty of frustration.

He started out fast, though. The rehab and minor league tune-ups worked out on schedule. Wood returned to the Cubs in dramatic fashion on

May 2, 2000, against the Astros, by now his favorite team, in a night game at Wrigley Field. Throwing ninety-six pitches over six innings, Wood added his own special touch of drama by slugging a two-run homer off Jose Lima on the very first pitch he saw in his first at-bat in the second inning. Finishing the night with a yield of one run and three hits, Wood "gives us hope," Sosa said after the game.

But the next few months were rocky. Wood's command and velocity were inconsistent as he built back his arm strength. His record dropped to 3-6 in July. He also went on the disabled list for more than three weeks with a muscle strain in his left side. When he came back in late August, Wood began to right himself. In his last five starts of 2000, Wood struck out thirty-one in thirty and one-third innings, allowing just seven earned runs. He rallied to finish above .500 at 8-7 on a horrid Cubs team that went 65-97 overall.

Not even a 1-4 start in 2001 could stop the forward momentum that began near the end of the previous season. Wood returned almost all the way to his 20-K form on May 25, 2001. He threw a one-hit shutout against the Brewers, striking out fourteen while walking just two, nursing the thinnest of margins to a 1-0 victory. The day before, Cubs pitcher Jon Lieber had one-hit the Reds, making the stingy outings only the eighth time in big league history teammates had thrown back-to-back one-hitters.

Over his last twenty starts of 2001, Wood was 11-2 with a 2.71 ERA. He would have been even better than his final 12-6, 3.36 ERA performance had he not missed a month with shoulder tendonitis. The disablement caused yet more panic in Chicago with daily bulletins about Wood's condition. Former Cubs Cy Young Award winner Rick Sutcliffe, a sometime confidant of Wood through his friendship with Mark Grace, even stirred up a firestorm when he suggested on a Chicago radio show that Wood was more seriously injured than advertised. Wood angrily denied Sutcliffe's report and vowed he wouldn't soon talk to him. The two made up, though, and Wood returned to the mound in September.

If Wood's dominance hadn't been proved in 1998, then 2001 erased all doubts. He struck out 217 in 174$\frac{1}{3}$ innings. Meanwhile, he held opposing hitters to a major league low .202 batting average.

Wood now was in the up cycle of his career. All the while, the positives of his personal life were outpacing his professional comeback, almost out of sight of the always-prying eyes of the media.

◆ ◆ ◆

Wood may have been dropped from the sky with his raw talent. But once he alighted on earth, he had to achieve a certain grounding in his life to propel himself forward emotionally. Man was not bred to live alone. And through-out his early career, when he didn't accompany new-found buddy Mark Grace out on some of the latter's nocturnal rounds, he had just the four walls of his apartment in which to confide when the myriad frustrations of big league life enveloped him.

That all changed amid a rut in the middle of his comeback season. He met Sarah Pates. And ever since, Wood's low-key, off-the-field life has changed for the better. The relationship has had nothing but a positive effect on Wood's approach to his job. He seemed so much more sure of himself, a feeling that came across loud and clear as he and Pates exuded pure positivism at the café in Mesa on that picture-perfect late afternoon.

The couple first met July 6, 2000, at a bar named Cactus in downtown Chicago. Pates was waitressing there while working her way through nearby Columbia College, after having worked as a marketing associate for Price Waterhouse Cooper.

Fate seemed to intervene. Pates wasn't even supposed to work that Thursday night. And Wood wanted to stay at home to chill out before his start against the White Sox at Wrigley Field the next afternoon. But Grace and his buddies wore him down over the phone, luring him out.

"I told them, OK, I'll come up there, say hi to the fellas, and I'll have one drink and I'll leave," Wood recalled.

Pates and her fellow servers wore different-colored wigs this night. Hers was green. "I turned to Gracie's best man and said, 'Damn, she's got green hair and she still looks good,'" Wood said. "Of course, he's five or six [drinks] deep, walks over [to Pates] and says, 'My buddy wants to talk to you.'"

"I was so turned off," Pates said of being bugged. "When you wait tables, you're used to a lot of people trying to talk to you. Then there was this drunk guy with his arm hanging over me saying, 'My buddy wants to meet you.' He [Wood] was sitting there quiet, laid-back like me."

Wood wanted to leave after two Crown doubles, but Pates kept them coming, apparently at the behest of Grace's crowd. Now why would Grace want to get his teammate tipsy, at the minimum, the night before he pitched?

"I must have been going bad, so he did it to get me out of a funk," Wood theorized.

Pates didn't know who Wood was. She wasn't even a baseball fan.

"I thought he was one of Gracie's buddies from out of town," she said. "I was at a couple of Cubs games as a kid [a native of Waukegan, forty miles north of Chicago]. I knew that name [Grace]. But all I knew [about the Cubs] was they kind of stunk."

So why did Wood stay at Cactus?

"I was telling the guys, 'See ya later.' But she said, 'You're not leaving, you've got another drink coming.' I said, 'I'll have a drink if you'll do a shot.' She does it again. I gotta go, but she keeps bringing them."

After "seven or eight," he quit, somewhat weak-kneed, and went home. Somehow, Wood got to his feet the next day to pitch eight innings of two-run ball, walking four and striking out six, against the White Sox. That game marked just the first time since his elbow surgery that he had gone eight innings in a game.

Following that game, Grace and Co. returned to Cactus and told Pates that Wood would come back to meet her. She doubted that. "Gracie said, 'You're Woody's girl.' I said, 'Who's Woody?' I didn't think I'd ever see him again."

Wood initially was of a like mind-set. "I was debating whether to go back," he said. "I didn't want to feel like a schmo, a stalker. But all the guys were there again."

Pates was bet $100 from her antagonists that Wood would show up. Grace and his friends frantically called Wood again. He soon arrived, tired from his day's work, but somehow invigorated by the betting action regarding his presence.

"At the end of the night, he pays for the tab, adds $100 to the tab [covering her wager] and says not to bet against him," Pates said.

She lost her bet, but gained her soulmate.

"She got off work, the whole group went out to play pool and we realized we're very similar," Wood said. "We started seeing each other regularly."

After Pates hit it off with Wood's family in suburban Dallas on Thanksgiving 2000, the couple moved in together at Wood's offseason home in Fountain Hills, Arizona. Wood now had training in domestic culture; as a bachelor living alone he used parts of cardboard cartons in lieu of draperies in his windows and crammed the living room to overflowing. "I just eye-balled it and ordered too much furniture," Wood said. "Six couches in one room. Gawd!" Pates added. Now learning, Wood helped properly outfit the house, played with the couple's new puppy, and took guitar lessons. Most important, he had someone with which to share his hopes, dreams, and fears.

"You go from not having anybody to talk to, to having someone you can tell anything to," Wood said. "We're best friends. We haven't hidden anything. We talk to each other about anything and everything. People who see us together expect I'll change as a person. It will calm me down and make me grow up. I'm not twenty-one years old, living in a house with a box in the window. I'm lucky to find the one I was meant for. Some people don't ever find them."

Pates had to get used to the baseball life while taking a crash course in the sport's nuances and history.

"I almost wished he was a plumber so I could see him more often," she said. The legend of Wood's twenty-strikeout game wasn't even known to her until she was informed about it while on her second road trip with her guy. Pates developed into a necessary sounding board for the pitcher of the house.

"She handles everything well, good press or bad press," Wood said. "I let off steam [when he was disabled for a month in 2001]. She knows I'm frustrated because I'm not pitching. She's very good at not taking offense if I'm in a bad mood. I talk to her about everything. I talk to her about pitching to guys. She'll go through lineups with me in the morning."

Pates persuaded Wood, who carried some baby fat with him early in his big league career, to work out more diligently in the winter of 2001–02. While not a couch potato, Wood admittedly had "never been a big fitness, workout guy."

"Kerry has an immense amount of talent," Pates said. "As our bodies start to change [with maturity], he can't just go off on his talent."

In turn, Wood and Pates have developed a value system in which sheer financial worth is not the end-all to their life, despite his $3 million-plus salary in 2002.

"We feel money is the root of all evil," Pates said. "I still buy him Hawaiian shirts at Target. It could end at any time. We're smart. A lot of guys out there aren't smart at all. We live in a $200,000 house, and we love it. We take pride in it and he's working on it. It's bigger than anything we grew up in."

"I got $1.265 million [as a signing bonus out of high school]. I put it in the bank, bought a truck and a boat," Wood said. "I didn't need to go out and buy all sorts of fancy things, jewelry, houses, and cars. I was eighteen years old and I put it away. I bought the one thing I wanted—a boat. My mom and dad got cars and bills paid. Obviously, our lifestyles will change as we make more money. You're going to get a bigger house, but we're not going to have twelve cars and four houses.

"I didn't come here for the money. I love the game. Whether you have $3 million or $30 million, what's the difference? You could live off either one of them. Yeah, at twenty-four I was financially set for life. Amazing."

"You could live off $100,000," Pates interjected.

Wood continued his line of thinking when asked if he would try to break the bank with the Cubs when the time comes to reward him with a multi-year contract after a big season and to keep him out of free agency.

"I will never press for more of anything," he said. "They know what's fair, we know what's fair. If we can get that knocked out in the first conversation, then we're settled. I'm pretty easy to deal with. I'm not going to battle for an extra $200,000 or an extra $1 million, as ridiculous as that sounds. You work out deals and meet in the middle."

Wood does not favor indiscriminate amounts of money being thrown at players in the game, particularly coveted youngsters.

"What I think might have to be worked on is guys coming out of college or high school who haven't even faced a minor league player, and now they're up into ridiculous amounts," he said. "I don't know how many guys I've seen in the minor leagues hurt their arm. If you sit and look at it, eventually it has to stop."

But if anyone wants Wood to comment in the offseason on the latest signing that pushes the megabucks contract envelope even higher, they will have to go through ballclub screeners to reach the pitcher—if he'll want to talk. Wood and Pates like to keep their private life private. His home number is not usually available to any media types, even those he knows.

"When I leave the field, my business is done," Wood said. "I don't have to go to work again or deal with [the media]."

"I've noticed that a lot of women really get wrapped up in the season," Pates said. "But to really strengthen him on the inside, we spend a lot of time together in the offseason. We really value the offseason as a couple. We're in our sweats, going to the grocery store and being normal people."

In Chicago, the couple live in a Lincoln Park apartment Pates described as "a little nook."

"We don't go out at all," she said. "We go to Lawry's [a steakhouse], see our favorite waiter, go to Joe's Stone Crab, and that's about it."

Wood refused endorsement and national-media appearance offers after his twenty-strikeout game. Even in spring training 2002, he preferred to keep to his baseball business and private life with Pates. When approached in the HoHoKam Park clubhouse in Mesa by a Cubs official about reading a radio commercial liner for the team, Wood politely declined. "I'm not a commercial guy," he said.

Wood goes even further in advocating his low-key style. Not only should a player's private life stay out of the limelight, but part of his work routine also should be off-limits to the media, Wood reasoned.

"I look at it this way," he said. "You guys have five minutes [after the game]. Most of the time I can bullshit my way through five minutes and tell you what you want to hear. I never read the papers.

"I think the media sometimes goes too far [in clubhouse coverage]. Some things don't need to be printed. If a guy's trying to play through an injury, has an ice bag on a part of his body it's not usually on and a reporter sees it, he'll blow it out of proportion."

But what about the fans' right to know about injuries?

"We'll let you know if we're injured," Wood said. "The public has a right to know about the game, what's going on. If the player wants to talk about things other than the game, that's at the player's discretion. There's a difference getting hurt and being injured. If you're injured, you're out, you can't play. If you're hurt, and a lot of guys play hurt, you deal with it.

"The concern with your progress [rehabbing an injury], being updated with the progress, that's one thing. Questioning and having doubts about how an organization is handling a player through rehab, whether it's too fast or too slow, is different."

Wood ended up at the forefront of the biggest Cubs clubhouse blowup in memory in the waning days of the 2001 season. Word leaked out that pitching coach Oscar Acosta was going to be forced out due to personality conflicts with manager Don Baylor. At the very same time, another story broke that the majority of Cubs players rebelled against the workouts and speeches of Mack Newton, Baylor's hand-picked fitness guru/motivator. The two stories merged into one giant conflagration. Taskmaster Acosta, a former Newton backer, had criticized the workout routine. The coach was tight with Wood, Lieber, and several other key veterans. Wood was so distraught about Acosta's situation that he suggested he would not make his scheduled final season start on October 4. Reportedly, Cubs official Jim Hendry talked Wood out of any sitdown-strike thoughts.

"I'd say there is [clubhouse] division," Wood after the start, a six-inning, ten-strikeout no-decision in a scoreless game.

"There's definitely got to be some trust won back," he added, referring to Baylor's offseason work in bringing the Cubs back together. Whatever effort was undertaken eventually proved unsuccessful in 2002.

So should the media have reported the Acosta-Newton-Baylor rhubarb the way they did? After all, the mild-mannered Lieber was so incensed he called the Acosta sacking "bullshit" on WGN-Radio, the team's flagship station. The comment aired uncensored.

"You have a situation where a group of players was adamant about something," Wood said five months later. "You're not going to have a whole group of players do that unless it's justified.

"But to be honest, I don't think fans should know about anything going on in the clubhouse. If a player doesn't like another player, it's none of the fans' business. That's just the way it is—guys don't get along with other guys, coaches don't get along with other coaches. When relationships are thrown into the papers, a lot of that could be kept in the clubhouse. Fans want to read about the team, the game. I'm sure the fans want to know about the players. But I don't think the fans would want reporters coming to their offices and asking about their personal lives."

The Acosta/Newton affair did not end Wood's plain-speaking stance. He ended up sounding off to some twenty reporters on the night of May 13, 2002, at Busch Stadium, assuming a role as unofficial team conscience when the Cubs totally collapsed going into the season's second month.

Wood kept a stream of consciousness going after he suffered a tough 3-0 loss to Cardinals ace Matt Morris:

"It's just getting real fucking tired of hearing the same shit every time the game's over: Just fucking keep your head up, we'll get them tomorrow. That shit ain't working. It's just frustrating."

"It's getting more frustrating as we go along."

He was asked whether his teammates shared his frustration.

"I hope so. Shit, I hope so. There's nothing more that I can say other than it's frustrating and it's getting real fucking old."

Wood was not pleased with his teammates' apparent cashing-it-in attitude so early in the season.

"We're playing like it's August and we're fifteen games under, and we're playing like we're already out of it. So if you can't get up for a Cubs-Cardinals series, then you got some problems. We're dead. We're flat.

"The whole team, we're 13-22 or whatever the fuck we are as a team. I think everybody needs to look in the mirror and see if they can honestly tell themselves that they're giving it all, myself included."

Finally, Wood was asked what factor would prompt a change in the clubhouse attitude.

"I don't know. I have no clue," he said. "I haven't seen any sign of anything, of any life. Somebody's got to step up and do something or collectively as a group we gotta step up as a team, and we just haven't been doing that."

Wood respects the work of most baseball beat writers. Columnists, though, are another story.

"There are different types of reporters," he said. "One who tries to make a name for himself. He hides behind a desk and comes to the clubhouse twice a year. Then there are reporters who are there day-in and day-out who understand what you go through, understand situations and are able to talk to you on another level, as opposed to a guy sitting at his desk downtown writing his own opinion."

Wood took issue with *Chicago Sun-Times* columnist Jay Mariotti's analysis of his Busch Stadium comments. He believed Mariotti changed the focus of the diatribe, making it look like Wood was taking shots at then–Cubs manager Don Baylor. The issue then escalated into a hissing match between Mariotti and rival *Chicago Tribune* columnist Rick Morrissey, who took him to task for allegedly twisting Wood's statements.

Wood will not shy away from speaking up when necessary at other opportune moments.

"Right now I feel like I always have," he said. "I'm laid-back, get along with everybody and can have a conversation and joke with anybody on the team. I feel like I belong because I've been in the organization the longest.

"I'm not going to have a team meeting every day. I will go around individually and ask them what they think of the situation and give them my opinion—right to the point."

One opinion Wood is not shy about expressing is an increasing feeling the Cubs have finally turned the corner from their unwanted image as baseball's lovable losers.

◆ ◆ ◆

During some dark days in 1999 and 2000, while he struggled to come back from surgery, Wood was none too pleased at how the Cubs conducted their business, on and off the field.

The team had become an embarrassment after their surprise wild-card playoff season in 1998. In August and September of '99 and '00, the Cubs tried to set all-time team records for late-season nosedives. In one stretch in '99, the Cubs were 10-40, even worse than a horrid division title–busting post–All-Star break slide of 10-33 back in 1973.

But after team president Andy MacPhail came down from the "Mt. Olympus" that he had sarcastically referred as the team presidency to take over from Ed Lynch as general manager, the Cubs' fortunes slowly began to improve. Confidence was the first shot in the arm, as Lynch had been unpopular with most players and could air-condition the clubhouse just by passing by. In contrast, MacPhail had long been one of baseball's most respected executives. The third-generation baseball man could move in any circles, make a deal with anyone. His talents had been wasted for more than five years up on the mount as team president, supposedly allowing the inexperienced Lynch to make all the day-to-day personnel moves.

Even factoring in the Cubs' horrid start in 2002, Wood is more optimistic than ever about the franchise's future, thanks to MacPhail's presence.

"Andy's a baseball man, he came from a baseball family, and he's very good at his job," Wood said. "He's a player's guy. He talks to the players. His door is always open. I think players need that kind of image of their GM and their upper brass, knowing they support the team and the players, knowing they want to win."

The Cubs improved to 88-74 in 2001, even holding down first place for two and one-half months through mid-August. MacPhail then made the biggest up-front free agent signing in team history by snaring outfielder Moises Alou. That move confirmed the feeling in the eyes of Wood and other teammates that the losing syndrome so long associated with the Cubs was being swatted away.

"We showed the fans we wanted to win [in 2001], getting Fred McGriff," Wood said. "The only move we could have made that would have been better than what we did was getting a season ticket for that [billy] goat, and I'm still thinking of doing that."

Wood might consider buying early for the goat. That's the most common curse supposedly afflicting the Cubs and causing their decades-long journey in baseball wilderness. According to the legend, a local tavernkeeper named William "Billy Goat" Sianis tried to take his seats at the 1945 World Series at Wrigley Field in the company of his mascot goat. Ushers refused the animal admission, so Sianis supposedly put a curse on the Cubs, hexing them until a Sianis goat was allowed into the ballpark. Starting in 1982, numerous goats were brought onto the field by Sianis's nephew, Sam, but the Cubs' fortunes haven't really changed.

But even with yet another pratfall, with a $75 million payroll, the most expensive in team history in 2002, Wood still is optimistic about the overall trend of his franchise.

"I think it [team attitude] is changing. They had a losing tradition, the worst streak in any sport. It's known. For a long time, people knew if you came to the Cubs, there's a pretty good chance you're not going to win. You saw some of the players the Cubs brought in. They did not go after the best available.

"Today, the front office changed people's opinion on the will to win. That was the big question mark for a long time. I even had that, to be honest with you. But now there's no question marks. Without a doubt, there's a statement we are turning things around and are serious about winning."

But winning just one year won't totally change the Cubs' image. Wood will discount any one-year wonders.

"One year winning is not going to change everything," he said. "In order to change a losing tradition into a winning tradition, you can't just win one year. You have to be the Yankees, Atlanta, the Mets. You have to prove you can make it there and deserve it every year."

If the Cubs ever do become a consistent winner in the near future, guess who will logically be in the forefront, throwing the ball at nearly triple-digit speeds, serving the intimidator's role that Randy Johnson and Curt Schilling had for the 2001 Diamondbacks? There's only one player on the Cubs who qualifies.

He's eager for the role. Kerry Wood has always dreamed of taking the mound during the World Series. He has all the confidence in his heart he'll do it in Cubby blue. And if that happens, once again all eyes will be on Kid K, same as they have since that rainy May day against the Astros in 1998.

"Every player in baseball has thought of being in Game 7 [of the World Series]," Wood said. "We've been doing it since we were five years old, playing in the backyard with a tennis ball. That's what everyone shoots for. I can't wait to be in that situation. I had a chance in '98 to be in a playoff atmosphere, and I can't wait to get back in it. You want the ball in that situation, just like the shortstop wants to make a diving play in the eighth."

Even if it's last raps in Yankee Stadium, with Wood bearing the crushing weight of wiping out all the curses, jinxes, bad karma and every other crazy thing that has happened to the Cubs over the better part of a century?

"Let's do it, strap it on, let's see who's better today," said the pitcher with a storied past, but who can also see clearly into the future.

9

⚬⚬⚬

THE CRAFTY LEFTY

You'd figure the duel would be a mismatch: slowballing Jamie Moyer of the Seattle Mariners against the powerful, World Series–tested New York Yankees in Game 3 of the American League Championship Series on October 20, 2001, at Yankee Stadium. Just another stop on the way to another Fall Classic title for the Yanks. The thirty-eight-year-old Moyer would run out of gas after the long season, right? And the lineup of professional hitters would certainly time Moyer's pitches well by the second time around the order, to be sure.

Yet the mismatch didn't go the way most figured. Using his trademark changeup that should be easy to hit but isn't, and factoring in the left-hander's guile and fearlessness, New York's bats were no match for Moyer.

He had just racked up two victories against a potent Cleveland Indians lineup in the American League Division Series. He had allowed just eight hits and two walks while striking out ten in his twelve innings of work. An encore would give the Mariners a shot in the most hostile of postseason environments.

New York had perked up right off the bat when Moyer served up a two-run homer to Bernie Williams in the first. But at the same time, the Yankees could see what Moyer under control could accomplish. He fanned Chuck Knoblauch on a 72 mph change-up. Calling Moyer a "cagey pitcher," TV color analyst Tim McCarver said scouts could use a thermometer instead of a radar gun to time Moyer's pedestrian-paced pitches. Sure enough, a fastball a few innings later was timed at all of 82 mph.

Moyer makes liberal use of his defense and every inch of the ballpark. In the third, left fielder Stan Javier leaped at the faraway fence in the deep part of Yankee Stadium to bring back a potential homer by Alfonso Soriano.

Moyer was in the midst of retiring twelve straight hitters after Williams's blast.

"I felt like once I got into the fourth inning, I got a second wind," Moyer said.

He held the Yankees long enough for the Mariners' offense to wake up on a fifth-inning two-run single by Bret Boone. Opening the sixth, John Olerud homered off the right field foul pole. Seattle went on to score six more runs in the inning.

Moyer decided to toss in his own personal change-up. He went to the clubhouse "to change our luck" during the big inning.

"It's a little game I play sometimes," he said. "Even when you score runs at times, I feel like I try not to get caught up in the celebration or the guys talking in the dugout and things like that."

One more inning of work, and manager Lou Piniella dismissed Moyer for the day. He rarely let him finish anyway with just eleven complete games in his six years as a Mariner. But he had dictated the emotional pace of the game. The Yankees hitters would become frustrated, which has become the modus operandi of Jamie Moyer after sixteen years in the majors.

Jamie Moyer delivers during the 2001 American League Championship Series against the New York Yankees, holding the powerful Bronx Bombers to two runs over seven innings. *Getty Images/M. David Leeds*

"We certainly felt that we had the chance to do some good things," Yankees manager Joe Torre said. "And I think you have to credit Jamie for keeping us right there at two runs."

Moyer's final line was seven innings, four hits, two runs, one walk and five strikeouts.

"He can carve up the best of the lineups," McCarver told his national TV audience.

Moyer would not get his chance to pitch in a World Series. The Yankees' postseason experience somehow canceled out the sheer team brilliance that marked the Mariners' unforgettable, 116-victory season in 2001. The whole world would not get to observe the triumph of old-school values, dedication and perseverance that makes up the pitching package of Moyer, who sported an 85-40 record for the Mariners between 1996 and 2001, and a 151-117 big-league overall mark through 2001.

By now, everyone in baseball knows all about Moyer. Even those who doubted him early on, who found it easy to cast him aside, who discriminated against him because he doesn't possess an above-average fastball, had to tip their caps to Moyer.

Brains and heart go a long way for pitchers if properly used. And Moyer was merely following a well-worn path that dates back to antiquity in the game. If you don't possess sheer speed and power, then technique and savvy can be adequate substitutes. It's seemingly even more pronounced if you're a left-hander.

Moyer is the living baseball embodiment of that old adage that the race often belongs to the tortoise, not the hare. You can hurry up to end up going nowhere. Take your time. That applies to both Moyer's pitches and the long, circuitous journey, spanning the continent, he undertook to become a twenty-game winner and earn the respect of an entire sport.

◆ ◆ ◆

For some age-old reason, left-handers don't have to throw hard to succeed. In fact, they can almost lob the ball into the catcher if they have fine control and location. Crafty left-handers can survive and prosper, and do both for a long time, if you simply examine the numbers in the *Baseball Encyclopedia* or other record books.

"We're a right-handed–dominated world," Jamie Moyer said. "Go to any Little League or college program. It's proven that a lefty who has a selection of pitches can succeed."

If a right-hander tried the same strategy, he'd usually be hammered and wouldn't last long. Soft-tossing right-handers simply aren't part of the game.

Whether it's the way their ball breaks in relation to the predominately right-handed corps of hitters or the relative scarcity of left-handers of any ability, the southpaw who relies on movement, location and smarts always seems to have a job in the game. Other than Mike Morgan, the record-setter with twelve teams on his baseball card, the most well-traveled group of pitchers were left-handers.

And these lefties who meander under the speed limit aren't awesome specimens of height and heft. More cerebral than physical, they can appear as Everyman. Moyer is six-feet, 170 pounds—same weight as in 1988—and is still somewhat boyish in appearance. At thirty-nine, he hardly appeared to have aged since his early years with the Cubs in the mid-1980s. The Mariners' knowledgeable ace, though, is a hulk compared to some of the southpaws who have preceded him. Being pint-sized at five-foot-six, 139 pounds did not stop Bobby Shantz from winning twenty-four games for the 1952 Philadelphia Athletics. Fred Norman, five-foot-eight and 155 pounds, won 104 games from 1970–80 for the Cincinnati Reds and several other teams. Yankees craftsman Eddie Lopat was comparatively beefy at five-foot-ten, 185 pounds when he held forth as "Steady Eddie" for Casey Stengel's early dynastic teams.

"Usually these guys have to basically pitch more with their heads than with their arms," Seattle Mariners general manager Pat Gillick said. "These guys really have to calculate and strategize with every pitch."

"They keep the ball down," longtime baseball executive Roland Hemond—now with the White Sox—said, "and have action on their pitches to make the ball sink, then push you off the plate inside to show it to you and work the outside corner a lot. They get strikes a little off the plate."

But there's a caveat. Almost every pitch of a soft-tossing lefty has to be finely-tuned. If they're left out over too much of the plate, disaster is waiting to happen.

"He's got to be razor-sharp and he can't afford to fall behind," then–Mariners manager Lou Piniella said. "And he can't pitch the middle of the plate like a lot of these guys who have an overpowering fastball."

The crafty left-handers' knowledge of the game actually was once more widespread to more of the pitching brethren. Piniella said the old-fashioned pitchers had to emphasize brains as much as brawn, even if they had great fastballs. That archetype is less common at present.

"They had to be, because they pitched longer in ballgames," he said. "They had to face a hitter three or four times, sometimes five times in a night. They had to make adjustments where they had to face that hitter the fourth or fifth time. That's why you don't see pitchers think as much as they used to. Now the reliever comes in. Then they had no pitch counts. Unless a guy was really, really tired, he stayed around."

The left-handers served as role models for those who followed in their wake. When he was a young pitcher who thought he could get by on raw ability, Jamie Moyer's first choice was to follow a pitcher with both power and guile, whose very nickname was "Lefty."

"I grew up in Pennsylvania," Moyer said. "Steve Carlton was my idol."

But he also took notice of southpaws who did not have the ability to blow hitters away with 94 mph fastballs.

"I also watched guys like Frank Tanana, John Tudor, Tom Browning, Jim Deshaies, Randy Jones, Tommy John," Moyer said. "Also Bruce Hurst and Bobby Ojeda.

"I used to love watching Jimmy Key. I'd come out early in the King-dome and watch him throw. When he was on the mound, I wouldn't take my eyes off of him. There were things that you could pick up."

Moyer reminded some of baseball's best minds of smart southpaws of the past they had witnessed.

"There's quite a bit of Tommy John in him," Hemond said. "There was also Jim Kaat and Ed Lopat. I was a big Red Sox fan and Lopat used to hand-cuff the big Red Sox sluggers with off-speed pitches.

"Frank Tanana, once he hurt his arm, he became an off-speed pitcher who spotted his fastball quite well," Piniella said. "He had a good changeup and a good curveball. Then there was Geoff Zahn, the closest I've seen to Jamie, comparison-wise. Larry Gura was another one."

Gillick cited Gura in particular along with former Mariner Dave Flem-ing and Steve Mingori.

One day some left-hander, cerebral and full of motivation to make full use of stuff that won't light up radar guns, may be compared with Moyer.

"He's a throwback, he really, really is," Piniella said. "He doesn't give in to hitters. He depends on change of speeds, and guile and location rather than velocity. He's got his own book on all of them [hitters].

"He wins. What can I tell you?"

♦ ♦ ♦

What's the old saying—"I throw the ball just as hard, but it doesn't get there as fast?"

That was true when applied to Jamie Moyer. But he has a dream of being able to wind up and actually throw a classic hummer or three to his catcher.

"Every now and then, I see a dominant pitcher pitch a game, a Curt Schilling, a Randy Johnson, a Kerry Wood, a Dennis Martinez. I say, 'Wow,

I wish I had a 92 mph fastball.' I don't know what I'd do with that, if for one day, God gave me the ability to reach back and throw 92, 94 mph. To have that kind of arm, though, comes with a lot of other problems. When guys throw that hard, hitters sit on the fastball.

"I don't know how many times guys who throw that hard come up to me and say, 'I'd love to have your changeup.'"

If Gaylord Perry could author a book entitled *Me and the Spitter,* then Moyer could update the tome and change the name of the pitch to "Change-up." And there'd be nothing illegal about his offering. Only deliberate—and amazing.

Change-ups are the majority of hurlers' third- or fourth-best pitch. They often desperately need the slowball to offer hitters something radically different from their typical "Number 1"—the fastball. In many cases pitchers simply never master the nuances of the change-up, thrown with a fastball motion, but arriving at the plate some 15 to 20 mph slower than the fastball.

For Moyer, though, the change-up is more than just an "out" pitch. It's his lifeline to survive and prosper in the major leagues. Lacking a fastball that could crack 90 mph and a knee-buckling, "12 to 6" curveball, he had to come up with another tack to win.

"He knew how to pitch, and had an outstanding change-up then," scout Bill Harford said of Moyer in the mid-1980s, when Harford was the assistant farm director for the Cubs. "It complemented his fastball very well. The difference in velocity made his fastball look a lot quicker than it was. But his fastball was a little greater than it is now."

Eventually, Moyer picked up a cut fastball while further refining the change-up. He now executes the pokey pitch perhaps better than anyone else in baseball.

"I figured out how to use each pitch to set up another pitch," Moyer said of the change-up. "I feel I've gotten better at that. I fine-tuned the thing. I've thrown as many as 60 change-ups in a game."

Combined with an extensive book on hitters' tendencies and his own natural determination and intelligence, Moyer uses the change-up to outfox the majority of hitters.

"Hitting is timing," he said. "The art of pitching is to break up timing. There's a large gap between 95 and 80 [mph]. Hitters are creatures of habit. Everyone can hit a fastball. The object is to stay away from the speed limit. If you're below that range, you rely on location—like real estate—and movement on the ball.

"The hitter tells you how you're pitching by how he's reacting to the pitch. It's like a chess match, moving the pieces around. You're trying to read his mind, his body language. You try to read the hitter, try to read his confidence, read what an opposing manager does. Is there someone in the lineup who tries to pull off-speed pitches? I'm trying to observe the hitters' reactions to the pitches."

Quality hitters past and present confirm Moyer's analysis, starting with Lou Piniella, his manager in Seattle.

"It was the hardest pitch for me to hit, especially a left-hander's changeup that sort of moved away from me every so slightly," Piniella said. "He [Moyer] would have been tough on me. You have to have patience, and had to hit the ball to all fields, not just pull it. You had to take the change-up away from him, hopefully the first two at-bats, hit it hard and make him throw you other pitches."

Mariners first baseman John Olerud has to bring his "A" game mentally to hit the game's best change-ups.

"The thing that makes the change-up such a good pitch is that everything about it makes it look like a fastball," he said. "It's the type of pitch that you could look for, and it's still hard to hit. The first reaction is to a fastball, and you go after it. That tells you why he's so successful, because he has such a good change-up.

"I think it's a great pitch, and that's the reason he's had so much success because it looks like a fastball."

Can you time a change-up?

"Yes, it's possible. You can do it. You have to force yourself that I'm not going to start my swing until he's just about let go [of the pitch]. A lot of times you start your swing when he's getting ready to throw it. It slows you down to where you have a chance. But if he throws a fastball, you've got no chance to hit it because you'd just be too late. Somebody has a real good change-up, mixes it up well, it's tough to hit."

Olerud had to develop a strategy against Moyer when he batted against him as a Toronto Blue Jay.

"My approach was to try to hit him the other way," he said. "A lot of times lefties don't like to throw change-ups to left-handed hitters. Sometimes lefties have better success because left-handers aren't throwing their best pitches against them."

The latter theory has been tried by none other than the switch-hitting Carl Everett, who batted left-handed against Moyer. "It takes away the sinking ball from him," Piniella said. A similar tactic was employed by switch-hitter Brian McRae, who batted left-handed against Braves southpaw Tom Glavine in the mid-1990s.

Rest assured, hitters need to research Moyer as much as he preps against them. Be it the change-up, what remains of his fastball or any other pitch, a lifetime of having to outthink hitters has made him ready to craft any sequence of pitches against opposing hitters.

"I'm always preparing," he said. "After I pitch, for the next four days, I'm preparing. At a game, I'm watching opposing hitters. I'm watching our pitcher, I'm watching their pitcher. I go back in my notes, try to sit down with my catcher to work up a game plan."

Moyer could probably teach the art of pitching and preparation better than anyone this side of old teammate Greg Maddux. He was offered that chance while still in his twenties. But there was more pitching left in his arm, even if it didn't seem that way at the time.

◆ ◆ ◆

Jamie Moyer, a graduate of Souderton Area High School in Pennsylvania, was good enough coming out of St. Joseph's University in Philadelphia to be drafted in the sixth round by the Cubs in 1984. Taken ahead of him were Morehead State (Kentucky) pitcher Drew Hall, a fellow lefty, in the first round and a skinny high-schooler named Greg Maddux out of Las Vegas in the second.

The doubters that would dog him his entire career were present and accounted for in 1984.

"I was told out of high school that I don't throw hard enough," Moyer said. "I've been told that all my life."

Moyer realized almost immediately that he'd have to outwork his competition to make the majors.

"When I went to mini–spring training after I signed with the Cubs, you could see the guys with the great arms, throwing 90-plus," he said. "I saw Maddux, Hall, Jackie Davidson, Carl Hamilton and Jeff Schwarz. Stacking myself up against those people, there was no comparison."

But there was one important difference. Moyer knew how to win. He was 9-3 in low Class A Geneva the remainder of 1984 after signing. In 1985, he was a combined 15-8 divided between high–Class A Winston-Salem and Double-A Pittsfield.

Moyer still has vivid memories of the lessons he learned and the people who taught him in what was then considered one of baseball's most productive farm systems run by the courtly player development guru Gordon Goldsberry. The likes of Moyer, Maddux, Rafael Palmeiro, Mark Grace, Shawon Dunston, Joe Girardi, Davey Martinez, and several other notables who played effectively more than a decade into their careers, beyond the 1990s, came out of that system.

Goldsberry would later help shepherd Moyer's career back on track with the Orioles after it derailed in 1991–92. Beloved by almost all with whom he had professional and personal contact, Goldsberry died of heart trouble early in 1996 while preparing to attend spring training in Arizona as an Orioles scout.

"There were all these great players developed by the Cubs," Moyer said. "Gordon Goldsberry is looking down on us and smiling."

Given tremendous latitude by then–general manager Dallas Green, Goldsberry had hired good instructors, empowering them to use a good cop/tough cop style when necessary. The minor league folks lit a fire under Moyer.

"My first year at Geneva under [manager] Tony Franklin and Bill Ballew, the pitching coach, taught me that this has become my occupation, not my hobby," he said. "Tony gave me the nickname 'Vern.' I was very fortunate to be around professional people early in my career. I started to see and realize I could pitch at a high level. Each level I had some success. I felt pretty good about myself, about pitching.

"But I didn't necessarily become a student of the game until I got to Double-A. I learned about the inner half of the plate. That's when the light went on for me. When I got to Triple-A, I learned more from the manager, Larry Cox, and Jim Colborn, the pitching coach. Jim Snyder [the taskmaster who doubled as coordinator of instruction] was a big help.

"I was never touted as a big prospect, so it was instilled in me that I had to work. When you live that work, work that way around that environment, it brought out the best in you. All the PFPs, running, circle jerks, that prepares you. They wanted to push each and every player to get themselves to the big leagues."

The feeling was mutual. Goldsberry and his aides put Moyer on a fast track toward the majors.

"Jamie was a terrific kid, a great worker, great personality," said Bill Harford, then assistant Cubs farm director. "He's still probably one of my favorite players as far as makeup."

A combined 6-3 record split between Pittsfield and Triple-A Iowa in 1986 led to his call-up to the Cubs on June 14. "I was behind Johnny Abrego and Steve Engel," he said of two trivia answers in Cubs annals. "Whenever Engel moved up, I moved up. I was very fortunate to be in an organization that was pitching-deprived at the major league level."

Moyer's advancement indeed might have been a little fast. The parent team was racked with injuries and ineffectiveness from the likes of Rick Sutcliffe, Dennis Eckersley, Steve Trout, and Scott Sanderson, who had all earned lucrative free agent contracts after the Cubs' astounding National League East title in 1984. Moyer displayed the inconsistencies of youth with a 7-4 record, but also a 5.05 ERA and 107 hits allowed in 87⅓ innings.

"Sutcliffe and Sanderson took me under their wing," Moyer said. "Jody Davis was good to me. So were Steve Lake and Manny Trillo. Early in my career, I walked a lot of people after I thought I had good command in the minors. I was in awe, playing against guys I had watched growing up."

Moyer showed more signs of progress in 1987, but wore down somewhat in the season's second half with his softer stuff, and an apparently juiced-ball season of hitters and a team that sagged badly after Labor Day. He finished 12-15 with a 5.10 ERA, allowing 97 walks and 28 homers in 201 innings, after he had been 8-4 with a 3.76 ERA as late as June 22. He had taken a no-hitter with 12 strikeouts through eight innings at Philadelphia on April 13 before Juan Samuel led off the ninth with a single. And on July 3, he set a then–Cubs record with seven consecutive strikeouts against the Giants at Wrigley Field.

Moyer seemed to improve his overall performance in 1988, but it wasn't reflected in his won-lost record. He had three complete games and his second career shutout, but lost a series of low-run contests, thanks to a suddenly power-short Cubs offense. Each 4-2 or 3-1 defeat seemed to further annoy new manager Don Zimmer, never a friend of pitchers. Moyer finished 1988 with a 9-15 record to go with a good 3.48 ERA and just 55 walks allowed in 202 innings.

"With Zimmer, I have no idea what happened," Moyer said. "There's still some things that baffle me about him. Low-run losses happen to a lot of left-handed pitchers."

Zimmer's old Cincinnati chum, Cubs general manager Jim Frey, already had become dissatisfied with Palmeiro's perceived lack of power and run production, despite the overall drop of power numbers throughout the league. "I want guys who can hit the shit out of the ball," was Frey's mantra then. Now Moyer was lumped into the discard pile. The rushed trade of stopper Lee Smith a year earlier combined with Goose Gossage's failures as his successor pressured Frey into combing for a new stopper. Eventually both were packaged along with former prospect Drew Hall in a deal for the Wild Thing, Mitch Williams, and five other major- and minor-leaguers from the Rangers.

"I really didn't get to know Frey and Zimmer as people," Moyer said. "I really didn't know the nuts and bolts of what they were trying to do. It was very different compared to the Dallas Green–Gordon Goldsberry regime. I was a big believer in both of them. But they [Frey and Zimmer] let some pretty intelligent baseball people go. There was a lot of disarray."

Moyer seemed to find a new home at Arlington Stadium. He struck out a career-high thirteen in eight innings in his first 1989 start against Toronto on April 8. He was 3-0 with a 2.28 ERA in his first four starts. But his left shoulder began to ache and his performance quickly declined. Moyer was placed on the disabled list May 31, not to return until the rosters were expanded September 1. He finished 1989 at 4-9 with a 4.86 ERA.

His first serious bout with arm trouble pushed him out of the Rangers' rotation for 1990. Moyer made just ten starts among his thirty-three appearances, going 2-6 with a 4.66 ERA. Leaving Texas as a free agent, he joined the Cardinals in 1991. But he declined even further. Opening the season in the St. Louis rotation, Moyer was 0-5 with a 5.74 ERA. He was optioned to Louisville late in May. Little did he know at the time that he would not pitch in another big league game for two years.

After spending the rest of the '91 season in Triple-A, Moyer was released. He tried to hook on with the Cubs in spring training 1992, but he did not have a good camp and was released on March 30. However, Bill Harford, by now the Cubs' farm director, had another idea about how Moyer could contribute. He offered the twenty-nine-year-old a job as an assistant pitching coach, almost a coaching "intern" job.

"He didn't have a good spring," Harford recalled. "We offered his contract to all the other clubs. They could have had him for nothing, and nobody wanted him. His career was almost over."

But Moyer wouldn't give up. "Jamie, to his credit, said, 'Bill, I think I can still pitch.'" He went home to South Bend, where he resided with wife Karen and then-infant son Dillon. The experience was morale-busting.

"We were home for six weeks, after we had just built a home in Indiana," said Karen Moyer, daughter of former Notre Dame basketball coach Digger Phelps. "He couldn't go anywhere. He tried to get unemployment after his release from the Cubs. He went home and sat by our phone. Every day it was something new. We thought we were going to Italy to play. We thought about Japan.

"My dad was trying to find him another job with Skyline Corporation in Elkhart, which built mobile homes. But he didn't yet have his college degree."

Finally, on May 24, Moyer signed a minor league contract with the Tigers to pitch at Triple-A Toledo.

"It was for $150 a week," Karen recalled. "It was peanuts. We went to

Toledo for the summer. We lived in a one-bedroom apartment with Dillon and our two Samoyed dogs. Our life was at the minor league park."

Moyer went 10-8 with a 2.86 ERA at Toledo, but did not get called up to Detroit in September.

Yet within weeks after the end of the '92 season, Moyer's luck began to turn. There was an advantage in being Digger Phelps' son-in-law. You got to meet some interesting folks.

People like then–Orioles GM Roland Hemond. Moyer turned out to be in the right place at the right time.

"Ed Farmer [White Sox announcer] took me to South Bend to see a Notre Dame–Penn State football game," Hemond said. "I talked to a base-ball group run by coach Pat Murphy in the morning. Then he said, 'Let's see Digger Phelps, there's a basketball game that night.' Jamie Moyer was in his office. I had a chat with him, and I was impressed with him."

Hemond then talked with one of his special assistants. Again, Moyer was fortunate. Hemond's aide was Gordon Goldsberry, who knew Moyer better than most baseball types after having supervised his minor-league development. Goldsberry had been fired by Jim Frey late in the 1988 season before hooking on with the Orioles.

Hemond's recollection of the conversation: "Gordy said, 'We ought to give him a chance. I've always liked Jamie. I don't think he pitches quickly enough. I was always on him to not waste time between pitches.'"

Moyer got his chance. Baltimore signed him as a six-year free agent on December 19, 1992. He started the 1993 season at Triple-A Rochester, the Orioles' top farm club.

"I saw him pitch against the 'Dream Team' of Richmond [the Braves' top affiliate] with Chipper Jones and Javier Lopez on a real, real cold day in Rochester," Hemond said. "He handcuffed them that day. Two or three weeks later we brought him up to the big leagues and the rest was history."

Moyer and his family were fighting their own deadline at this point.

"We had decided if he was not called up to Baltimore by May 31, we'd put our house on the market. We needed the money," Karen Moyer said. They beat the deadline by one day. Moyer was called up with his sparkling 6-0 record and 1.67 ERA while his wife burned up the miles driving between Rochester, Baltimore, and New York packing up an apartment with their two small sons in tow. The rest of their lives began.

♦ ♦ ♦

Reinvigorated, Moyer was 12-9 with a 3.43 ERA in twenty-five starts the final four months of the 1993 season in Baltimore. His performance would slip in the next two seasons, fractured by the debilitating strike. But he had now re-established himself in the majors, albeit as a pitcher who required razor-sharp control to succeed.

Tempting the age-old fate of southpaws at Fenway Park, Moyer signed as a free agent with the Red Sox after the 1995 season.

"I had a so-so year with the Orioles and they weren't interested in re-signing me," Moyer said. "Dan Duquette called, and said he'd like to sign me as the fifth man or swingman, or as a long reliever. I said that's fine. I didn't start the '96 season in the rotation. But we were in Kansas City and all of a sudden they said I'd start. I pitched well, won, and then went back to the bullpen for a couple of weeks. Then a spot start, back to the bullpen, and I was a mop-up guy. I went to [manager] Kevin Kennedy on numerous occasions. Boston was having a horrible first half, underachieving miserably on a Mo Vaughn–led team.

"When we pitched well, we didn't hit. When we scored ten runs, we'd give up twelve. It was a team effort to play badly. I went to Kennedy and told him I just wanted him to know if he needed another starter, I'd want a spot start. Each time I thanked him. They kept calling up guys from the minor leagues to spot-start. Finally I pitched well against the Yankees. I got a chance to start on a regular basis around the All-Star break. By now I'd heard that the Rangers were interested in me, the Mariners were interested in me.

"One day I was supposed to start against Kansas City. I was supposed to stretch, but I was told Kevin wanted to talk to me. I figured something was going on. He said I was traded to the Mariners for Darren Bragg. I got on the phone with Dan Duquette and he gave me his song-and-dance."

In reality, Moyer was enjoying the biggest break of his career. On July 30, 1996, he took his 7-1 record to a still-developing team that really needed his moxie.

"Lou [Piniella] put out his hand out and said he's looking for someone to pitch," Moyer said.

Piniella got more than he bargained for. Moyer finished out the '96 season as the tortoise to Randy Johnson's hare, his 6-2 record and 3.31 ERA elevating him to true crafty-lefty status. And to prove '96 was no fluke, Moyer went 17-5 with a 3.86 ERA for the Mariners in 1997. He was particularly dominating in the cozy Kingdome with a 12-2 record and 3.63 ERA that season.

"You figure out a way to pitch in all ballparks," Moyer said. "I didn't mind pitching in the Kingdome. I felt that was an advantage I had. Guys came in complaining about pitching in the Kingdome."

Moyer began dictating the pace of the game, even if his pitches were among the game's slowest.

"One of the things Gordy [Goldsberry] told Jamie that he has applied, is working fast," Bill Harford said. "He's never going to be an overpowering guy. Keep your infielders in the game, throw strikes, work fast. I saw one game where he sprinted to the mound before Bartolo Colon left the mound."

Moyer couldn't master every hitter in the game.

"Guys that hit me well were Manny Ramirez and Bernie Williams," he said. "I had a lot of success against Chili Davis in the National League, but I couldn't get him out in the American League."

By the end of 1998, Moyer became Seattle's ranking lefty after the monster trade-deadline deal of Johnson to the Astros. He didn't disappoint with 15-9 and 14-8 records in 1998 and 1999, respectively. Moyer now ranked as one of baseball's top control pitchers. Between 1997 and 1999, he did not walk more than forty-eight batters in any one season.

All the while, he did not forget who helped him along the way.

"He sent me an autographed baseball when he won his 100th major-league victory," Hemond said of one 1998 Moyer triumph.

Halfway across the continent, Harford, by now a scout, watched Moyer in admiration. No doubt the lefty never second-guessed his decision not to take up coaching in 1992.

"A decade later, and a lot of money later, he's done extremely well," Harford said. "He's made millions after turning down that coaching job. It's a credit to him, his perseverance and his makeup."

Moyer would stumble in the 2000 season, his 13-10 record belying a fat 5.49 ERA as his performance nosedived in August. Trying to get back on track as the Mariners advanced to the American League Championship Series, Moyer suffered a hairline fracture of his left kneecap while pitching a simulated game on October 7. His season was over, but his overall career still had a lot more steam than one of his fastballs.

Despite his troubles in 2000, Moyer now was a near-institution in Seattle. Taking his place in the rotation in 2001, he proved that age and experience are often the strongest allies for a crafty lefty.

Moyer's 20-6 season with a 3.43 ERA was slightly submerged among the astounding team achievement by the Mariners: a record-tying 116 victories that made an early shambles of the American League West pennant race.

Showing that he wasn't about to coast while the Mariners had everything locked up, Moyer pitched even better as the dog days commenced. He went 11-2 to finish up the season with the American League's second-best second-half ERA of 2.22.

Obviously, Moyer's season proved that any pitcher need not have over-powering stuff to win twenty games. Nor do they necessarily require youth to be on their side. At thirty-eight, he was the oldest major leaguer in history to win twenty games for the first time.

"I think it can be done by anybody," he said. "As a pitcher, you've got to do a lot of the right things. But I also believe you've got to be surrounded by a lot of good people, and I was. We played very good defense, we scored a lot of runs, we had a lot of timely hitting. That's why I won twenty games, that why we won 116 games. We played as a team, we won as a team, we lost as a team. The whole season was a team effort.

"I try not to put any kind of parameters on what's going on. You go out and work hard between your starts. You just go out and pitch. Once you set limits on yourself, once you start to reach some of those goals, you tend to slack off a little bit. I leave that [limitations] up to the media, they seem to be pretty good at that."

Moyer started off hot and never looked back. He was 5-0 after a victory against the Red Sox on May 3. Later, he would tie a Mariners record of ten consecutive victories in a thirteen-start span between July 23 and September 24. On October 5, he won his twentieth game, allowing four hits in seven innings in a 6-2 victory over the Rangers at Safeco Field.

All along, Piniella managed Moyer's workload carefully.

"One thing about Jamie is the pitch count," Piniella said. "He gets to a certain pitch count in the game, the ball starts coming up and that's when he's more prone to get hit. So we watch his pitch counts very, very carefully. If we have the good fortune of giving him a good lead, we might shorten him up [in innings] so he's stronger for the next two or three starts."

Moyer brought his "A" game against baseball's premiere franchise, becoming a Yankee-killer in the process. He was 2-0 in three starts against the defending World Champions, allowing just three runs and twelve hits in twenty innings.

Such mastery merely built on confidence that had long existed. Moyer felt no need to gaze over at the Yankees dugout to give the "I-told-you-so" look at bench coach Don Zimmer, the man who ran him out of Wrigley Field thirteen years earlier after managing the lefty for just one season.

Moyer had professed to be puzzled about Zimmer's negative reaction to his pitching style. But there are few vindictive bones in his body. He will not lay awake nights thinking about why he couldn't please "Popeye," nor plot ways in which he can show him up today.

"Everyone's entitled to their opinion," Moyer said. "Everybody does what they feel they need to do. It's just part of the baseball experience. I think I've grown a lot, matured a lot. To hold things against people, to feel certain ways toward people, to me is a waste of time and effort. I could direct my energies in more positive directions than that.

"It's just the way the game is. Every organization could say, coulda, shoulda, woulda. We let this guy go, and now look at what this guy has done. For every organization, there are probably ten, fifteen to twenty players over the course of their history where they say, 'Geez, we should have held on to them.' Sometimes a change of scenery becomes a good thing for players. I've had my fair share of those."

One player who forced a change of scenery for himself in 2001 was Red Sox center fielder Carl Everett. The talented but flawed Everett had been the trigger of a number of incidents during his Boston tenure, but none potentially as inflammatory as several at-bats against Moyer on August 14, 2001, at Fenway Park.

In the first inning, Moyer complained that Everett was positioned out of the batter's box as a result of the location of his front foot to home plate. In close-ups of Everett's feet, ESPN television cameras confirmed the foot placements. Moments later, Moyer hit Everett with an inside pitch. Everett jawed in the direction of Moyer as plate umpire Mark Hirschbeck escorted him to first base. There, Everett continued shouting at Moyer and twice pointed to the bleachers.

Everett was trying to call his shot, according to Mariners first baseman John Olerud.

"He was upset because he got hit and told him that he was going to take him deep. He said it twice."

Two at-bats later, in the fifth, Everett made good on his gestures, but went too far. He did connect for a homer. Still angered at Moyer, Everett grabbed his crotch and spit in the direction of the mound as he rounded the bases.

"I was embarrassed for Carl Everett and the Red Sox organization," Karen Moyer would say months later. "I'm glad my boys weren't watching it."

But Moyer himself professed to be unmoved. He never gave Everett a second glance.

"My job, whether it's at home or on the road, is to pitch, and to pitch effectively," he said after the game. "Why get involved, or get into any situation? My job is to focus and to stay on focus. I'm not going to play into any situation."

The pitch that hit Everett was one Moyer was trying "to drive inside." Since it was the first inning, Moyer implied that intentionally hitting Everett wouldn't make much sense. "I was trying to establish both sides of the plate—just trying to make my pitches. To me, it's a non-issue."

From the hindsight of the 2002 season, Moyer still downplayed the Everett confrontation.

"To me, it wasn't my incident," he said. "My personal thing is I don't try to go out and embarrass anybody or show anybody up. What other people choose to do, that's their choice. They have to live with their actions or reactions to what they do on the field or off the field. I look at it, it's his issue, his problems, his career, and he has to deal with it however he's going to deal with it. I'm not going to get caught up in it. Once it was over, it was over. You can't take it back. You move forward."

Everett was dispatched to a repository of troubled players, the Texas Rangers, after the 2001 season. Moyer continued on with the Mariners, a franchise that had now established unusual stability after losing three superstars—Randy Johnson, Ken Griffey, Jr., and Alex Rodriguez. Such departures might have crippled most teams, but the Mariners only got better—better than any other American League team in regular season history.

But in Moyer's view, the roster from top to bottom was dramatically improved after the superstars' departures. No longer did Seattle have to depend on a small core of players who were far better than their teammates.

"You hate to lose players," he said. "One was via a trade, the other two were via free agency. But this organization has been very resilient. A lot of it is the reflection on the organization. They brought in a lot of great quality people.

"They filled the voids maybe not with players maybe not putting up the [same] individual numbers, but with a group of players that put up the same numbers if not the better numbers than one person as an individual. To me that's probably the difference. No disrespect to any of those three, but one guy does not make a ballclub. When it does, that ballclub finds itself in the middle of the pack because one guy gets to hit only four times a game. One guy gets to pitch nine innings only once every five games. You can only contribute so much. That's why it's a team game."

But despite all the franchise's attributes, and even though the Mariners breezed through the American League like none others in 2001 before getting off to a roaring start the following season, the most important aspect of a team's competition level was sorely lacking: a World Series in Seattle.

Despite Moyer's masterful Game 3 performance, the Mariners lost the 2001 American League Championship Series in five games to the Yankees. That was one game less than New York needed to upend Seattle in the 2000 ALCS. The Orioles nudged the Mariners out of the AL Division Series three-games-to-one in 1997. The memorable 1995 Division Series, in which the Moyer-less Mariners rallied from a two-games-to-none deficit to upset the Yankees in five games, was followed by a six-game ALCS loss in which the Indians won the final three games.

Close, but never a cigar.

"It's difficult to get there," Moyer said of the World Series. "I don't feel a sense of frustration. I feel a sense of accomplishment because we've had at least some success to get to the playoffs [with different groups of players].

"Look at the short history of this club, twenty-five years, it has a nice little history behind it. There are some organizations that have never gotten to the playoffs or haven't had a great deal of success. I think this organization has done some nice things in the Northwest for the game of baseball. You try to do your best. If you have a good season and are fortunate to be in the playoffs, that's icing on the cake. There are twenty teams sitting at home, wishing they were in the playoffs.

"I don't regret anything. It's been a great ride. It's not easy to get to the World Series. You've got to be at the top of your game when you get to the playoffs. When you're not, you find yourself sitting at home."

What if Seattle isn't rated as well as it can be if it does not reach the Fall Classic?

"That could be a historian's way of looking at it, and the media may follow historians," Moyer said. "But those of us who've lived it as a team know what we've done and it's no small thing. Nor will it be diminished by what happened from here on."

◆ ◆ ◆

Through seven teams and fifty-five moves, by her count, Karen and Jamie Moyer have developed a very well-grounded perspective on their impact on life and ability to help those less fortunate.

"We're different people than we were when we were with the Cubs in 1988," Karen said.

The couple met while Karen was an intern at WGN-TV in the summer of 1986, when Jamie was first called up. Cubs announcers Harry Caray and Steve Stone introduced them.

They were married after the 1988 season, when Karen worked for Ohlmeyer Productions in New York. Then she worked production for NBC and produced a weekly basketball show for her father, Digger Phelps.

The Moyers are now the parents of four and relocated from South Bend to Magnolia, an island in Puget Sound. They have all the material possessions they ever desired and are overjoyed to live in a community that "has opened its arms for us," Karen said. But even while they struggled to pay the bills during Jamie's career low point in the early 1990s, they believed in giving of themselves. The couple's long interest in charities has evolved into the Moyer Foundation.

"You do what comes natural to you," Moyer said. "When you deem it necessary to do things, then you do it. I don't think you can force it. You can't act in a way that you're not yourself. You've got to be genuine to help. As a group, as a club, as a pro athlete, as a human being, it's our way to help.

"Our emphasis is on children's charities and helping children. Our hope is to continue to move forward, not grow too fast. Help in a responsible way. Help in a productive way. I think we're moving along nicely. We made some addition to staff. It's all about helping people in less fortunate situations."

Established formally in July 2000, the Moyer Foundation raised $500,000 for Pacific Northwest charities in its first year. Mariners wives were enlisted to help in the worthy causes. An annual bowling party was set up, promoting organ donation programs. The foundation obtained a luxury suite at Safeco Field to host parties.

But early in year two, the foundation had to shift into high gear to help children who lost parents in the September 11 terrorist attacks. The Moyers started the process of setting up bereavement camps in New York to help the children.

"We were naming the camps after Tom Burnett, who was on Flight 93 and helped take down the terrorists," said Karen, who administers the foundation. "Counselors come in to talk to the kids. The bereavement period is the year after. The shock has worn off, and the reality sets in that Daddy is not coming home."

Compared with the life-and-death issues of September 11, organ donation and others, the troubles of Moyer's game are miniscule. But the same passion that he applies to helping others in need is also directed at desiring a more ideal game of baseball for all people the sport touches.

"I'd like to see a way for this to not outprice itself for fans," he said. "This is entertainment, we are in the entertainment business."

Moyer dreams of a world in which labor peace is declared in baseball. The contract agreement of September 2002 can only be termed a truce.

"It would be nice to see management and the union somehow get on the same page," he said. "It's got to start at the top. Have a commissioner that everyone agrees on, where one side doesn't have an advantage over the other side. It's not for the union or the owners."

Reporting on the labor strife is an often-cynical sports media. Moyer wants to see more baseball reporters as well-prepared in their profession as he is for his starts.

"I love the media," Moyer said. "It's the responsibility of players to respect the media. There are a lot of great media people in the game. But there also are a lot of people who hang around, who punch in and punch out. They're very unprepared. It shows in the questions they ask. I don't know if they don't take pride in that. The reason I feel I can make this kind of opinion is I see this all the time in the clubhouse.

"When I broke in, beat writers took it upon themselves to learn about you. I don't see that anymore. When I broke in, beat writers flew on the team plane. Fred Mitchell [of the *Chicago Tribune*] was one of the most enjoyable people around."

Perhaps labor, management, and media could benefit if Moyer stays in the game after he throws his last change-up. Bill Harford, who saw Moyer's coaching potential and made that 1992 job offer, said the game "would benefit from somebody like that staying in the game and teaching kids how to pitch."

Moyer, who believes both players and front offices under-appreciate minor league coaches for the effort they put in under sometimes mediocre playing and training conditions, would consider sharing his considerable knowledge down the line. But, first, "I might have to get away from the game for a little time" to spend more time with his family.

When he does return, Moyer said he might "strongly consider" front office work to really make an impact.

"I would like to be at the point where I can speak my opinion," he said. "Not change the game, but keep the good values in the game. Keep the positive progress going.

"When I walk in the door, I have to feel I can give a great effort today. I don't know if you still see that all the time today. There are more agents, more money involved. People go through the motions saying this is my job, I can cut this corner."

The only corners Moyer ever cut, even when his heart and head seemed in better shape than his left arm, were on the edges of the strike zone. He proved once again that brains and guile can triumph over raw power almost any day in a thinking man's game.

10

THE TEAM PLAYER

Everyone who picks up a bat and ball starts out with the same dream.

They're using every ounce of strength and sinew to bash the ball as hard and as far as Ruth or McGwire. They're flying through the air with the greatest of ease to make that basket catch with their back to home plate, á la Mays. And they wind up, almost effortlessly, the ball breaking warp barriers to arrive in the catcher's mitt just like Ryan or Koufax.

Gradually but inevitably, reality sets in and the weeding-out process begins. The least talented will drift away after Little League or sandlot play. Others will continue on to play high school and Legion ball, but their baseball ambitions start to peter out by college. A smaller group will be fortunate enough to gain baseball rides to college. Even cozier is the bunch that get picked in the June amateur draft or sign as free agents.

The talent pool winnows down even further. The majority of minor leaguers never make it to the majors. Only a tiny fraction of those that do become stars. Some have the proverbial "cups of coffee" in the Show, others exist for years on the back nine of rosters, and even more settle in to somewhat comfortable roles as regulars, some of whom flirt with stardom in certain seasons.

In the latter two groups, there are a goodly number who are invaluable to their teams, and not just for what baseball skills they can contribute. They are good around the clubhouse, possessing attitudes that help foster team chemistry and harmony. They bridge the gap between the inevitable locker room factions, they're wise about the game and they'll usually subjugate their own statistical goals for the greater good of their ballclub.

In short, they're "team players." Another term is "consummate professional." They've spanned all the generations of the game. And they range in talent levels from utility players like Jeff Huson all the way up to Hall of Famers like Tony Perez.

They've all had their childhood dreams of glory, but now they've altered them. It's a more practical goal, being invaluable to their club not as a superstar, but as good guys to have around. Teams can't live in harmony or win without them.

Move the clock back two decades, and Ellis Burks had a combination of the slugger's goal and the Mays whiz-kid-in-center ambition. And for good reason. Experts rated this prime Boston Red Sox prospect a five-tool player. He could run, throw, field, hit, and hit with power. The BoSox finally would have a "30-30" player—an all-everything who could hit thirty homers, steal thirty bases, and breeze past the old, ponderous, and often lily-white image of the venerable franchise.

But Burks's career took turns he never expected. Controversies and injuries in Boston ended what he hoped was a lifetime career at Fenway Park. He'd be on the move, first to Chicago's South Side, then to Colorado, San Francisco, and, most recently, Cleveland. Burks would only once achieve the 30-30 goal despite some fine seasons. On the verge of superstardom at mid-career, he instead evolved into a professional hitter and clubhouse role model. Everywhere he went, he made friends and influenced people. Managers and front office types admired him. He'd always have a job as long as he'd be able to avoid hobbling about due to the long-term effects of injuries.

Childhood dreams of glory gave way to a reality that was not unpleasant at all. Burks got into the age-old rhythms of baseball, and that provided him a career that may have been longer lasting than he could have ever figured.

◆ ◆ ◆

Chicago gossip columnist Irv Kupcinet hosted a longtime TV talk show that had a tag line, "The lively art of conversation." Ellis Burks is a practitioner of that kind of art. When he takes a dugout seat more than three hours before a game, he puts his companion at ease immediately. One feels he can talk with Burks for hours, way past game time, not just about baseball, but about any subject affecting the human condition.

Burks has arrived very early anyway, long before most Indians teammates, to treat his myriad of aches and pains. Old-school guys like him don't mind hanging around the ballpark for half their waking hours. So he has time to put his own career life in perspective, about a dream deferred, but never a passion denied.

His career has far fewer years ahead of him than behind. Burks's outfield time is diminishing. Designated hitter duties will be largely his fate from here on out.

But pride shines through when the dignified Burks speaks. He knows his bat, combined with his clubhouse stature, always will be prized.

"I never considered myself a superstar," he said as the ballpark slowly comes to life around him at mid-afternoon. "I never liked that title. I'm a team player, and I want to be a part of the team. I want to be one of those guys you can count on in key situations.

"On all the teams I've been on, there's been a superstar to fill that role. In Boston, there were Jim Rice, Dwight Evans, Tony Armas. Chicago, Frank Thomas. Colorado, Larry Walker, Dante Bichette, Andres Galarraga. In San Francisco, Barry Bonds and Jeff Kent. It's never been a problem with me to settle in and be a part of a team."

The 30-30 dreams are for younger men with egos, budding stars trying to make impressions, get their first big contracts. Burks has no need for such astounding numbers. His seasonal goals are that of a number five or number six hitter, the type teams need to round out the middle of their order. Not the main man by any means, but a player they cannot live without.

"I like the idea of being a consistent player," Burks said. "Somewhere around .300, twenty [homers] plus, eighty [RBIs] plus."

He's gone way beyond those goals on occasion. Burks has belted as many as forty homers and driven in as many as 128 runs in a season. Twice he has batted as high as .344, an impressive number for a right-handed hitter in any season, in any era. Burks set a record, later tied by Fred McGriff, of hitting homers in forty different big-league ballparks.

In spite of his accomplishments, raw numbers are far from Burks's main motivation.

The team player portfolio he has accumulated through the years is far more important, and was endorsed by his managers.

"He's a real solid player, a very underrated player," said Mets coach Don Baylor, for whom Burks played for the better part of five seasons. "If not for injuries, he really would have put up some numbers. He would miss enough time to where he wouldn't have a big year. He's a very good player, but he should have been a great player.

"He always knew how to hit. He is a great mistake hitter. Like Tony Armas, he was a great hanging breaking-ball guy."

But the Baylors and Dusty Bakers of the world prize Burks as much for his character and professionalism as for his hitting mechanics.

"He's as good a guy as you'll want to know," then–Giants manager Baker said. "He's a man in the real sense of the world. You need someone like that on the field and in the clubhouse. I still talk to him. He still talks to guys on our team."

Long ago, Burks realized teams can go far in this game if they possessed an excess of team players and a minimum of individualists.

"Baseball's become such a lucrative thing for players and owners," he said. "Everything depends on stats. It's all about the money, the security. A lot of people forget about the team aspect. If you win as a team, you'll get the big prize, which is the postseason, where everyone makes their money. Everyone gets a piece of the pie.

"My coach, Jack Allen, at Ranger [Texas] Junior College, said, 'Son, I don't care if you can throw a strawberry through a battleship, or run a hole through the wind, if you don't hustle on my team, you won't be on my team.' And that's the last time anyone had to say that to me. You've got to be a team player, because those individual stats will come."

"I play every game like it's my last. You run out ground balls hard, you'll never see me jogging. And I've always said to lead by example. I go out there and take the game with pride. I love coming out here each and every day. I do the little things it takes to be a big league player. It's an honor to be here playing."

Burks's value system predated his success in baseball.

"My mom and dad brought me up saying, 'Treat people they way you want to be treated, and you'll be treated fine,'" he said. "Respect people, and you'll get your respect. You never think you're better than anyone else, no matter who much you're making."

Burks's wife, Dori, first met him while he played at New Britain, Connecticut, in the Red Sox chain in 1985–86. The Burks on display early in the twentieth-first century would have been recognizable to the eighties model.

"I don't think he's changed at all," Dori said. "That's why people view him as so upstanding. People expect others to change when they get more money. They can't see why some people remain the same. I'm not surprised at all he hasn't changed. He's kind of complex. Ellis is a real deep person who thinks before he acts.

"He's even-keel all the time. He never comes home with his job."

Burks knows how to deal with some of the more testy characters in baseball. He does not have to possess five years' seniority in one team's clubhouse to act on the courage of his convictions.

The younger Barry Bonds was a touchy person with which to deal, be it teammates, Giants staffers, or especially media. Bonds could be as articulate and deep as Burks, but they digressed from there. Standoffishness, suspicion, and pure arrogance prevented Bonds from developing a large admiration society in the game.

Burks set Bonds straight one day a few years back, not long after Burks was traded to the Giants in 1998.

"I've talked to Barry Bonds about certain stuff," Burks said. "Barry Bonds is Barry Bonds. There was one of the trainers he happened to say some things about. I didn't particularly like it when I heard it. I pulled him aside and told him I didn't like what you said to the trainer.

"I felt it was an honor on my part to play with a guy like that. But it doesn't really take much to treat people right. I looked at it like this: I'm a new guy on the team, but I'm also an established veteran. You cannot talk like that. I've been around just as long as you have. Maybe my numbers aren't quite as good as yours, but we are the same."

As Burks advertised, he'll treat everyone the way he'd want to be treated—superstars or nervous novices. If they don't live up to certain professional standards, he won't hesitate to speak up.

"I will say something," he said. "I've said things to different people. I've pulled guys aside and said, 'You're a rookie this year, this is not what you should do.' You should come out each and every day, stretch with the team, be quiet and listen to them [veterans].

"If they want a professional opinion, they all come to me. They know I'm going to tell the truth and I'm going to come straight."

Burks's reputation had preceded him when he came to the Indians in 2001. In his last year as Cleveland GM, John Hart believed he had acquired a good baseball citizen.

"Hart came up to me and says, 'You have a tremendous relationship with the other players,'" Burks said. "I don't form cliques. I try to get along with everyone, the Spanish guys, the white guys, everyone. I am a people person.

"I've been all around the country, lived in all sorts of neighborhoods, gone to predominantly white schools and predominantly black schools. I've mingled with everyone, poor and rich. You can drop me off here, I'll be fine. You can drop me off there, I'll be fine."

Burks's ability to get along with all types was tested when Hart picked up reliever John Rocker not long after he got into hot water for opening his mouth. After Rocker's racially insensitive remarks, Burks could have been excused for wanting to keep his distance and reacting with revulsion on the left-handers' arrival in Cleveland.

But Burks builds bridges instead of burning them.

"I said I'll react the same way, play the same way," he said. "I won't go out there with animosity. A lot of people say things they don't mean. A lot of people say things in the heat of the moment. When I met John Rocker when he was traded over here, he was a very nice guy. A lot of things happen throughout one's life. You say you made a mistake, and then move on.

"That's what makes the world go 'round, the difference in opinion. Everyone can't be the same. I don't think you'd want everyone to be the same.

"But I thank God and thank my parents for the way I am."

◆ ◆ ◆

Burks is living testimony to the value of children being raised by two parents at home.

His mother, Nettie, divorced his father, also named Ellis Burks, when their son was three. Two years later, she remarried, to James Terry. The stepfather stepped up with his inherited parental duties.

"He took the responsibility of being my father at the time," Burks said of Terry. "He raised me according to the way he was raised. He taught me a lot of the values in life. He was one of those quiet men where you walk softly, but carry a big stick. You listen to people. You could tell a man's personality by listening to him."

Burks comes from a large extended family in Vicksburg, Mississippi. The kinfolk are so far-flung that he has a cousin in the big leagues—former Cubs outfielder Roosevelt Brown, who confirms that the person Burks has become had firm roots among the family in Vicksburg.

"He's always been the type of person who enjoys life," Brown said. "He enjoys it to the fullest. He's always been like this since he's a kid.

"He's straightforward with everyone. We grew up and had nothing. His grandmother lived in Mississippi, along with his dad and his favorite aunts. I see him a lot during the holidays. The family was close-knit because it's so big."

The upbringing in that huge Vicksburg-based family was largely the reason for Burks's diplomatic talents.

"He's non-confrontational," Brown said. "He's a perfect person to get along with people. That's me, too. Ellis can make friends with everybody. It was because the older people in our family take people in. Every house is open to the relatives. You can live with any relative. He goes back home, everybody's your mom, everybody's your dad."

Burks was literally a homebody as a child growing up in Texas. "My mother made me leave the house one summer," he said. "I'm in the house every day. She said, 'Why don't you join the Little League team practicing around the corner?' They needed a shortstop. That's when I started playing baseball. I don't know what I would have done [otherwise]."

"We'd play family games, and he wasn't that good," Brown remembered. "But when he left to go to Texas and came back, whoa. He played summer ball. Before, he probably wanted to chase turtles. Find turtles and examine them."

After starring at Everman (Texas) High School as a shortstop and pitcher in his senior year, then moving on to Ranger Junior College, Burks was selected in the first round of the since-discontinued January draft in 1983 by the Red Sox. Boston's first pick in the regular June draft that year was fellow Texan Roger Clemens.

Still relatively raw, Burks did not start racking up numbers until his fourth pro season, at Class AA New Britain, in 1986. He stole thirty-one bases while batting .273. The Red Sox had some promising home-grown kids headed by Clemens and a slew of position players.

"When I first was drafted by Boston and going through their system, there was a lot of expectations upon quite a few younger guys on the roster," he said. "You had Sam Horn, who they considered to be the next Willie McCovey. Mike Greenwell was a great line-drive hitter, and they compared him to Fred Lynn.

"They thought I was going to be the next Willie Mays, a 30-30 player every year. I was one of the first kids in their organization who could hit for power and steal bases."

Burks was better statistically when he finally made his Red Sox debut on April 30, 1987, against Seattle. On June 10, he got BoSox fans' tongues wagging with a two-homer (including a grand slam) and seven RBI performance at Baltimore.

The dream of 30-30 seemed close at hand by season's end, just after his twenty-third birthday. Burks had slugged twenty homers and swiped twenty-seven bases, an unprecedented combination of power and speed in Boston. He was the first Red Sox rookie and only the third Boston player in history to belt twenty homers and steal at least twenty bases in the same season. His club-leading steals total was the most by a Red Sox rookie since Tris Speaker's thirty-five in 1909. Already, Burks was being linked statistically with an all-time great.

"My first year, I hit twenty homers and stole twenty-seven bases, planted the seed in their mind that was going to be my destiny in my career in Boston," he said. "And Boston was definitely a place where I wanted to spend the rest of my career.

"If everything went right, I thought I'd be a consistent .290 to .300 hitter, with twenty or thirty homers a year. I was a leadoff hitter for six years in the big leagues. I thought those were good numbers for a leadoff hitter."

Projections of glory were not out of line.

"The Red Sox are probably no different than a lot of other teams when they labeled their own player as a 30-30 guy," said Baylor. "That's what the label was on Ellis early in his career."

Arthroscopic surgery to remove bone chips in his right ankle late in spring training 1988 did not derail Burks from enjoying a fine sophomore season with 92 RBIs, a .294 average and twenty-five stolen bases. He slugged a pair of grand slams and enjoyed a career-best fifteen-game hitting streak. The Red Sox seemed to be set with a Mays-like player in center for years to come.

But health problems and a peripheral involvement in some Red Sox controversy started to crimp Burks's dreams of a long tenure in Fenway Park.

He separated his right shoulder, losing two months' playing time. That ruined the momentum of a season that could have been greater, Burks having hit .303 when he was able to play.

Burks's image of a glorious Red Sox tenure was tarnished in his own eyes when two prominent African American Red Sox teammates began having problems in a city that seemed to have less progressive racial attitudes toward its athletes of color than many Southern cities. The Red Sox, of course, were the last big league team to integrate, back in 1959. And with few exceptions, African American players never have seemed to be the centerpieces of the franchise. No wonder Burks, possessed of all the five-tool talent, was regarded as a wunderkind; fans had scarcely seen his likes in town prior to his arrival.

First pitcher Dennis "Oil Can" Boyd got mired in controversy. Burks was not happy with the way he was treated.

"They were saying Oil Can was involved in drugs," he said. "I never knew Oil Can to be involved in that. Oil Can was like a big brother with me. He took care of me" when Burks first came up.

A bigger hurt was the treatment accorded slugger Jim Rice, the most prominent African American Red Sox of all time. Rice got into a rhubarb with then–Red Sox manager Joe Morgan after slap-hitting infielder Spike Owen was sent up to pinch-hit for the slugger. Rice ended up on the loser's side of the confrontation.

"The fans turned on Jimmy, the media turned on Jimmy," Burks said. "That affected me. Jim Rice was my childhood hero. I see this happening to Jimmy, and that affected me. I don't think that was very fair."

Burks tried to soldier on. In 1990, he was named to the American League

All-Star team, but didn't play due to a hamstring pull. Burks finished the season with 21 homers, 89 RBIs and a .296 average, while winning a Gold Glove for his outfield play.

The injury bug began to bite hard in 1991. Burks had another hamstring injury in May, had tendinitis in both knees in July and ended up severely hampered for seasons to come when a bulging disc was discovered in his back near season's end. The disc problem finally forced him to the Boston sideline for good near the end of June, 1992. He would never play another game for the Red Sox.

"In junior college, I had back problems for three weeks, but the Red Sox didn't have any issues with my back," Burks said. "After I made it up to Boston, it started bothering me again. That's the one thing I couldn't control—injuries."

Concerned about his health and by now watching their pennies at times, Boston management did not offer Burks a new contract for 1993.

"It hit us when the Red Sox didn't tender a contract," his wife, Dori, said. "We were crushed."

Almost immediately, the White Sox swooped in with a one-year offer. Burks took it. Then the Red Sox came calling.

"They came the next day and offered the same deal as the White Sox, thinking I'd come back to Boston," Burks said. "But it was a day late. I felt I wasn't wanted anymore. The worst thing you can do with a player is make him feel he's not wanted."

Burks made the Red Sox look foolish. Playing right field, he was a key contributor to the White Sox's 1993 American League West title season with 17 homers and 74 RBIs. He collected his first postseason homer against Juan Guzman of the Blue Jays in Game 5 of the American League Championship Series.

But Burks's stay in Chicago was brief. Always trying to economize with part of his roster, Sox owner Jerry Reinsdorf offered just a one-year deal. The Colorado Rockies, flush with cash after a boffo inaugural season in 1993, came in with a three-year offer. Burks took the longevity and security.

"It was a new organization and a fresh start in the National League," Burks said. "I figured maybe that would be helpful to me."

The White Sox ended up with a succession of annual right fielders—Darrin Jackson in 1994, Mike Devereaux in 1995, and Danny Tartabull in 1996. They might have done better keeping Burks. Despite more injuries, he would develop into the indispensable good man around the clubhouse as a Rockie.

◆ ◆ ◆

Despite their New England moorings, the Burks family loved their new homestead out West.

"We got used to moves," Dori said. "After that [Boston], it was a business. It worked out well for us. We settled in Colorado in 1994. It's just a way of life for us."

Burks had more family time than he desired, though, during the 1994 and 1995 seasons. As if he needed more parts of his body to inflict with injuries, this time he hurt his left wrist—spraining it in '94, then undergoing surgery just before the '95 season. Burks played in only 145 games total during the two seasons.

Then Burks must have summoned all his emotional concentration to cast off the pain, if for just one season, in 1996. The year he always had the inner confidence he could amass, the season for which Red Sox fans had always dreamed, became reality. For one season, even amid the homer-happy high plateau air of Denver, Burks flirted with superstar status.

Playing center field in the most powerful lineup in the game, Burks racked up numbers that netted him a third-place finish in the NL Most Valuable Player balloting.

Playing 156 games and coming to bat 613 times—both by far the most of his career—Burks slugged 40 homers, added 45 doubles, collected 211 hits overall, batted .344 and drove in 128 runs. He also swiped 32 bases. He finally was a 30-30 man, with plenty of room to spare, while joining an all-time exclusive club. He became only the second major leaguer in history, after Henry Aaron in 1963, to accumulate 40 homers, 200 hits and 30 steals in the same season.

Burks's 142 runs scored, 392 total bases, 93 extra-base hits and .639 slugging percentage paced the league. The total-base total was the most in the National League since Aaron's 400 in 1959.

"It was awesome," Burks said. "It's one of those years that any member of a team should experience. Everything went right. It was a lot more fun, and it made you feel like coming to the park was easy."

Another Burks talent caught Baylor's eye. "Ellis was the best baserunner besides Larry Walker I had as a manager," he said.

But Burks's fate was not to stay at this exalted level of performance. More injuries prevented a repeat of '96 the following season. Burks suffered through a sprained left wrist and a sprained ankle. A strained groin, always a balky injury, forced him into the disabled list at midseason. When he returned to the lineup, he finished the season strong, ending up with 32 homers and 82 RBIs in 119 games. Projected out to a full season, the numbers would have nearly duplicated 1996s lofty output.

By now, the Rockies began to think of retooling, their awkward combination of a powerful lineup and horrific pitching in Coors Field condemning them to middle-of-the-pack status after a brief foray into the postseason in 1995. Now thirty-three, Burks was suddenly attractive to other contenders. He informed the Rockies he could no longer be a regular center fielder due to the toll that had been taken on his body.

For the only time in his career, he was involved in a trade. At the deadline on July 31, 1998, he was dealt to the Giants for three players. Burying his ego as always, Burks batted .306 in 42 games the rest of the season as the Giants fought right down to a wild-card berth qualifying game against the Cubs the night after the regular season ended.

He worried that his career was in jeopardy due to his physical problems.

"I'm a survivor," he said. "There were times when I thought I'd retire. Like in 1998 when I got traded to San Francisco. I thought that was it. It was one of the times when the agony and pain was there every day with my bad knees. I thought that was it. I had surgery at the end of that season, but here I am now."

"You can't quit," said ballplayer-cousin Roosevelt Brown. "You quit, you're beat. If you say you're done, you're done. If you don't quit, you can do anything you want to do. He's very, very persistent in what he does."

Burks re-signed with the Giants as a free agent, and paid dividends despite increasingly sore knees. In only 390 at-bats spread over 120 games in right field in 1999, he slugged 31 homers and drove in 96 runs. Burks was one of baseball's best clutch hitters, batting .378 with 45 RBIs with runners in scoring position.

By now, Burks had adopted an extensive game preparation routine to get balky knees ready from a true throwback type.

"I'd be at the ballpark at 2:30 for a seven o'clock game to get prepared for that particular night," he said. "What I do reminds me of what Andre Dawson did to get ready. Andre called me the year before he signed with the Red Sox [1993] and asked about Boston, where he should live, how did I get along with everybody. We talked and it was great. When I got to the National League, I'd see him with the Marlins. He gave me all these different ideas about [working out] his knees. He helped me out a lot the past four years. I could just imagine what he would have done in his career with good knees."

The same went for Burks. Dusty Baker marveled at his professionalism at the plate and in the clubhouse as a lineup complement to mainstays Barry Bonds and Jeff Kent in spite of his physical limitations.

Coming to bat officially 393 times over just 122 games in 2000, Burks matched his career high with a .344 average. He drove in 96 runs while slugging 24 homers. But Burks increasingly had trouble playing the field on his bad knees.

"It's best for him to be in the American League where he can be a DH part of the time for his knees," Baker said. "It got difficult for him to be in the National League."

The Giants let Burks go after the 2000 season. He signed with the Cleveland Indians, who had a perfect role for him shuttling between DH and left field. Better yet, then–Indians GM John Hart needed an upstanding individual in the clubhouse after Cleveland had endured the likes of Albert Belle and other less-than-pleasant egos over the past decade. He was signed to a three-year deal with a club option for a fourth.

"It's stepping your game up another level," Burks said. "Don't try to hit home runs every time or get four hits. There's no extra pressure. The good thing about this club, everyone got along great. There were no confrontations."

Burks fit in comfortably in Cleveland, and produced again in the middle of the lineup to round out the production of Robbie Alomar, Juan Gonzalez, and Jim Thome to push the Indians to yet another American League Central title. But that batting order combination lasted only one season. Hart left for the Texas Rangers after 2001, replaced by longtime aide Mark Shapiro, who was under pressure from new owner Lawrence Dolan to cut the team's always-high payroll. Shapiro also had his own ideas about team building, centered around pitching depth and more youth. Shockingly, Alomar was traded as part of a huge deal with the Mets, while Gonzalez was cut loose. Thome and Burks had to shoulder the power burden alone in 2002. And then there was one, Burks, after Thome's off-season departure as 2002 ebbed.

"It was a shock to me," Burks said when he learned from Shapiro himself in a 7:30 A.M. phone call that the GM had dealt Alomar. "I knew some things were happening. It was a tough thing to swallow. I don't care who you could have gotten in a trade. Robbie is Robbie, a Hall of Famer on the first ballot and a ten-time Gold Glover."

But bridge-builder Burks also appreciated Shapiro's management style.

"He's been a standup guy since I met him in the offseason [of 2000–01] with John Hart," he said. "He's been totally honest with me. He said that in any given year that if I felt the Indians were not living up to their bargain, not winning, feel free to come in and talk about it."

Burks may one day take Shapiro up on his offer. And if he does, it will

The Cleveland Indians signed Ellis Burks in 2001 both for his ability on the field and for his positive clubhouse presence. *Cleveland Indians*

be accomplished in conversational style, an exchange of ideas, no contentiousness, and kept out of the media. Shapiro would be advised to listen, if not bring Dolan into the meeting. They will have a man good enough to be a front office exec in their midst, and his analysis of baseball cannot be dismissed.

♦ ♦ ♦

Ellis and Dori Burks and their four children—daughters Carissa, Elisha, and Breanna, and son Christopher—live a comfortable lifestyle in the Denver suburb of Englewood. But if you didn't know Burks was a ballplayer, you wouldn't think he and his family were anything special or enjoyed a privileged status in life.

"My family, we don't think we're any different than anyone else," Burks said. "We're just normal people. I don't call ahead of time and want a table for four at a bar or club. You wonder about people like Michael Jordan or Michael Jackson. I couldn't do that."

"I grew up dirt poor in New Britain," said Dori. "I didn't grow up with a silver spoon in my mouth. My nature is to not blow money. My kids have to work for their stuff. Sure, my husband has nice cars and a nice home. But I'm not buying $2,500 pants. I still go to the Gap."

Burks himself will still dress like a million dollars, which of course he possesses. He'll show up at a restaurant on the road dressed for dinner in a suit, like he was the team owner.

"He's neat," Dori said. "He's the only guy who can make a warmup suit look like a [business] suit."

Burks looks at quality of life, on and off the field, as his motivation instead of the pursuit of every last dollar.

"In '96, when I had the best season of my career, I could have gone to the Mets or Indians for twice as much money," he said. "I chose to stay in Colorado, and stay here with my family. I loved playing in Colorado. Everyone complimented me on that. I did that because I thought that was right."

Burks has some ideas about what he believes is right for baseball. The one aspect the game cannot afford is continued confrontation between owners and players over dividing up an enormous financial bonanza.

"I don't know how long this can go on as far as salaries and contraction talk," he said. "The game will survive. But we, as players and owners, have to come together and work together. We have to do something. It's tough to fathom anyone making $10 million a year, and then go on strike. They'd say, 'You're crazy, take that money.' We all realize the fans make the game go. You can't be that ignorant.

"When owners are giving out salaries of $25 million, I sit back and wonder, 'Wow. Where is this going, where does it stop?' I think back to the time when I was in college. One scout said I had a chance to make a million dollars in this game. That sounded unbelievable at the time."

Ensuring that Burks remains well-grounded in his practical attitude toward life is the flow of current events.

He was born September 11, 1964. On his thirty-seventh birthday, he awakened in Kansas City after the team had flown in from Cleveland in the post-midnight hours.

"I woke up that morning happy," Burks said. "It's my birthday. I turn on the TV and saw the report of the planes hitting the buildings. To lose all those people, and it wasn't a war. It was the worst thing I had ever heard or seen."

The Indians' "people person" felt the pain of millions. But Ellis Burks didn't need September 11 to heighten his sensitivity to his fellow man. That's part of his being, part of his job.

But he'll only have a limited time to win more friends and influence more people as an active big leaguer. Burks knows there's an end point to his career, and it's not far off in the future.

"If I'm still playing well, I have [2002] and next year, then an option year, and that will be it for me," he said. "I won't keep playing past forty. I won't be hanging on. I want to be remembered as, 'This guy got better as he got on. He was more.' I'll do it on my terms."

Baseball will be that much richer if he continues in the game after Burks's body finally gives out in the next few seasons. He'll be welcomed in many quarters.

"If he wants to stay in the game, he'll have no problem staying in the game in any capacity," Dusty Baker said.

The capacity of Ellis Burks, people person, may be good enough.

11

⚬⚬⚬

THE SCHOLAR-ATHLETE

We always looked with envy at those who could decipher the riddles of algebra and calculus, or who easily aced the chemistry and physics exams. They truly were brains, set apart from most of the rest of us. And, hey, the government wanted more of these whizzes anyway to keep up with the Soviets after they embarrassed the United States by launching Sputnik in 1957.

So it turned out that those who were good in math and science in school ruled the world. Far better than controlling the centers of government power, they ruled the centers of wealth, counting, analyzing, and moving around money like it was second nature. The math-science Einsteins could combine the best of new technology and capitalism to create fortunes for themselves and prosperity for the majority of others. Occasionally, they'd turn to the dark side, as in the Enron implosion, but the system of rewarding those who conquered the tough high school and college courses worked more often than it didn't.

The competitive end of athletics in the millennial era was largely exempt from this trend. Modern sports' emphasis was getting the prime beef out of the classroom and onto the field, court or rink as fast as possible. None of the major sports desired quality prospects hanging around colleges to get their degrees; they'd grab them as soon as their rules allowed, and then kept changing the rulebook so that even younger athletes could be signed.

Many teams shied away from top Colorado high school pitching prospect Scott Elarton in 1994. Price was a factor, but also word got around that Elarton would take his college ride due to the influence of his parents, who were both local educators. Few scouts bothered to check out Elarton's burning desire to play pro ball while still getting his education. The Astros had an in, though, understanding the kid and swooping in to draft Elarton.

College, and sometimes even the tail end of high school, merely gets in the way of an orderly talent flow. The NBA began skipping the college process altogether to sign high school man-children, while Major League Baseball would take kids as young as sixteen out of Latin American countries. Possessing a college degree, especially from one of the country's better schools, along with the academic, analytical, and even social-awareness skills that go along with it, were last on the list of priorities of the talent-mongers.

No wonder Doug Glanville was sometimes misunderstood when he started his climb through an otherwise talent-bereft Cubs minor league system in the early 1990s. Then, again, anyone who could skillfully add brains to the usual package of brawn was looked at oddly. To be sure, there were always scholar-athletes in baseball and other sports, but they were advertised as the unusual types, somewhat at odds with the flow of the game. The image of the almost-totally physical specimen was the norm. Intellectual reading would be the box scores in the *Sporting News*.

Glanville, the Texas Rangers outfielder, managed to transcend the normally disparate realms of academics and athletics. He didn't want to rule the world from the top of a corporate pyramid even after obtaining an engineering degree from the Ivy League's University of Pennsylvania in 1993. He had a variety of interests, goals and dreams that did not require as much money accumulated as fast as possible. And while he was skilled and passionate in baseball, his favorite sport, it would not be an end to a means. Baseball would get its proper turn at bat in the emotional lineup of Glanville's life, but it would not be the controlling, push-everything-else-to-the-sideline factor.

He would be accepted for the total person that he had become through a young manhood spent with a loving, forward-thinking family that wanted him to go through as many life experiences as possible. And if he was shunned, well, he'd eventually move on to the next phase of a hoped-for rich existence.

"From where I am at this point, I found I have a niche within the baseball community," Glanville said. "In a way, surprisingly, where I come from, I feel like my background has been embraced. Not so much on the field, but in the clubhouse and in communities I play for. The communities around these teams are looking for someone to pass on certain messages to kids. They're looking at a role model.

"Once you get established, a lot of stigmas fall by the wayside. People have an opportunity to get to know you. You prove you have their back. You pass these macho tests."

But those tests were nothing like the ones on which Glanville used to excel in high school and college. Having a mind in the game is perceived as unsettling, if not dangerous, by those in power. Glanville found that out in minor league outposts like Daytona, Orlando, and Des Moines.

"In the minor leagues, that's a complete 180 from where I am now," he said. "In the minors, there are all these levels, the rites of passage. You haven't been in the game long enough for people to know how you are. You're changing cities, coaches, and managers every half-season. People bring in these perceptions. People say you're too smart, you ask too many questions. There's a fine line between asking questions and challenging authority. It can come out in a negative way."

Shreds of negativism about Glanville's academic prowess still crop up even as an established major leaguer. None are serious enough to bring anything but smiles to his face. "Rocket scientist and Einstein, those were the main things in Chicago," Glanville said of teammates' nicknames for him as a Cub in 1996–97. Another incident took place early in his Phillies tenure in 1998 when he was in a slump. He already had gained some notoriety for co-crafting a Penn project that dealt with traffic patterns around a new Philadelphia stadium.

Glanville recalled thusly: "The fans hollered: 'We heard you designed a stadium. Why don't you design a stadium you can hit in?'"

That gibe would have received at least a "B" if Professor Glanville was teaching a class in humor, Philadelphia-style. Everyone from an Ivy Leaguer to the house nitwit will get their razzing, and be able to give it back in kind. Some things never change in baseball.

Glanville's brainpower now blends in with a reputation as one of baseball's best defensive center fielders who can hit a lick, too. They always look askance at baseball's scholar-athletes, who always have to prove that they can truly fit in with the boys. Almost always, they do.

◆ ◆ ◆

Educated ballplayers always have had to work harder to fit in among the more ignorant masses who majored in balls and strikes, the Babe and babes, and computing discounts on Red Man.

Players like second baseman Eddie Collins were labeled "college men," often in a not-so-complimentary manner. Yankees manager Joe McCarthy tried to ban pipe smoking on team trains, as if the pipes were the sign of an intellectual or "egghead." Perhaps the more formal school learning you possessed, the less baseball macho you would have had, went the prevailing wisdom of the day. The rural and urban blue-collar base of baseball talent earlier in the twentieth century did not exactly attract scholarships from the finest schools in the country. In reality, education and baseball were in many

Doug Glanville graduated from the University of Pennsylvania in 1993 with an engineering degree, leading to nicknames such as "Rocket Scientist" and "Einstein" early in his career. *Mattie Glanville*

ways synergistic, but try telling that to the typical baseball pepperpot of days gone by.

"Billy Martin said you can't hit with a fuckin' diploma," said entertainer/crazy man/center fielder Jimmy Piersall, no magna cum laude himself.

Nevertheless, well-educated players with higher ambitions than baseball filtered into the game. Yankees infielder Bobby Brown went to medical school, becoming a cardiologist prior to his 1990s tenure as American League president. Tigers sidearmer Elden Auker had planned to go to medical school at the dawn of the 1930s, but opted out when he discovered that baseball still paid more than most college graduate jobs in the early Depression days. A prominent Padres pitcher of the 1970s was continually referred to as "Dr. Steve Arlin," since the right-hander was practicing his touch and command in dental school at the time.

Other players broke into the literary world, drawing mixed reaction within the game, while they were still active. Jim Brosnan had curious teammates lined up to contribute to *The Long Season,* his groundbreaking realism-baseball book in 1959, although some tradition-bound baseball writers scoffed at the effort. A decade later, Jim Bouton became a pariah with the Yankees due to his authorship of *Ball Four* and all its revelations of frathouse behavior by idols such as Mickey Mantle.

One flaming intellect actually was mislabled as a flake or screwball, according to Hall of Famer Fergie Jenkins.

"They called Bill Lee the 'Spaceman,' but he had an IQ of 160," said Jenkins, who along with Lee and outfielder Bernie Carbo were a counterculture thorn in the side to baseball war-horse Don Zimmer when he was Red Sox manager in 1977. "He was the smartest guy in the game. When someone had an opportunity to meet Bill Lee for the first time, they'd say he's strange. He wasn't. He just was smart."

Northwestern alums Joe Girardi and Mark Loretta have not done badly for themselves in the majors. But thriving most of all is Doug Glanville, who was fated for a life of emotionally expanding horizons long before he mastered his first engineering-school exam at Penn and found out he was good enough to be a first round big league draft choice. How Glanville was able to fit in, overcome some loutish handling by minor league managers and coaches, relate to the brutes in the locker room and come out on top as a quality major leaguer was perhaps preordained by the life his forward-thinking parents laid out for him early on.

The key to his ability to transcend all groups is not being able to decipher a technical manual, but to read people for what they are and relate to them on their level.

"There are plenty of guys I can talk to," Glanville said. "You're trying to get away from the whole dumb-jock idea. People like Randy Wolf and Marlon Anderson are very sharp. In spring training 2001, Wolf and I talked about Twenty-one Questions, and had the whole team doing it. I haven't found myself intellectually starving.

"There are lot more [smart players] than people think. They show they have academic desires and interests. You have an interest that's different, and there are people who appreciate it. I like astronomy. They might have some questions on it."

Cecil and Mattie Glanville ensured that their second son would never tilt one way or another toward academics or athletics. Somehow, he'd toe-dip in both, a piano lesson dovetailing with Little League practice, the two activities complementing one another rather than fighting for young Glanville's time and passion.

Perhaps the best lesson Glanville learned from his father, a psychiatrist who grew up in Trinidad, was that all brains and no experience are a bad mix.

"Intelligence doesn't necessarily have to do with survival and street smarts. And my dad was a survivor," Glanville said of a man who has fallen ill in recent years.

The laboratory for the younger Glanville's full, rich-in-experiences childhood was Teaneck, New Jersey, across the George Washington Bridge from Manhattan.

"Teaneck was incredibly diverse," Glanville said. "I prided myself in being able to get along with everybody. I don't think getting along with anybody was ever an issue."

Glanville got lessons in mind and body through the efforts of his parents. Cecil Glanville wasn't just advising patients on the analyst's couch or prescribing depression-fighting drugs; he shared his own wealth of experiences having played cricket and soccer both in Trinidad and at Howard University. Mattie Glanville passed along her math genes to her son, having taught math in junior high school and at Teaneck High School for twenty-one years.

"I think Doug had the benefit of a very loving family," said Mattie. "Our value system is predicated on what our religion is. Also our educational background. We have a strong sense of community. We also have a very hands-on family with grandparents and nieces. Even though we may be [physically] distant from each other, whatever values that were taught in the home are reinforced in the larger community."

The Glanvilles found out very early that Doug would not be an ordinary child. He was academically precocious.

"He knew his alphabet before he was two years old," Mattie said. "He wanted me to teach him algebra before his time. It was sixth grade. He was too young, but he really wanted to do it. Around eighth grade is normal. He always was on an accelerated math track."

But one activity in which the Glanvilles ensured their son would participate was a weekly African American educational program in Teaneck on Saturdays. He started attending at age three.

"They taught African American history and culture, critical thinking skills, a sense of community in caring and sharing—giving back something," Mattie said. "They also had dance, drama and computers. Doug was there through his junior year in high school for some twenty weeks a year."

Thanks to brother Ken, baseball would soon vie for its own place in Glanville's increasingly crowded schedule of childhood activities. Time management became a skill he'd learn quickly.

"My brother had me out there the moment I could hold a bat," Glanville said. "I was playing since I could walk, basically, going through all the levels. Baseball always was my first love, so I always found time to grab a bat or ball and get a little work in. When I was in Little League, I played shortstop and second base, and pitched. Later on, in high school, I switched to the outfield.

"But all along, I also did academic things. I was playing piano. I was always busy. The best thing I learned from that was balancing your schedule. I had so many things going on that I had to be disciplined to keep everything at a high level. That taught me a lot, and I had that instilled in me early."

Glanville and his parents sought some balance. Some summers he'd stay home to play baseball. Other summers he'd attend camp at home. One summer Glanville went away to a physics camp near Springfield, Massachusetts. He'd squeeze in a little softball while at these camps.

There was lots more. Glanville went to a workshop at Columbia University in New York. He also attended a special academic program at Duke University. This, on top of Sunday school and participation in the choir, along with status as one of the co-editors of the Teaneck High School yearbook.

"We never had to be heavy-handed about things," Mattie said. "He wanted everything. He would never be one-dimensional."

"At an early age, I took on a lot of things that normally would be done by someone more mature," Glanville said. "That helped me a lot as a player down the road. You have to be careful not to be burned out as an eight-year-old, but I think anybody can do it. It's a matter of your focus.

"I was competitive because I had my brother ahead of me. But whatever you get out of life, you have to juggle a lot of different things—it might be kids, it might be school. To get that lesson early, it's good preparation."

Glanville earned mostly As and Bs on his grade school report cards. He boosted his GPA to more than 4.0 in high school.

"I was good in math and science," he said. "I kind of liked everything. My versatility was my strong point."

Glanville's academic performance would provide him with an entrée into any school in the country. But he also could have garnered an athletic scholarship off his all-state (New Jersey) baseball feats. Starting a college-long pattern, he opted for academics. His parents had to pay the full tuition at the University of Pennsylvania, where the baseball program was lucky to squeeze in thirty to forty games a year in the cold Northeast springs. He rejected the thought of trying out for the U.S. Olympic baseball team, not wanting to miss classes after his parents had written the hefty tuition checks.

"You have to give credit to players at those types of schools," Glanville said. "You're really out there because you love to play. There's no incentives—not a lot of fans, no athletic scholarships. That aspect became a big asset to me, because I was able to develop the work ethic of balancing all these things. Once I understood, I applied it to baseball and it made me a better player."

While Glanville earned some notoriety playing baseball at Penn, he enthusiastically immersed himself in the engineering-school curriculum. Penn had been trying to encourage minority enrollment in engineering since the early 1970s to boost employment in a field that had largely been closed to African Americans previously.

Glanville was just the right role model that Cora Engram, director of minority and academic support programs, in charge of recruiting and admissions, wanted for the engineering school.

"He was the epitome of the ideal student we wanted in engineering," Engram said. "He was very determined. He knew what he wanted. He loved baseball, but knew education was most important. In this school, it's hard to get As. You have to work very hard to get good grades.

"Doug was articulate. He was well-disciplined. He was active in the society of black engineers. He also served as a tutor. He was always in my office. When you have students like that, you give them academic aid."

Glanville managed to boost his GPA over 3.0 in the punishing academic program. All along, he resisted the urge to leave school early to pursue baseball. Glanville would not let baseball hurt his academics. One day, he missed a game against Temple to take an engineering exam. "He got a 98 on it," Mattie said proudly.

Glanville's favorite class and professor was an introduction to transit engineering course in his junior year, taught by Vukan R. Vuchic.

"The moment I took the class, I liked it," Glanville said. "I liked maps and cartography. Professor Vuchic travels the world [studying transit systems]. He's a big public transit advocate."

"I was impressed," Vuchic said. "You didn't see him lose interest. He said he loved baseball, but what really was his goal in life? He told me had a lot of time of play baseball, but he had to finish his degree. It was his ability to think far ahead."

Glanville also worked on a senior project on commuter railroads for Vuchic. The professor had him make a presentation at a Society of Civil Engineers meeting.

"He enjoyed writing the paper," Vuchic said. "He did the analytical work and performed the computations. He wrote it well. If he hadn't had a baseball future waiting for him, he could have gone to a good starting job in the field, in a transit agency or streets department."

If Glanville pursues a transportation engineering career after he's through with baseball, he'll definitely be from the Vuchic school of public transit advocacy.

"Driving is a freedom thing," he said. "It's the American way. You're independent, you control it, you can go wherever you want. The professor said people are mad when they're stuck in traffic, but they really wish everyone else is off the road so they can ride quickly.

"It can be difficult to set up the proper [public] transit patterns. There are periods where the city is the hot spot and draws companies in. Next you know, they flee to the suburbs. Every society has its priorities. China and Japan economize space. Europe has a phenomenal rail system. I'd recommend high-speed rail for here, something comparable to the car."

Glanville's involvement and commitment to Penn's engineering school did not stop with his 1992 graduation with a degree in science and engineering. He serves on the school's board of overseers, attending several meetings each year. He stays in touch regularly with Vuchic and Engram. And students may be surprised when the hometown center fielder suddenly shows up to talk with them at their dorm.

To Glanville, students going through the system can't get enough of the same math and science aptitude that has served him well. He believes the high educational system has to ensure all its participants are computer-literate.

"Computer science is the driving force now," he said. "They can't hold enough classes to keep up with demand. Penn introduced a course in Practical Computing. It filled up so fast they couldn't keep up."

Turning to baseball, though, it did not compute to Glanville why such a well-rounded view of the world made so many coaches and managers uncomfortable when they first encountered the only Ivy League product in the Cubs farm system in the early 1990s.

◆ ◆ ◆

Despite the relatively skimpy schedule he played in the Ivy League compared to the weather-friendly environment of players coming out of Sunbelt schools, Glanville still impressed Cubs area scout Billy Blitzer with his all-around tools at Penn, which advanced to the NCAA tournament in both 1989 and 1990.

Blitzer's word counted a lot in the Cubs organization when scouting chief Dick Balderson made Glanville the twelfth pick in the 1991 draft, when the outfielder finally relented to play pro baseball for a $300,000 bonus one semester before graduation. Unlike many player personnel mavens, Balderson didn't often go out in the field to personally scout prospects. He relied heavily on his regional talent procurers.

Strangely, Glanville was the antithesis of the player then–Cubs GM Jim Frey coveted. Frey liked musclemen who "hit the shit out of the ball," and Balderson had made a huge blunder two years previously in picking raw country-kid Earl Cunningham number one for projected power that never panned out. Frey had criticized Balderson's predecessor, Gordon Goldsberry, for stocking the Cubs farm system with fast, athletic types without a lot of bash-brothers ability. "Midgets," Frey called them.

Even though he was not a power guy, Glanville had the full backing of Balderson and farm director Bill Harford. He thrived at Geneva in the low–Class A New York–Penn League, batting .303 and stealing seventeen bases in twenty tries in just thirty-six games. *Baseball America* named Glanville the second-best prospect in the league.

But Glanville started to encounter turbulence in his career in 1992. Promoted to high–Class A Winston-Salem, he hit just .258, although he stole thirty-two bases and performed exceptionally in center field.

Almost immediately, Glanville endured a tough-love relationship with the controversial Jimmy Piersall, then in the middle of a long tenure as Cubs minor league outfield instructor. Piersall liked what he saw in center field, but not at the plate or on the bases.

"He picked up all the [outfield] fundamentals I taught him in a hurry," he said. "He had a great arm, better than mine.

"But he had to work on his baseball instinct. The [baseball] thinking part did not come easy for him. There were no books for it. He was a terrible baserunner for a long time, and tried to hit too many home runs. He had to play awhile, he had to learn how to play out there."

The analytical, sometimes introspective Glanville and the quasi-crazy, profane Piersall would get along fine over the next few years. But Piersall soon would be outnumbered as a Glanville advocate. In July 1992, Jim Frey's GM successor at Wrigley Field, Larry Himes, fired both Balderson and Harford. The moves were made to clear the way for hiring Al Goldis, Himes's longtime associate from their White Sox and Angels days. Goldis, then working for the Brewers, would head up both scouting and player development and bring in his kitchen-cabinet of managerial, coaching and scouting cronies. Goldis formally took over in September 1992, vowing a parade down Michigan Avenue celebrating a Cubs' World Series victory at some juncture in the future.

"The people who drafted me were gone so quickly," Glanville said. "As a center fielder and leadoff guy, you're expected to do a lot of things. If you're a one-dimensional player, you only focus on one aspect. But in my position coming up through the minors, you have to hit, put the ball in play, steal bags, run, and play defense. It takes a long time to learn all of that, and master it all.

"I ended up playing for three different [minor league] organizations with the Cubs. It's very difficult. You don't know where you stand. Things can change overnight. There's different teaching philosophies. What you're doing right for one organization, you're doing wrong for the new one."

Two sets of thoughts soon emerged on Glanville. Publicly, the Goldis-led player development regime was not going to trash a recent number one pick. But privately, word began filtering up to Chicago that Glanville was tentative and not aggressive enough.

The attitude of the new management seemed curious. Longtime scout Goldis had gained notoriety for four straight number one draft picks that clicked from 1987 to 1990 with the White Sox—Jack McDowell, Robin Ventura, Frank Thomas, and Alex Fernandez—when he ran that team's player development system under Himes. He prided himself on not only an eye for talent, but some nontraditional methods of player development. A potential renaissance man like Glanville and supposed innovator like Goldis should have clicked, but the relationship remained tenuous for the two full seasons that Goldis ran the Cubs' farm system.

Years later, working as a scout for the Reds, Goldis tried to put the best spin possible on Glanville.

"I was from Columbia and he was from Penn," Goldis said. "I tried to make a connection that way. I tried to talk positively to him. A lot of people were down on him."

Piersall, a constant thorn in Goldis's side, heard differently. He remembered Goldis complaining that Glanville "didn't have any guts, that he'd quit."

Glanville—who in his conciliatory manner said he "didn't have a problem with Al," a man who "worked tremendously hard"—believed his style of desiring explanations to management orders was misunderstood as offering excuses instead. In addition, his inner fire and dedication was not always expressed by an emotional style on the field.

Goldis's initial impression of Glanville filtered down to his staff.

"Goldis respected my background, but felt how I applied it on the field was too tentative," Glanville said. "In '93, in Daytona, I got beat over the head for being too tentative. So I tried a new tack, threw helmets and things like that, but it didn't do anything for me. Then [Ryne] Sandberg came down for an injury rehab stint. I watched him like a hawk. That's the way I wanted to go. Ryne killed you quietly, softly. I could relate to that.

"It's a double-edged sword. If you're too quiet and low-key, you're not tough enough. You're loud and screaming, then you're wild and out of control. It's better to stay true to yourself. At least you can say that was me instead of being someone else."

Glanville's offensive style also was irritating management, but the player insisted that they wanted to rubber-stamp him into a mold.

"You have to give the player some creative leeway," he said. "I was a high-ball hitter. Coming up in the minors, it's always: 'You can't swing at that, lay off that, you'll never be able to hit that in the big leagues.' That's a personal thing. If that's your strength, you have to go after that. Your coach is a source of information, and should give a player a chance to try things. If it works, go with it. If it doesn't, try something else."

The constant carping caused Glanville to "go into a shell for a time." When he'd ask questions, "everything came out the wrong way."

Unimpressed, Goldis kept Glanville at Double-A Orlando for one and one-half seasons. He did not give management reason to promote him to Triple-A, let alone to the Cubs. Glanville hit just .264 in 73 games for Orlando in 1993, then stalled out at .263 in 130 games the next season at the same Southern League outpost.

Glanville's misery quotient only worsened in 1995 when he was finally promoted to Triple-A Iowa. Goldis was no longer in charge of the farm system as Andy MacPhail took over as Cubs president and Ed Lynch as GM in the fall of 1994—the third Wrigley Field front-office regime in four years for Glanville. But a Goldis appointee, Ron Clark, who had been the farm system's coordinator of instruction in 1994, was appointed the Iowa manager. Clark, whose instructional lineage dated back to Dallas Green's stewardship of the productive Phillies farm system in the 1970s, was an old-school tough guy. The personalities of Clark and Glanville were like oil and water.

Clark got on Glanville. He was talking about "tough, tough, tough," the center fielder said. The relationship went sour. Piersall didn't like Clark's handling of Glanville. "I said to Clark, 'What the fuck are you trying to do to him?'" Piersall recalled. "Clark just didn't like the type of player he was. Glanville came off as easy-going."

Taking over from Goldis in supervising the farm system in 1995 was Jim Hendry, now Cubs general manager. "I think that Ron's intent was good," Hendry said. "Doug wasn't performing at the level he should have up to that point. Ron tried in his old-fashioned way to toughen him up. But Doug was also misunderstood. His nature was not outgoing or [outwardly] aggressive. Deep down, he played harder than people thought."

By now, Glanville especially needed the counsel of his parents. Cecil Glanville's perception of the human condition through his psychiatric training came in handy. The conversations were particularly heartfelt one night when Glanville didn't play and kept calling his parents throughout the game.

"We told him you can't change other people," Mattie Glanville said. "We told him it's a rite of passage. Parents want to shield their kids from pain, but can't always do it. He had to learn.

"We kind of understood it [management attitude]. If they're an institution, they have a right to set up the parameters. Baseball is such a small fraternity, they could stay very closed to ideas. They're a special club. They become insular. They allowed Pete Rose to self-destruct. They allow certain things to happen because it meant winning. The way they do things doesn't always work out positively."

A young life's worth of Cecil Glanville's good words had given him enough of a foundation.

"My dad's a pretty positive person," Glanville said. "He gave me advice on having inner strength. Don't let anyone else take you away from your destiny. Someone might try to bury you, but don't let that be a factor."

He was never at a point where he thought of quitting.

"I always said to my teammates that they'd have to run me out of the game to make me stop playing," he said.

Between his parental guidance and his well-rounded experiences, perhaps Glanville was in better position to handle an additional burden heaped on him during this period. Beyond the daily pressures of management, he and all of his minor league teammates had to endure an unusual training program mandated by Goldis and assistant GM Syd Thrift. If the program didn't retard their development, it certainly did not promote it the way the devices and methods were employed. Glanville's development certainly stalled out while the program was in place.

Some gizmos were decidedly low-tech. Players stood on rubber tires and 2-by-4 pieces of plywood, ostensibly to improve balance while hitting. Goldis even thought of using soccer balls to boost footwork. Meanwhile, Thrift, likened by some associates to a fast-talking Music Man salesman, instituted a program of special eye exams aimed at improving hitters' depth perception. Players looked into a "vectogram"—several pieces of plastic containing an imprinted image. The farther the player pulled the pieces apart, the more he had to focus on the image in the middle.

With his educational background, Glanville found the training system "interesting to say the least. They had so many different ideas and different gadgets to try to work on aspects of the game. I understand what they were getting at. They were going to the root, trying to say, 'Balance is important to a hitter, so let's come up with balance drills.'

"But the bottom line in the game is the game. There's certain fundamental things by playing that you have to develop. If you get too far away from it, you might lose that focus. His [Goldis's] philosophy is probably the most unique I've ever seen. It turned out it didn't work well with that organization."

The players began to chafe under the extra work. Pitching instructor Lester Strode said later the minor leaguers began to dread coming to the ballpark. Spring training was "military-style, structured," Glanville recalled. The rubber tires and 2-by-4s were distributed throughout the farm system for use in pre-batting practice workouts. With the extra drills, players wondered if they'd have anything left for batting practice and the game itself.

"We'd be doing these drills in the heat at 2 P.M. in Florida before batting practice," said then-outfielder Robin Jennings. "When it's ninety-five degrees and one hundred percent humidity, you're doing all this early work and with all the minor league travel, it takes away from your concentration. To have it mandatory to do these extra things was too much. It's not like you have plush clubhouses to take a break in after these drills."

"I know they were tired," Goldis said. "We tried to build them up to where they were physically and mentally strong. They were never conditioned to playing the entire season. A lot of guys [in other organizations] worked harder than the Cubs guys. Do hockey players get tired? In the long run these guys built up their physical and mental endurance."

MacPhail disposed of the tires, 2-by-4s and vectograms in 1995. Soon Goldis, who in a new role as scouting director was unhappy with the new management, was gone, too. But Glanville remained, wondering where his career was headed. He was twenty-five, getting up there in baseball years in relation to not yet appearing in a big-league game. Under Ron Clark, he had languished again with a .270 average and just thirteen stolen bases at Iowa in '95.

The spark to get him going, though, was not to be found in the farm system. Glanville found it in the Puerto Rican winter league, playing for a team managed by longtime baseball man Tom Gamboa late in 1995.

"I had to help him win in Puerto Rico; he wasn't in the business of developing players," Glanville said of Gamboa. "It turned out better than I could have dreamed."

Gamboa was a 180-degree turnabout from many of Glanville's previous managers and instructors.

"Tom is a positive person, and he's patient enough to understand where you're coming from, your personality," Glanville said. "He doesn't hold grudges. I'm the type of guy who needs that [positive reinforcement]. If someone goes off on me for errors, I tend to back off a bit. That's where the criticism came from about being tentative about my speed. You're ripped for being thrown out, so you don't go back and try it again immediately. Tom told me that I was too much of a people-pleaser.

"It wasn't any specific instructional thing. It was more of a philosophy. He said he knew I'd been through a lot, but just to come down there, play my game, don't be afraid to make a mistake and be aggressive. He just let me play. Tom always used to say, 'Never let anybody take you away from your destiny, just because someone may not like you.' I got the opportunity to play against good competition. Once you start succeeding against good competition, you start to believe in yourself more.

"I did believe in my heart when I walked away from Puerto Rico that I could play every day in the majors."

He was only one year off in his own analysis. Glanville showed enough improvement in his game and confidence to make a big impression in spring training 1996. Although top 1993 Goldis draftee Brooks Kieschnick, a slugging prospect with few other baseball skills, had the weight of expectations at the time, talk around the Cubs camp was that in reality Glanville was closer to the majors, and a better player than their other minor league outfielders such as Robin Jennings and Pedro Valdes.

Sent back to Iowa, Glanville thrived with a twenty-one–game hitting streak in May. His overall quality of play earned him his first promotion to the Cubs on June 9 for fill-in and late-inning defensive replacement duties. Although he was optioned back down at the end of July, Glanville definitely had the brass' attention. A seventeen-game hitting streak late in the season ensured a September callup. He has never returned to the minors since.

Going into 1997, Glanville seemed assured of no worse than a platoon role in left field, the right-handed half of a planned grouping of a left-handed hitter chosen from among Kieschnick, Jennings, Valdes or Brant Brown, a reluctant émigré from first base to the outfield. But when the Cubs lost a National League–record fourteen in a row coming out the gate while Kieschnick and Brown were found wanting, Glanville found himself with the full-time left field job. Center was closed to him due to the presence of incumbent Brian McRae. He had to stay in left when the slumping McRae, whose criticisms had irked management, was traded in early August to the Mets in a package of players that included center fielder Lance Johnson.

Glanville quietly impressed the Cubs—and other teams. In his first full year in the majors, he hit an even .300. He was finally able to use his speed to his benefit with twenty-five infield singles, including four bunts.

But the Cubs lacked power beyond Sammy Sosa. In the offseason, they traded for left fielder Henry Rodriguez, making Glanville an extra man on the roster with Johnson's continued presence in center. At the same time, the Cubs lacked a second baseman after having let minor leaguer Miguel Cairo go in the expansion draft to Tampa Bay. Newly-appointed Phillies GM Ed Wade informed the Cubs that if they were willing to trade Glanville, he'd deal them second baseman Mickey Morandini, a favorite of fans and teammates.

On December 23, 1997, the trade was consummated. Only three years previously, Glanville was a nowhere man. Now he was a mainstay. Christmas presents come in unusual packages. He would play in the city in which he had excelled so much in college.

◆ ◆ ◆

Whatever else Phillies management, fans, and the media have thought of Glanville, they could never question his status as one of the game's best defensive center fielders.

"What he doesn't do offensively, he more than makes up for it in the outfield," manager Larry Bowa said in 2001. "He saves tons of runs each year. He's right there with [Andruw] Jones in Atlanta. He's got great speed, he plays shallow and gets a great jump on the ball."

"Doug saves 100 runs a year," shortstop Jimmy Rollins gushed.

Glanville immediately won over the often-skeptical core of Philadelphia writers in his first spring training with the team in 1998.

"The first time we noticed how good he is came in an exhibition game in Bradenton," *Philadelphia Daily News* beat writer Paul Hagen said. "He went way into the left-center field gap to take a hit away. We all sort of shook our heads."

Jimmy Piersall's confidence in Glanville's glovework was well-founded, and the early tutoring paid off. Glanville's shallow style allows him to take away dying-quail hits while still having the blinding speed to plug the gaps.

"He didn't believe in diving unless it's absolutely necessary," Glanville said. "I don't throw the extra hotdog into it.

"I'm very proud of my defense. I'm very happy with what I can accomplish. I study hitters and where to play people. I work hard at it."

But, perhaps expecting a throwback to Phillies favorite Richie Ashburn, along with a dash of Willie Mays, the always-fickle fans seemed to want far more offensively out of Glanville than he was able to give them. They desired the perfect leadoff man, a quality that he did not possess.

To the purists, Glanville's problem is that for a top-of-the-lineup man, he doesn't take enough walks. He has never walked more than forty-eight times in any season, holding down his overall on-base percentage.

Otherwise, Glanville has been productive enough for what a leadoff man is supposed to contribute, with an often-laggard Phillies lineup behind him. In 1998, he recorded an NL-leading 678 at-bats, batted .279 and scored 106 runs. Then he blossomed with his best season to date in 1999. He did not need to walk much with a .325 average and 204 hits. Also included were 11 homers, 38 doubles, 73 RBIs and 34 steals in 36 attempts for a majors-pacing 94 percent success rate.

But Glanville's inability to match his dream '99 season in the ensuing two years was a point of contention for the critical observers of Philadelphia baseball.

"When you're fast and steal bases, you need to hit the ball on the ground," Glanville said. "I'm a kind of a bad-ball hitter, and can handle the balls out of the strike zone. It's been a career-long struggle [selectivity at the plate]. I can get defensive and hurt myself.

"I don't walk a lot, but I swing at pitches I can handle. There's the pressure of being a leadoff batter, trying to be patient and seeing the ball. My lifetime average is in the .280s. In stealing bases, I'm very proud of my selectivity. I still carry over the Triple-A thing of being very exact when I stole. I do have a reputation of minimizing mistakes."

During the stretch drive in 2001, Larry Bowa dropped Glanville down from the top of the lineup to the number six slot.

"Every time we don't score runs, the paper says it's because Doug Glanville doesn't get on base," Bowa said at the time. "That's not the case. We have a guy who will probably be our leadoff man for the next ten years in Jimmy Rollins. Doug can hit second, he could hit sixth, he could hit anywhere.

"I like him the way he is. You're not going to change an aggressive hitter to be a patient hitter. That's just the way the game is. There's not any more prototype leadoff hitters with 100 walks. The game has changed."

Bowa's decisions were fine with Glanville. "I have versatility," he said. "I have had success at number two, and at number six and eight. I can fit a lot of places. I don't fight it. If the manager wants me to be here, I'll do it."

Glanville would not get criticism for his offensive style in Paul Hagen's *Daily News* stories.

"I think they're very happy from what they get from Doug," Hagen said in 2001. "One year he had star quality with more than 200 hits. They've been forced to make him a leadoff hitter. He doesn't hit a lot of home runs. He doesn't steal a lot of bases. But he does a lot of little things. He's a tremendous complementary player.

"You don't want to have two guys at the top of the order with a low on-base percentage. Doug's not going to have a great on-base percentage. But he can do so many other things to help you win a game. If you bat him down in the order, he can drive in a run. He's hard to pitch around, particularly if the ball's up in the zone."

It's a good thing that the philosophical Glanville is a people person, who has seen the worst that baseball has to offer. He could have clashed with the emotional Bowa, baseball's closest relative to a bantam rooster, who had vowed to tone down in his second go-around as a manager with the Phillies in 2001.

But as the heat was turned up in the division race against the Braves in the second half of 2001, player grumbling about Bowa began to surface in Philadelphia media accounts. One line of thinking was that victory had a happy father in Bowa, but defeat was an orphan, disowned by the manager.

None of the dissent seemed to come from Glanville.

"We're cool. We get along," he said of Bowa during his final Phillies season in 2002. "We have no issues. I always felt I could work with anybody. If people want to work with me, I'll be happy.

"He's volatile, aggressive, a guy you knew wants to win. If I can get respect from him, that should tell you something. He said at the end of the year, he was really happy with what I did.

"After playing in Triple-A for Ron Clark, in my mind it can't get too difficult."

◆ ◆ ◆

Now firmly in his thirties and playing for a new team, the Rangers, Glanville will "try to ride the wave as long as he can" in baseball. But he does not believe he will have a carefree life just because he's affluent.

"The good thing about baseball, the thing that makes it special to me, is the dues you have to pay to get to the major leagues," he said. "You make no money, but you learn life's lessons. You don't forget that experience.

"When you break it down, guys still love to compete. Money doesn't guarantee your future, your life, your health. The fact I made more money than ever starting in 1999 and 2000 didn't stop my father from being sick.

"I'm conservative [managing money]. That's partially me, partially my parents. I don't know how longer I will play this game."

Mattie Glanville has all the confidence her son will choose his course wisely.

"We're there to remind Doug what he's there for, what he stands for," she said. "He can remember to keep the fabric of his life. Family is number one. The other is having a great sense of right and wrong. It doesn't mean because you have more money, that means you can be less responsible. He can see how he can use his position as a celebrity, to be more powerful, to help others.

"He said, 'Mom, I'm not all that interested in money per se. Sure, give me my CDs and electronic games, a nice house and car, but after that I'm not so sure.'

"If other African Americans hadn't come before him, if his family didn't back him up, he may not have what he has. There's a lot of things he's standing on. He has to give back [to the community]."

No longer does he have to try to change to fit the classic mold of baseball, all brawn and little brains.

"I remember him calling me, telling me that [Jimmy] Piersall said to him that baseball has to replace everything," Mattie said. "But he would never be one-dimensional. In their minds, the only [baseball] model is to want it worse than anything else. Doug proved it otherwise. He didn't have to wear it on his sleeve."

Glanville's post-playing life likely will be more of the same—everything under the sun, from analyzing the intricacies of getting a jump on a ball in center field to figuring out how to get people to leave their cars at home and take the train.

He has a lot of life's experience to pass on to others.

"He would be a dynamic teacher or professor," said college mentor Cora Engram.

"I'm prepared to work—hopefully, at something I've enjoyed," Glanville said.

He'll have a wide range of choices.

12

THE DIRTIEST HELMET IN THE GAME

Craig Biggio would be the perfect spokesman for a laundry detergent company.

Some endorsers are not believable or seem insincere. But Biggio is ideal simply because he'd need industrial-sized portions of the cleaner just to get his uniform in shape to play the next day. It's that scruffy and filthy, because the Houston Astros' lifer is just doing his job around second base and in the batter's box.

Biggio's never been a Clean Gene on the field. It's the only way he knows.

"I just like to play the game hard," Biggio said. "You're going to get dirty doing that."

"His uniform was the dirtiest of all our players," remembered Seton Hall baseball coach Mike Sheppard, for whom Biggio played in the mid-1980s.

"He's always in the dirt trying to make things happen," said former longtime Astros coach Matt Galante, now with the New York Mets.

But while his various pinstriped, orange, black and white combination of pants and jersey will start out each day clean, Biggio's batting helmet is another story. Stadium lights can scarcely reflect off the helmet since, again, it's the most stained, scuffed helmet in baseball.

"We got on him about everything, his superstitions," Galante said of his fourteen seasons with Biggio. "His helmet is one. He likes a dirty helmet."

In 2001, Biggio acquired a new helmet when he reported for spring training. "It was clean and shiny," he said. "You get pine tar on your hands [and in turn, on the helmet]. It's not anything I work on every day. It just happens."

True, but he never cleans the helmet.

"I just like it that way," Biggio said. "I'd be very upset if somebody took it—put it that way."

Uniform and headgear scruffiness has long gone hand-in-hand with scrappiness, determination, and hustle. It links back directly with the Cardinals' famed "Gashouse Gang" team of the early 1930s. Then, the player uniforms weren't washed as frequently as in the present day. They sweated profusely in the gray woolen road uniforms. Thus the stained, smudgy Cardinals appeared as if they had worked in a gashouse. But the dirty "unis" were more applicable for a take-no-prisoners, leave-your-body-on-the-field style of play.

"I don't know any of the Gashouse Gang," Biggio said.

But, like Cardinals second baseman Fernando Vina, Biggio is one of the main throwbacks to Pepper Martin, Ducky Medwick, Dizzy Dean, et al. Be it his propensity to get hit by pitches, his impressive leadoff-man power, his hustle on the basepaths, or the aggressive second base play by this converted catcher, Biggio is an old-school player who learned to play the game the right way from some interesting mentors. And he often does it with a smile emanating from a choirboy face that could make him the leading man on a daytime soap opera.

"I've been around a long while," Biggio said, "and had a chance to be around some special people, like Buddy Bell, Nolan Ryan, Bill Doran, guys who played the game the right way, guys who played hurt, guys who went out there every day. They did what they had to do to play the game.

"When the day's over, you can look yourself in the mirror. Good or bad, you at least gave 100 percent effort, and that's all you can ask for. Play the game the right way, and that's the only way I know how to play it."

Biggio has been playing the game the right way since he broke in on a veteran-laden Astros club as the 1980s drew to a close.

"It was a good opportunity to see how to approach the game," he said. "I was twenty-two years old, and the next youngest guy was thirty-one, thirty-two."

The lessons stuck, and others in the Astros orbit are impressed to be around a true throwback.

"He's certainly as much old-school as there is in the game today," Astros general manager Gerry Hunsicker said. "We're all products of our environment and experience. He's never forgotten how it was when he came up, the relationship of veterans to young players, the way a young player was supposed to act. He's been instrumental in helping young people coming up, and we've all benefited from that.

"It starts with respect for the game. Unfortunately, a lot of players don't have respect for the game like the players of the prior generation. He certainly subscribes to the old-time work ethic, where you leave your body on the field every game. You suffer through the aches and pains. You don't want to come out of the lineup. He was never on the DL until [2000] when he tore up his knee."

Astros pitchers know that Biggio's old-fashioned, all-around game provides them a comfort zone.

"He's definitely a true throwback as far as being hard-nosed and playing to win," said pitcher Shane Reynolds, who ranks second to Jeff Bagwell in length of service as Biggio's teammate. "He plays the game the way it should be played."

Two-time former Astro Scott Servais summed up Biggio succinctly.

"Craig plays at the same pace every day he plays," Servais said. "He does play at a different kind of pace than most guys."

Biggio's own definition of his style isn't much more complicated.

"I just try to play the game hard, give everything you got, the way Pete Rose played the game," he said. "Maybe it's from the days when I liked to play football and just got dirty and played that way. Maybe that was part of it, too. It's just a lot of fun to play the game. I just enjoyed playing sports in general.

"Football was my true passion. I enjoyed baseball, too. I tried wrestling, but I wasn't very good at that. Football was a lot of fun for me. I was a running back. I was kind of fast. I could run really well. I wasn't going to try to run anybody over, but if I had to, I would. Walter Payton was my hero. If you had an extra yard to gain, run the guy over instead of run out of bounds. Emulate him and run like him.

"I'd much rather have done that [continue to play football], but things didn't work out for me in that profession."

The name "Pete Rose" and concept of running over someone to move forward are interesting. Biggio isn't the only one who conjures up Charlie Hustle's name in describing his style.

"I've said he's Pete Rose with more ability," former Astros manager Larry Dierker said. Dierker may have had to take issue with Biggio's opinions about his managerial skills in the clubhouse and with Astros owner Drayton McLane, but he can never question his on-field demeanor.

"Rose made the All-Star Game at five positions," Dierker said. "If you had asked Biggio to play another position, he probably would. He's got desire and the fire burning inside him that Pete Rose had, that made him a special kind of player."

Astros coach Jose Cruz also dropped Rose's name.

"Craig hustles like Pete Rose," he said. "I've never seen him slow down. He could have played when I did. He's one of the toughest players I've ever seen."

Dierker and Cruz also said Biggio can hark back to Joe Morgan as an all-around player, combining power, speed and defense. "I don't think Joe Morgan would take offense at that comparison," Dierker said.

But after fifteen years of Gashouse Gang–style play, perhaps one day future scrappers and hustlers will be compared to Craig Biggio.

◆ ◆ ◆

Coming up through the game, Biggio had two outlets for his style. He was a catcher. And with his stance hugging home plate, he became a target for pitches.

Somehow the two aspects, along with his childhood love of football and contact, have merged into one powerful baseball package. Converted to second base after his third full big league season in 1991, Biggio still brings a catcher's mentality to all parts of his game.

"One thing about catching, you really have to know where everyone is on the field," Biggio said. "You have to have an idea how you want to pitch. As a young guy, if you had an older staff, they knew what kind of game they wanted. When I went out to second, it was beneficial, but it was different. I had to learn all over again. But being a catcher helps when you're hitting, because you try to think along with the catcher and see what he's calling.

"The catcher has to be the field general," Gerry Hunsicker said. "When I think of Craig Biggio, I think of a guy who's focused on every single pitch. He's always thinking ahead. His mental toughness is linked somehow to when he was a catcher."

Catchers spend their professional careers in pain, nursing minor injuries to their hands and other body parts on which the strain of the position takes its toll. Although Biggio was relieved of that burden back in 1992 to preserve his offensive skills, he also lives with pain from the number of times he has been plunked by pitches.

If consistency is a Biggio byword, then taking it for the team was his constant companion from 1995 to 1998. In each season Biggio was hit by pitches at least twenty-two times, with a team-record and National League–high thirty-four in 1997. After being plunked twenty-eight times in 2001, he totaled 197. And yet after all those black-and-blue marks, the threat of bro-

Now a center fielder, Craig Biggio still applies a catcher's mentality to the game with his focus, toughness, and smarts. *Houston Astros*

ken bones always close, here was Biggio still holding forth as the Astros' leadoff man in 2002.

"I don't go up there with the intent of trying to get hit," he said. "I understand that pitchers have to pitch inside. But if I think about moving, I can't be half the hitter that I am. I understand I'm going to get hit. I just can't move. By the time I get my leg up and down, the ball is three-quarters the way on me. I can't move to get out of the way."

Get one thing straight, though. Biggio is no masochist or glutton for punishment; he's not possessed of some off-the-chart pain threshold when ball meets flesh and/or bone.

"It hurts," he said. "It hits you on the elbow, it hurts. It's part of the game, it's going to happen. I'm not using it to get on base, I'm using it to protect myself. You try to play the game right. It's playing the game hard. It's the only way I know how to play."

Comfortable in football padding as a running back at Kings Park High School in New York, Biggio had no problems encasing his arm and elbow in padding and armor. Eventually, Major League Baseball banned all the layers of armor, permitting some old-fashioned padding covering oft-injured areas. But the powers-that-be wanted to ensure that players didn't intentionally shield themselves like their football counterparts as a way to get hit by pitches without paying a price.

Biggio defended his use of armor, insisting that he merely was trying to protect himself from the inevitable.

"If you continue to get hit in the same spot," he said, "and get hit in the elbow twice on consecutive days, you can't hit for a week, two weeks, and you have to continue to go out there to play.

"Nobody cares. Pitchers don't hit you and say, 'I'm sorry' as you go down to first. If you can wear something to keep from continuing to get injured, why not wear it? I've been beat up on my elbows and triceps over the injuries over the years. It's hard hitting after they swell up."

Shane Reynolds can get into both Biggio's head and those of his pitching brethren on other teams to see both sides of the story.

"That's part of Biggio's game," he said. "He wears the armor, he's not going to move much. Against some pitchers, he'll take that part of the game away from them, pitching inside. You know he's not going to move, and if you leave it over the plate he's going to hit it.

"That pisses a lot of people off. People hit him because of that. I don't blame them at all. It makes you upset at times. Once they hit him, he's on base, he might steal a base, score a run. He knows what he's doing."

Hunsicker did not lose sleep worrying about losing Biggio for a month or more as a result of a ball breaking a bone.

"I never really feared that," he said. "I feared more his aggressive style of play, that injuries would catch up to him on the field. He knows what he's doing with a bat in his hand up there. I have all the confidence in the world he can handle the situation."

Putting himself in further peril, Biggio likes to slide head-first. The risk of injury is greater, especially to the hands and wrist being jammed or stepped on.

"I suggested to him not to do it," Dierker said. "But it was a real good slide for him. With that last push, he gets into the bag more quickly than with a conventional slide."

Biggio obviously handles all the pain along with the usual wear and tear of a long season well. In his fourteenth consecutive full season as an Astros regular in 2002, he had played in fewer than 149 games only four times. The first occasion was his first year in the lineup, as a catcher, in 1989. Two more abbreviated work schedules came in the strike-shortened seasons of 1994–

95. The only significant time Biggio lost to injury was the final two months of the 2000 season, when he injured the anterior cruciate and medial collateral ligaments in his left knee on August 1. The Marlins' Preston Wilson had crashed into Biggio as he attempted to turn a double play.

Freed from catching duties, Biggio became a true ironman. He played all 162 games in 1992, his first year at second base. Biggio did not miss a game in both 1996 and 1997. He played in 160 games each in 1998 and 1999.

"I just think I was lucky," he said of his uncommon good health. "[2000] was my year to pay the price. It's nice. If you're going to get hurt once every fourteen years, I'll take that."

"That's one thing you can say about Craig, he's out there every day," said Jeff Bagwell, his fellow longtime Astros "Killer B." "That's impressive about anybody, to go out and do it."

Helmets sure get dirty if they're used in every game—and are not cleaned. You can drill Biggio, knock him down, try to wear him out. He keeps coming back for more.

♦ ♦ ♦

Biggio did not start out his baseball-playing life standing in the way of pitches and rubbing his nose in the dirt to smother a grounder. He was a typical middle-class kid who simply loved playing.

He started at age five, playing T-ball. Eventually, Biggio played shortstop and outfield, and caught for two different teams in Little League.

"I think I was really good," Biggio told Dusty Destler of *Junior Baseball Magazine*. "My dad started me young, and he said if I couldn't handle it, he'd wait and let me play with kids my own age. But I ended up playing with the kids above me. I held my own and did OK.

"My dad was very supportive. He pushed me, he made it fun, and he taught me that if you're going to be good at the game, or whatever you do, you're going to have to work hard at it. Same as in life, if you're going to be successful in life, you're going to have to work hard at it."

In high school, Biggio made the Kings Park varsity as a sophomore. Not long afterward, he started attracting the attention of college baseball recruiters. Foremost among them was Seton Hall coach Mike Sheppard.

"He was the big deal guy in high school," Sheppard said. "He played middle infield then. He was also quite a wingback in football. We wanted him flat-out because he was a baseball athlete. I always tell kids, play baseball, don't get put in a set position."

Sheppard recruited Biggio to play the infield or outfield, but found out he had also caught in high school. Out of necessity, he switched Biggio behind the plate. "He caught almost every inning of every game for two years. He wanted to play all the time," Sheppard said.

"His enthusiasm for the game is outstanding. He just loved the game, and had the same disposition if he was 6-for-6 or didn't get a hit. His enthusiasm rubbed off on others.

"He was always a pepperpot on the bench. I'd tell him to sit down on the bench. He'd always be up talking. I'd want him to rest. But if I took him out, he'd be at another position.

Biggio batted third in a lineup that included two other future major leaguers: Mo Vaughn at designated hitter and John Valentin at shortstop. First baseman Martese Robinson, who led the league in hitting, was drafted by Oakland. Robinson is now director of pro scouting for the Cardinals. Sheppard's son, John, played second base.

"It was a great offensive team, and might have gone all the way [to the College World Series title] with some pitching." Fueling the run production was Biggio's speed. "I always gave him the green light to steal," said Sheppard. "He had blinding speed in college."

While at Seton Hall, Biggio played in the summer Cape Cod League, an incubator for big league talent.

"Apparently all the best prospects at that time go to that league to play, and I figured that I had a chance because I held my own with them," Biggio told *Junior Baseball Magazine*. "You evaluate yourself, think that maybe you have a chance, maybe you'll get lucky, and I did get lucky."

The hustle and hard work paid off. Biggio was named first-team All-America in his junior year in 1987 after batting .407 with 14 homers and 68 RBIs. That cemented the Astros' opinion of him. He was selected in the first round of the 1987 draft.

Biggio played only 137 minor league games in Class A and Triple A before the Astros called him up on June 26, 1988. He remained a backup to Alan Ashby the rest of the season, but earned his first offensive milestones against big-name pitchers. Biggio's first major-league hit was against eventual Cy Young winner Orel Hershiser on June 29; his first homer was a game-winner at Wrigley Field off Goose Gossage on August 22.

"When he came up, we knew he'd be a good player," Matt Galante said. "I didn't think anyone thought he could be a Hall of Fame–level player. How good it would be would be up to him."

Finally inserted as the regular catcher when Ashby was put on waivers May 11, 1989, Biggio immediately made an offensive impact on a contending Astros club. He slugged 13 homers, drove in 60 runs and flashed uncommon speed for what was normally position for plowhorse players. Biggio recorded a string of eighteen straight stolen-base attempts, dating back to 1988, that was finally broken on August 1, 1989. On September 9, he became the only the seventh catcher since 1900 to steal twenty bases in one season.

At the same time, Biggio began to show the nimbleness in the field that would pave the way for his eventual switch to another position. He played the last five games of the '89 season in the outfield, including four in center field.

Biggio played 113 games behind the plate and 50 in the outfield in 1990, batting .276 with twenty-five steals. Then he jumped another level in performance in 1991, becoming the first Astros catcher ever named to an All-Star team. For good measure, he became the first player ever to be charged with catcher's interference in the Midsummer Classic while Paul Molitor was batting.

By now, Biggio's offensive potential as a speedy, top-of-the-lineup man was established. He had batted second or third frequently in 1990–91. In the latter season, when Biggio batted a team-leading .295, he was the second-hardest National League player to double up, grounding into only two double plays.

Team management by now figured his future still up the middle, but on the other side of the infield. On an experimental basis, Biggio played three late-season games at second in 1991. The conversion went full-bore the following spring training.

"One of the reasons we made him an infielder is longevity, the ability to steal bases, to be able to work more on his hitting," Galante said. Also, he'd be able to play 150 games instead of 125 games [as a catcher] and avoid getting hurt."

"I didn't have one of the greatest arms in the world, so the organization thought that it would be better for the [team] if I moved to second," Biggio said.

Biggio dived into the process of converting to second like anything else in his game—full speed ahead.

"It speaks volumes about his desire," said Dierker, who witnessed the conversion as an Astros broadcaster. "He came out about an hour ahead of the workout every day in spring training to take ground balls at second base. He accelerated the process. He never missed a beat."

With fresher legs from not having to catch, Biggio had far more spring in his basepath steps in 1992. He swiped thirty-eight bases, slashed thirty-two doubles and scored ninety-six runs. Biggio also earned notoriety as the only player to make the All-Star team at catcher one year, then at second base the following season. And after ranking as just an average defensive catcher, he began to excel at second with a .984 fielding percentage and just twelve errors in 1992.

"He had great range and speed to both sides, covering a lot of ground out there and saving a lot of hits against us," Dierker recalled.

"Things worked out ten times better than I ever could have imagined," Biggio said.

He couldn't have summed up what was ahead of him any better.

♦ ♦ ♦

Biggio and a young first baseman named Jeff Bagwell suddenly became the cornerstones of a retooling Astros franchise under new owner Drayton McLane in 1993. Bagwell hadn't yet fully established his formidable power credentials in '93, so it was left to the five-foot-eleven, 180-pound Biggio to muscle up, such at it was, in the cavernous Astrodome.

He elevated his offensive game to the level he maintained for the next decade in '93. Biggio's twenty-one homers led the Astros, the most-ever by a Houston middle infielder (including Joe Morgan).

Despite his increased strength and production, Biggio never considered himself a power hitter.

"When I try to hit home runs, I can't do it," he said. "I try to hit the ball hard, hit it up the middle. You get lucky and get fifteen to twenty a year."

"I'm somewhat surprised at the power he's generated late in his career," Hunsicker said. "That's really set him apart from virtually every other lead-off hitter in the game."

"He just used his ability," Bagwell said. "He used to pretty much get out in front of the ball and just run while he was hitting it. Then he stayed back more and started driving the ball.

"After [Ryne] Sandberg, he was the guy who revolutionized the position at second base with power. Nobody had come along where a guy could steal fifty bases, hit twenty home runs, drive in eighty to ninety runs and score 120 to 130."

He dropped to six homers in the strike-fractured 1994 season, but came back smoking when play resumed in 1995 with twenty-two to go along with 123 runs scored. Among his other '95 accomplishments were four stolen bases in one game and his second consecutive Gold Glove Award as the revived Astros were nosed out by the Rockies for the NL wild-card playoff berth on the season's final day.

His baseball portfolio almost complete, Biggio was set to cash in on his first megabucks contract after the '95 season. It seemed touch and go that he'd return to Houston, as owner McLane was keeping tight rein on team payroll. The Rockies and Cardinals were rumored to be in hot pursuit of Biggio's services. Near season's end, he expressed a liking for Wrigley Field, and perhaps the Cubs should have tried to land him; McLane could have never competed dollar-for-dollar with a Tribune Company that had opened its exchequer. But then the Cubs got word that team icon Sandberg, who had retired in June 1994 due to his collapsing first marriage, wanted to come back.

Everyone returned to where they were supposed to be. Deep down, Biggio had developed a strong sense of loyalty to the Astros. McLane re-signed him to a lucrative five-year deal.

"Certain guys leave and move on," Biggio said. "It's important for the fans to have someone to cheer for their whole career. Tony Gwynn in San Diego, Cal Ripken, Jr., in Baltimore. It's important in the community to have someone to look up to and watch year in and year out, rather than watch a guy for two, three years and he moves on. It's something in the game you wish you'd see more of."

Biggio immediately began earning his new contract.

After another great all-around season in 1996, Biggio entered his true prime the following two seasons. Dierker, just named manager to succeed Terry Collins, moved Biggio to the leadoff spot full time after floating in and out of that lineup slot for years.

But Biggio began hitting like a middle-of-the-order hitter. He slugged 22 homers and drove in 81 runs while batting .309. He stole forty-seven bases. His major-league-leading 146 runs scored were the most in the NL since Chuck Klein's 152 as a Phillie in 1932. Batting 619 times, Biggio also became only the third player ever (after Augie Galan of the 1935 Cubs and Dick McAuliffe of the 1968 Tigers) to go the entire season without grounding into a double play.

Then he showed he could get even better as the Astros became an elite regular-season team with 102 victories in 1998. Adding to career highs of 210 hits and a .325 average, Biggio became only the second big leaguer after Tris Speaker of the 1912 Red Sox to record fifty doubles and fifty steals in one season. Biggio recorded a club-record fifty-one two-base hits along with a career-high fifty steals in fifty-eight attempts.

"There's a lot of things I've been able to do up here that have surprised myself," Biggio said. "I played my 2,000th game [early in the 2002 season], and that's 2,000 more than I ever thought I'd play. Just getting better as the years went on came from maturity, learning and understand what the other teams are trying to do to you.

"I wasn't catching anymore. That had a lot to do with it. People don't

Shown turning a double play, Craig Biggio went the entire 1997 season without grounding into one of his own, only the third major league regular to accomplish that feat. *Houston Astros*

understand the physical toll that your body goes through catching day in and day out. Also, late in the game a lot of the times your last at-bat, you're giving it away because you're so fatigued. You're not trying to give it away, but you're just beat up. Playing second, I was able to stay fresher and stronger throughout the game and stay mentally sharp."

Biggio continued to run up the numbers playing in the Astrodome, a pitcher's paradise.

"The Astrodome is a great place if you're a line-drive, ground ball hitter, a gap hitter," he said. "The Astrodome took away a lot of home runs, but it made it up in different areas. I miss the Astrodome. It was a fun place to hit [as a home player].

"Guys hated to come there. It was dark. Teams had a hard time adjusting their sights to the ball until the last day [of each series].

In Houston's last season in the Astrodome in 1999, Biggio continued flirting with all-time offensive marks. He amassed 56 doubles, first major leaguer with that many doubles in one season since George Kell of the Tigers in 1950.

The daily firepower and on-base percentage generated from the leadoff spot fueled the most powerful Astros lineup in history, one that shrunk the Astrodome's distances. Bagwell had RBI totals of 120, 135, 111, and 126, respectively, from 1996 to 1999. When Moises Alou was traded to Houston for the '98 season, he had his best-ever RBI total with 124.

With Biggio well-established as one of the game's premiere players, McLane was not going to leave anything to chance as Biggio's free-agent season loomed in 2000. He re-signed his star to a four-year deal worth about $8 million annually.

"In baseball, there are no no-brainer decisions," McLane said. "You have to carefully think through it. But everything pointed toward re-signing Craig. He had just been a vital part of our franchise for ten years."

"There was concern whether he could play at that high level. You're paying players for what they did in the past. We wanted him to have the physical ability and motivation to play at a high level."

Hunsicker concurred with his owner's actions.

"I don't think it was ever really an issue," the GM said. "Drayton feels like every organization has one or two cornerstone players. Whenever possible, you keep those players.

"There was not much doubt as long as those players wanted to be fair to the organizations. They didn't take any hometown discounts to stay here. They're paid commensurate with other players."

Negotiations went as smoothly as megabucks deals could go due to the already-cordial links between owner and player.

"He and I have a very special relationship that made a huge difference," McLane said.

"I've been here for fifteen years," Biggio said. "I knew the first owner [John McMullen] for six years. If you can't talk to the owner, and I've been through two, three negotiations, then there's something wrong with it. There's nothing wrong with being able to talk to the owner. It's nice to see your boss around, good or bad. He understands the fact of guys going out to bust their tails every day. Good or bad, he's going to be there to support you. That means a lot to the players."

Although paid handsomely, Biggio vowed not to hold up his team for every last dollar. And he had a special loyalty to his adopted city.

"I'm making plenty of money," he said. "It wasn't about the money, it was about having the chance to win. I was close, I almost left, but we were able to work it out. I always wanted to stay. I don't need to be making all the money in the world. I'm treated very fairly. It's a lot of money. I make enough money for my kids and my family, and I get paid to play the game that's something that I never thought I would be able to do. I've been able to do it for fifteen years. It's something pretty special.

"It's [Houston] a great city, I've got some ties here. It's the only place I know. The city's been good to me, the organization's been good to me. To me, the ultimate thing would be to win a World Series with a middle-market club. To do it here would be special.

"You're a middle-market club. We know we won't have a $100 million payroll like the Yankees. The middle market is what we have, it's the reality. What they've been able to do here is tremendous."

Biggio's loyalty made a big impression on lifelong Texan McLane.

"Craig was very thoughtful, he really wants to be a Houston Astro, he wants to complete an entire career here," he said. "That happens so rarely in Major League Baseball these days. He could have gotten more money as a free agent. We met him more than 50 percent of the way.

"I've been in business forty-two years. The qualities I want rank this way. Personal integrity is number one. Loyalty is number two. Craig has a commitment to the Houston Astros as a franchise. He wants to play for one team his entire career."

Bagwell had been taken care of contractually in similar fashion by McLane with a deal that runs through 2006. A similar old-school character, Bagwell's lifetime 349 homers and .303 average through 2001 may have made him a co–Mr. Astro with Biggio.

"Both of those players wanted to stay in Houston," Hunsicker said. "We both feel like they're both future Hall of Famers. This organization never has had a Hall of Famer."

"I think we've both been pretty fortunate with management to be able to work it out," Biggio said. "To be able to work it out in this age is pretty special."

"We both play the game the same way. We play hard, play the game the right way, every day whether we feel good or bad. He's one of the best players to ever play the game. We run out balls, dive, steal bases. It's a lot of fun playing with a guy like that. We just know each other. We've played together twelve years, and in this day and age of no loyalty from management and players, it's pretty special."

The "Killer Bs" have had to make a few concessions to age.

"We both used to have more range," Bagwell said. "Now we both have to know where each other is at any particular time. The most important thing Craig and I have in common is our love for the game, to play the game

228

the way it's supposed to be played. Sometimes it's good enough, sometimes it's not. But we believe that everyone who plays here should feel the same way. To watch him do what he's done for the twelve years I've been here is impressive.

"We do have different personalities. But we're friends off the field. And when we come to the ballpark, we believe in the same things."

◆ ◆ ◆

You'd never connect the scrappy but handsome Biggio to the nitty-gritty of baseball politics. But too many in and around the Astros organization figured his major-domo status and close relationship with McLane put him squarely in the middle of the firing of two managers—Terry Collins and Larry Dierker—five years apart.

Collins had taken a team that had not progressed under Art Howe to a 66-49 finish in the strike-shortened 1994 season. The Astros were eliminated from the wild-card race on the last day of the season in 1995. They finished a disappointing 82-80 in 1996 with reports of displeasure by Biggio and Bagwell on the emotional Collins's handling of the team surfacing. Collins went; the Killer Bs, of course, stayed.

Dierker's laconic, self-deprecating style was in sharp contrast to that of Collins. The Astros seemed to respond, peaking at 102-60 and 97-65 records in 1998 and 1999, respectively. But the team imploded in the first two months of the 2000 in a rough adjustment to newly-opened Minute Maid Park, then known as Enron Field. The pitching staff, particularly volatile Jose Lima, was totally frazzled by the snazzy ballpark's short left field porch. By the end of June, the Astros were a horrid 27-52. Reports of clubhouse dissension and dissatisfaction with Dierker cropped up. Again, Biggio seemed to be in the center of it. He apparently began expressing his dissatisfaction with Dierker's game strategy and postgame candor via off-the-record remarks to reporters.

"It's something that you can expect on a team that's losing," Dierker said. "There's a buzz in the clubhouse. Sometimes it's hard to look in the mirror. It's a challenge to get along with everybody.

"Craig had a lot of passion, a lot of baseball intelligence. Those two things may cause him to respond in different situations a different way. I had more meetings in the locker room in the first half of 2000 than in my whole managing career combined. I started going to guys one by one. Most of the guys didn't want to talk. A few did."

But the granddaddy of the clubhouse buzz seemed to rise to a crescendo in the final days of the 2001 regular season.

The Astros had been a hot second-half club, moving from a 57-48 record and four-and-one-half–game deficit on July 29 to overtaking the Cubs for the National League Central lead on August 18 and a 90-60 mark and five-and-one-half–game lead on September 24.

But then Houston endured a major pratfall as the onrushing Cardinals caught them with one week to go, going 3-9 to end the regular season. Eyebrows were raised when Dierker refused to allow his pitchers to throw strikes to Barry Bonds almost throughout a three-game series at home October 2 to 4, before Bonds finally connected for his seventieth homer off rookie lefty Wilfredo Rodriguez into the upper deck in the series finale. Only a 9-2 victory in St. Louis in the 162nd game, officially giving the Astros the division title, provided a reprieve from the downward spiral. But the reverse momentum continued in the Division Series in a three-game sweep at the hands of the Braves.

When Dierker was fired at a Union Station press conference on October 18, 2001, despite a 448-362 regular-season record and four division titles in five years, Hunsicker called the driving force behind the move "leadership in the clubhouse."

"It's obvious some of [the players] were getting tired of me. And I understand that," Dierker said. "[Fans] may not appreciate the politics and power structure. I think fans believe that the manager has more power than he really does."

"If Larry was guilty of one thing, it was caring too much for people and expecting them to be as responsible as he is," Hunsicker said. "A lot of those he directed didn't share those same attributes."

The *Houston Chronicle*'s John P. Lopez aimed squarely at the heart of the team in an October 21, 2001, column fingering the ringleaders behind Dierker's departure:

"Biggio and Co. had as much to do with Dierker's forced resignation as McLane, Hunsicker, or any of the suits standing sullenly at Union Station . . . And maybe their call was the right call, considering the way the club was slipping away from Dierker in the final weeks of a dismal end to the 2001 season." Added Lopez: "The leaders of the clubhouse bypassed Hunsicker and went straight to McLane with their gripes and ultimatums. . . . It wasn't the first time McLane put his hands on the general manager's duties, taking the players' word as gospel over perhaps the best GM in the league."

Hunsicker claimed no players came to him insisting they could no longer play for Dierker. He added that a player the caliber of Biggio would not be consulted when he hired Dierker's replacement.

"The problem is," Lopez wrote, "Biggio or some other players might be on McLane's selection committee. Before the Astros find an answer to their managerial question, they need to figure out who's running the show, or else they'll be looking for a GM, too."

Almost a season after the Dierker firing, Biggio called the reports of his alleged king-making abilities "a bunch of BS."

"I wish I had that power," he said. "I never went to Drayton. What Drayton McLane does with his ballclub, it's his club. If people want to sit and point the finger to say, 'Jeff and I did this or that,' that's a bunch of BS. It's not the truth. I wish I had that power because we'd definitely have some changes.

"It's just ridiculous, people speculating making decisions and taking cheap shots at people. People want to say what they want to say. It would be pretty sad if the organization was being run that way."

Biggio professed to be concerned with only one issue during the Dierker administration.

"He penciled my name in the lineup every day; that's all I really care about. I played as hard as I could. As long as you put my name in the lineup, I'm fine. I play hard for everyone."

No matter what his off-the-field role, Biggio's endured ongoing frustration over the team's postseason failures factored into whatever behind-the-scenes politicking he did. The franchise was loaded with talent and momentum in the final years of the 1990s.

Never did the Astros seem as ready to advance to the World Series as in 1998, when Hunsicker pulled off a daring last-second, trade-deadline trade of his top minor league prospects to the Mariners for Randy Johnson. But despite two fine Division Series outings by the Big Unit, the Astros' hitters snoozed through a four-game victory by what was, on paper, an inferior Padres club.

Houston had similar offensive short-circuiting when the Braves swept them three in a row in the Division Series in both 1997 and 2001. It was only slightly harder for Atlanta in 1999 when they dispatched Houston in four games.

Biggio and Bagwell simply were different postseason players than their usual dominant offensive selves. They batted a combined .150 with no homers and five RBIs in 100 at-bats.

"You've got to get lucky," Biggio said. "You get a play here or there, a pitch here or there. We were victims of the off-days in 1998, where we saw Kevin Brown twice. The breaks have to go your way. You have to get a ball to fall in, a key call. That's the reality of baseball.

"In the World Series in San Diego, Tino Martinez looks at a pitch that looked like strike three. It's called a ball. The next pitch he hits into the stands for a grand slam."

Biggio at least was satisfied McLane and Hunsicker approved payroll-inflating moves, such as the Johnson trade, to boost the Astros' postseason chances.

"The reality of baseball is that you're not going to be in this position every year," he said. "When you have an opportunity to win and you don't go out and try to help the ballclub, that's not right. Every time we've had a chance to win, they've done that."

◆ ◆ ◆

Craig Biggio always has racked up an impressive community-service record while a high-profile major leaguer. He's actively involved in the Sunshine Kids, a support organization for children with cancer and their families. He also was the 1997 winner of the Branch Rickey Award for community service.

That's the soft side of the tough guy with the dirty helmet, who off the field is a father of two sons and a daughter.

"I'm proud to say that besides being a helluva baseball player, he's a good husband and father," said Mike Sheppard, Biggio's old college coach.

But Biggio's down-in-the-dirt style is so powerful that it will obscure all other sides of him as long as he plays. To be sure, there will be some slippage as his thirty-seventh birthday looms.

"He's changed a bit—he's willing to sit for a day game after a night game," said Dierker, his former manager. "He's still possibly the best leadoff man in the league, even though he doesn't steal many bases anymore. He does everything else.

"If he doesn't steal bases, so what—if he hits forty doubles and twenty homers? There was a time a few years ago when he could do all these things and steal bases. I thought then he was in the top five most valuable players in the league. Now he's dropped out of that group and in the top 25 in the league."

Biggio is not putting a time limit on the balance of his career.

"As long as I'm still having fun, enjoying the game and help some people," he said. "I thought about it at one time, having a time limit. I'll play it out as long as I'm having fun and physically I feel fine, let's see what happens. As long as there's still a fire to burn, I'm still going to try to play."

Old comrade-in-arms Jeff Bagwell is predicting a definite post-career Biggio destination that may parallel his own.

"He's a special player," Bagwell said. "He's a Hall of Famer."

13

THE GOOD OL' COUNTRY BOY

Despite Florida's status as one of the most populous states, there are a few places where you can simply get away from everything.

The hamlet of Mayo, in the far northern part of the state, is one such locale. Only 400 souls reside in the town. The surrounding Lafayette County, with about 4,000 residents, is the least populated county in Florida. Rustic and rural are the most apt descriptions of the area, far from the usual sub-tropical, sheltering-palms seashore image of the state.

"We're not in the panhandle and not in the peninsula," resident Herbert Perry said. "We're right where the 'hinge' would be. It can get cold in the winter. There were three different occasions where we had to fix the pipes, where it got down to the low teens. If it's thirty degrees in Gainesville, we're twenty-four. The gulf breezes don't come across where we are."

Mayo, according to Perry, exists "on a straight line" one hundred miles west of Jacksonville, and eighty-eight miles east of state capital Tallahassee. Gainesville, home of the University of Florida, is sixty miles to the south. The Georgia border is thirty miles to the north, with small-city Valdosta just beyond.

"Proctor and Gamble own most of the county, probably 75 to 80 percent, mostly pine trees," said Perry. "They own a million acres. If you go from the backside of my brother's [Chan] and my dairy [farm] and go a mile due south, you've passed the last houses you're going to pass for forty miles. It's just nothing out there. For people living here, owning land is huge. It's the measure of wealth."

Mayo, and the Perry family farms, are so far away from the symbols of urbanism that the family needed satellite receivers to pull in a choice of TV channels. The cable-TV system, available within the Mayo city limits, does not reach the Perrys' property.

Prior to satellites, the family had to hoist a rotating TV antenna atop a thirty-foot tower to capture the far-fringe reception-area video signals. "We had color TV, but we had only two channels, ABC and CBS," Perry said of life in the 1970s. "We didn't really get NBC. It was out of Jacksonville and watching it was like [picking it] out of a blizzard."

In such an atmosphere, without the leisure-time distractions and choices that most citified and suburban folks have taken for granted for decades, the Mayo residents adhere to the values and patterns of life of another age. Their community is almost placed under glass. It's a time capsule of the formerly rural life that used to predominate nationwide.

There are four evergreen pillars of the community—family, church, work, and sports. Life is simple and basic. This is the environment in which baseball became our national pastime in the latter half of the nineteenth century, an American Gothic image of six-day workweeks, church on Sunday mornings and "town ball" games between neighboring communities on Sunday afternoons.

Baseball was nurtured by entire families of kids playing in every spare moment in cow pastures and open fields. This was no fable of ghostly ballplayers emerging from a cornfield á la *Field of Dreams*. Instead, it was real life, the kids dreaming of the faraway big leagues, fantasizing themselves as great stars that they read about from a distance, fathers teaching their sons the fundamentals of the game, and fostering competitiveness among brothers as they squeezed every non-work or school moment in to play ball.

"Most of the great athletes of long ago grew up on a farm," said former pitcher Lindy McDaniel, who grew up in the 1940s and 1950s on an 800-acre ranch that raised cattle along with cotton and alfalfa crops near Hollis, Oklahoma, not far from the Texas border in the southwest part of the state. Many returned to the farm in the offseason, keeping themselves in shape with their normal daily chores in the fields or barns.

Deprived of any lures to other activities, the siblings would hone their talent to a high level. Some bird-dog might notice them, and report them to the full-time big league scout to whom he was loyal. More often just one player in a family would be signed, his long journey upward to the majors usually starting in some other backwater town in the old Class D leagues. But the scouts knew about heredity and family genes long before the medical researchers. If one brother had talent, why not sign up another?

Sometimes three brothers would be inked to contracts as in the case of the Boyer siblings—Ken, Clete, and Cloyd—out of rural Missouri. Earlier, the town of Lucas, Arkansas, produced the Dean brothers, Dizzy and Paul (later tabbed "Daffy" to play off his colorful brother), who were the one-two starters on the Gashouse Gang Cardinals of 1934. Two decades later, St. Louis went the same route in signing McDaniel, then younger brother Von off the family ranch.

But as farmland got gobbled up by developers and the lure of jobs in the cities depleted the rural population, this old talent pipeline dried up. The prospects would now come from baseball factories in high schools or colleges in the booming, suburbanized Sunbelt. Kids would play on manicured fields instead of makeshift basepaths among the haystacks. They'd be coached by professionals, not farmer-rancher/parents. Baseball would be regimented, with little of the ad-libbed joy of the rural past.

A few exceptions still exist, though. In isolated Mayo, it was possible to be a throwback. Herbert Perry followed that classic route to pro baseball, learning from his dad, hitting rocks in the field, carrying a ball and glove on the tractor, and sometimes competing against kid brother Chan. The Cleveland Indians drafted Herbert Perry in 1991. In tried-and-true fashion, the area scout was a believer in the gene pool, drafting Chan three years later. Herbert would carve out a decent career in the majors, hitting .300 with the 2000 White Sox before moving on to the Texas Rangers, while Chan finally made it to the big show with the Indians in 2000 before moving on to the Braves organization.

"We benefited from being in a rural environment," said Chan Perry. "When you're from a small town, all we knew was number one, the dairy, which was work, and number two, sports. When you got ahead of your work, you started playing the game you love. We were always playing sports. If you had ten minutes, you filled it up trying to hit a foam ball with a broomstick."

No matter where each brother's travels would take him, both would always return every fall to the farm in Mayo. They'd be true to their roots. The trappings of pro baseball were fine, but they were so well-grounded in family and farm. They could take the boy out of the country, but they can't take the country out of the boy—the old adage was so true. And in the process, a treasured piece of baseball that added the homespun aura to the game for 100 years was preserved going into the twenty-first century.

◆ ◆ ◆

In an out-of-the-way Deep South town like Mayo, all aspects of life seem to run together. And you hear about it and how things got to be the way they are in expansive detail through the natural storytelling talents of the natives. Mayo-ites can carry on a conversation, and Herbert Perry is no exception.

"That's the way people entertained themselves," Perry said of the tales, tall and small. "When I was five or six, I'd always go to the barber shop and listen. It was fun to hear all the stories and the things that were going on around Mayo. They were talking about the twenties and thirties, and the way things used to be. I can't imagine Mayo's changed much except people are driving cars and not pulling wagons."

Although the folks of Mayo can talk, they're also respectful and modest in a small-town way.

"If a kid's driving around with a Mustang with his music turned up loud or he's beaten' up and down the street squealin' his tires and stuff, people look down at that," Perry said. "Humility was one of the things that was drilled into you. To have an air about you or to be arrogant in any way where I went to school, your friends would ostracize you. People in Mayo weren't aggressive. If there was the last piece of food on the table, the Mayo mentality was to look around and see if anyone else wants it before you grab it."

Sitting down with Perry, you discover that a multi-generational family history, dairy farming, and sports are intertwined in a small town. Often, relationships are a little too close for comfort.

"If you're from the tenth cousin on down, you live in Lafayette County," Perry said. "It makes it real tough when it comes time to ask people out for proms, because there are only 4,000 people."

The past is prologue to the present, and the future isn't going to change much compared to today. Perry starts off the family tale with great-grandfather Arthur Perry, who started the line of dairy farming in the area.

This forebear was involved in an escapade. The short version is that Arthur was going home on a horse-drawn wagon one day. The horse was spooked by someone on a tree limb, and bolted along with the wagon through the front fence of a house. "They tore it up in the front yard. He kicked my great-grandfather's butt," Herbert Perry said of the property owner.

Next in the Perry line was Herbert Lee Perry. He in turn had another son named Herbert. Starting with Arthur "Artie" Perry, almost all the males in the family were known by nicknames or middle names. Herbert Lee Perry's son was named Herbert Edward Perry, and he became better known as "Edward" Perry. In turn, future major leaguer Herbert Edward Perry, Jr., became known as "Herbertson" because his father talked so fast. Chan Perry is not short for "Chandler" or the like. He was named after Chan

Gailey, once a University of Florida football star who went on to coach the Dallas Cowboys.

"My father had very little," Herbert said of Edward Perry. "Herbert Lee died when my father was nineteen. His youngest sister was three. He had to be the father figure of his three sisters. I've always watched him and always saw a sense of responsibility. If someone in the family is hurting, then we're all hurting. We're a close-knit family."

The family never strayed much from Mayo until Perry's sister, Diana, recently moved to Montana. "She's the first person in the immediate family who left Mayo," Perry said. He and his brother have always returned to Mayo, and Herbert could never get enough of the ol' homestead.

"I knew I was going to Florida," he said. "That's the closest school to home. I couldn't handle going somewhere three, four, five, six hours from home. I don't think I could handle it. Even at Florida, I was home two to three times a week. If I had three hours free and it was an hour trip home, an hour trip back, I'd spend an hour at home. I love Mayo. It's my little oasis. I think about it all the time."

Even away from Mayo, playing in the majors during the season, Perry sticks close to his family.

"I never go out after games," he said. "When I'm away from home and playing sports, that's all I do, play baseball. I'm not a partier. I don't enjoy being out. The only person I like being out with is my wife. I like it slow and I like it easy-going. Baseball is as hectic as I care for it to be.

"I always played with small-market teams. I've never really been comfortable with big cities. I dread the city more than the team. I'm not a big-city type."

Even as the Perry brothers' pro baseball careers got into full swing in the 1990s, they always had the dairy as their calling. None viewed it as back-breaking work, even though the business was virtually a 24/7 proposition. After all, the Holsteins had to be milked daily.

Early on, Edward Perry had put his sons to work handling all the farm chores. Eventually, Herbert and Chan acquired their own dairy farms adjoining their father's property.

"My dad was tireless," Herbert said. "When we could stand up and make that clutch go down, we were old enough to drive a tractor—at age seven. The boys handled the raking of hay."

Handling the livestock was the most challenging, but to the Perrys that soon became second nature. Edward Perry owns 900 head of Holsteins and between 400 and 500 head of beef cattle. Herbert and Perry own 800 head on their property.

A necessary part of dairy life was assisting in the birthing of calves. Edward Perry, of course, became teacher for his sons.

"It's not that hard to teach," he said. "It's tough to get inside to make sure everything is all right. Herbert watched several before he did it himself. Herbert was always the type to say, 'Let me do it, Daddy.' Chan was a little more laid-back."

Claiming he was "born and raised doing it," Herbert Perry estimated he handled some three hundred births.

"Most of the time with an older cow, the calf is upside down or backward," he said. "The toughest thing is when all four feet are trying to come through the [birth] canal at the same time. Or when one foot is dropped down and it's behind the head, where you have to go in there and turn it. It's amazing how tight things are in there to be able to move calves around. It's taken me as much as two hours to pull one."

Isn't the "midwife" afraid he'll get kicked by the mother during the seemingly difficult procedure?

"No, once the mother gets to that position and to that point, she's not going to kick," Perry said.

Outsmarting livestock also is part of the job description. Perry also learned how to bend the Angus and Brahmas to his will, but it wasn't easy.

"If they beat you at a gate one day, they're going to try to beat you there every day," he said. "When you're trying to pen up beef cows, they're a little wilder than Holsteins. They can outrun you. Even if you have horses, dogs or trucks, it doesn't matter. A wild cow is a wild cow.

"We've turned the water trough off for a day to make them thirsty enough so that when you open the gates, they'll want to go in there [to drink]. If they beat you today, you've just got to let them go and come back tomorrow to try to get them. That's where you get the attitude [in baseball] of let today go, come back tomorrow and get them."

"Rural kids make decisions on the fly," Oklahoma rancher and former pitcher Lindy McDaniel said of ad-libbing one's way through the daily farm routine. "In the city there are a lot more rules to follow."

The physical benefits of hard, manual farm labor also help an athlete. "When you go back to repetitive work, it's a lot different than going for fifteen to twenty minutes on weights," said McDaniel. "I think rural kids get more exercise overall through that repetitive work."

Sure enough, even a Hall of Fame pitcher like Warren Spahn touted the benefits of outdoor labor. He said he kept himself in shape to pitch effectively into his forties by working his own Oklahoma ranch in the offseasons of the 1950s and early 1960s.

But for a lot of budding down-home athletes, farm life was not all work, no play. The Perry brothers were fortunate. If farming was Edward Perry's profession, then baseball was his spare-time passion. Sports coursed through the family history in every non-work and church hour.

"In the war days, my daddy played on the town team, playing every Sunday," Edward Perry said of Herbert Lee Perry. "At lunch, I'd get somebody to catch me. During the fifties, I could have told you the lineups of all sixteen teams."

Edward Perry pitched and later coached local teams. "My dad was a really, really good pitcher and a good hitter, too," Herbert Perry said. "My dad and mother are great athletes. My kid sister was the best athlete of us all, but she could not stand being in front of people. She had a phobia about being in front of people. In high school, she could always outrun me and outshoot me. She's more like my dad, who is a better athlete than me and my brother."

It may not have been inspiration for Kevin Costner's character in *Field of Dreams*, but Edward Perry, described by Herbert as "tireless," carved out his own piece of baseball heaven out of his property.

"I put my own little field behind my house—very crude," he said. "We had a batting cage made out of chicken wire. We played ball in the yard. We also started the Little League program; we didn't have one when I was a kid. I'd take an hour, an hour and a half a day, five days a week, to work with the kids. I loved baseball that much.

"We worked with the kids from the time they were first moving around. He'd go on the road and get pebbles. Herbert used a tobacco stick and hit pebbles for hours. That's where he got a lot of his swinging ability. You see kids as something you weren't. I knew Herbert was special from the time he was six."

"I hit and hit and hit," Herbert Perry said. "That's what I loved to do. A lot of it came from hitting rocks."

"What we didn't realize at the time was we were honing our skills to hit," Chan said.

Edward didn't mind it in the least if his sons mixed chores and baseball.

"When we were raking hay and if we got far enough ahead of the person who was bailing it, we would jump off the tractor and play [in the middle of the field]," Herbert recalled. "We always had a bat and ball in the tractor."

"When we'd go hunting, they always took a football or a ball and glove," said Edward.

The proud father set up baseball as a kind of reward system for his offspring.

Herbert Perry honed his hitting skills as a youth out in the fields of the family farm with a tobacco stick and pebbles. *Brad Newton/Texas Rangers Baseball Club*

"Kids raised on farms have much better discipline [than their urban counterparts]," Edward said. "I told the kids that you keep your grades up and cause your mama no problems, you can play sports. If you don't do that, sports will be taken away. Sports is icing on the cake. If you're exposed to the outdoors, to nature, to wildlife, you know how to appreciate life, the little things that make things tick.

"One thing I told my wife: We were very blessed that we never had to worry about our children."

The Perry boys fired up their imaginations with dreams of mimicking the faraway major leaguers. With the Jacksonville NBC affiliate's signal buried in electronic snow, they could hardly enjoy the Saturday game of the week. Like their father in timeless Mayo, they'd get baseball information wherever they could, and apply it to their fantasy games.

"When you're so far removed from the major leagues and big-city life and you just catch a few games on TV, if you leave it for exactly what it is, play it for a game, you'll enjoy it," said Chan. "You're making yourself better and better and better. One day, you go to the University of Florida, and you playing alongside athletes from big [city] high schools. You play the same game as them, but you realize you're playing better. You get to that level by nothing but repetition. My success and Herbert's success is playing the game as a game, not getting caught up in success. We were nobodies, and nothing was expected from us."

But the Perrys themselves thought they were somebodies. They'd play against each other, despite their age difference. Not only did Herbert develop a quick bat, no small thanks to slapping those pebbles around, but he also had a strong arm off the mound. When they caught a game on TV, they noticed a certain fireballer on the mound for the Houston Astros.

"When you're from the country and follow a game on radio or TV, you can visualize yourself doing it," Chan said. "Everybody wants to be up there with the bases loaded, bottom of the ninth and two out, either as a hitter or pitcher. And whenever Herbert was pitching, he was Nolan Ryan."

Soon the older brother was racking up high school strikeout totals that were worthy of the Ryan Express.

♦ ♦ ♦

Sports was often the only spare-time activity in and around Mayo. As in many other tiny communities, the participation rate among youths was much higher than in big cities.

"Sports is a huge part of the culture," Herbert Perry said. "If you're good in sports, it gives you a bit of a podium where you'll be recognizable."

And in football-crazy Florida, Mayo became an island of baseball strength.

"Back in the mid–twentieth century, there wasn't a [high school] classification system in Florida like there is now," Perry said. "The reason baseball is as big as it is was the little guys could rise up [and beat large schools].

Same in basketball. Every now and then you could get five guys together who could compete against five guys from a big school. In football during my dad's generation, you'd compete against what's now 4-A [classification] teams and we would be 1-A [the smallest schools]. We had good athletes, but we were outmanned.

"If you had two good pitchers or even one good pitcher, you could beat anybody on a good day. And every year we had a horse for a pitcher."

Perry became just such an animal. He started in the Little League program his father helped nurture at age seven. By nine, he was playing on a team with twelve-year-olds. "When I was fourteen, I was batting third or fourth on men's softball teams," he said. "I led the league in hitting every year. My dad knew and I knew I was pretty good."

So did kid brother Chan. "He was twice the athlete that I was, an absolute stud," the younger Perry said.

A shortstop-pitcher at Lafayette High School, Perry hit ".440-something as a freshman, .530-something as a sophomore, .610 as a junior and .615 as a senior," he said. "But my pitching was better than my hitting. I still hold the state record for strikeouts in a single season. I struck out 210 and walked eight in my senior season."

Perry's storytelling talents kick into high gear.

"At the [1987] district tournament on a Tuesday, I faced six batters and struck out all six," he said. "I came back Thursday, struck out nineteen and pitched a no-hitter—no, that was the perfect game—and came back Friday and struck out twenty. I loved to pitch. I used to throw 91, 92 [mph]. If I could pitch, that's what I'd rather do. You control the game. I love to challenge people."

For good measure, Perry threw two other no-hitters as a senior. He also played quarterback and punted for Lafayette's football team. Keeping busy and being proper away from sports, he was the school's student council president.

Perry's all-around athletic talents led him to the University of Florida. He started out playing football. He was a Gators teammate of Emmitt Smith. But, eventually, Perry opted to concentrate on baseball only, quitting the football team four games into his junior season. Perry earned All-SEC honors in baseball in 1989 and 1991. He didn't allow his academics to slip, gaining academic All-SEC status in 1988.

Aggressively rebuilding their farm system at the time, the Indians drafted Perry in the second round in 1991, joining an impressive collection of young hitters being groomed. But the selection by Cleveland, where opportunity seemed to be knocking, did not turn out positively for Perry, who was moved to first base.

Perry hit well the further up the minors he played. In the middle of a .327, 70-RBI season at Triple-A Charlotte in 1994, he was promoted for a cup of coffee in Cleveland, just before the Indians selected Chan out of Florida in the forty-fourth round of the amateur draft. Then, on June 12, 1995, Perry was brought up again to replace the disabled Dave Winfield and spent the rest of the year on the parent club's roster. Perry hit .315 in fifty-two games and slugged two homers off Yankees lefty Andy Pettitte in a July 17 game, but could not crack the starting lineup full-time. He did not make a good impression with manager Mike Hargrove by going 0-for-14 throughout the 1995 postseason, including the World Series against the Braves.

"I was behind Jim Thome at third base and Paul Sorrento and Eddie Murray at first base," he said. "Mike Hargrove was a diehard righty-lefty guy [for making up lineups]. But I always hit righties better than lefties. I told people that, and they look at you like you're stupid. I'd always get up to see lefties, and that's something you had to get comfortable against.

"If you come up in an organization like Pittsburgh or Montreal, they can't afford to go out and sign free agents. In '95 as a rookie, I hit .315. But the next year in spring training, I had no chance to play and went back to Triple-A because they got a free agent in [Julio] Franco. Look at any team that wants to consistently challenge for the pennant, and you don't see rookies on the team. If you don't have a chance to be rookie of the year, you don't have a chance to start. You have to burn all your options to force them to play you every day or trade you."

Herbert and Chan Perry faced another drawback in the Cleveland organization. Neither were slugging prospects. The Indians were stocked with musclemen, and believed they had enough talent on hand to trade away the likes of Brian Giles, Sean Casey, and Richie Sexson.

"The team that signed us, we went against their prototypical player," Chan said. "We weren't guys who hit forty home runs."

Chan, a first baseman–outfielder, had one minor league season in which he hit the twenty-homer mark, at Class AA Akron in 1997. But like his brother, he was a line-drive, gap-to-gap hitter who otherwise did not exceed ten homers in any season in the minors. Like Herbert, he was hemmed in by power hitters at his positions in the majors.

But the worst problem was a seemingly endless series of injuries suffered by Herbert. He was on the disabled list for Class A Watertown as soon as he was drafted in 1991. A torn right rotator cuff wiped out the last two months of the 1993 season at Class AA Canton-Akron. A broken left wrist wiped out the last month of play at Charlotte in 1994.

One good season of decent health punctuated the pain in 1995. Then it got worse. Perry tore cartilage in his left knee late in June 1996 in Triple-A, missing the rest of the season after undergoing surgery. Then he was hit with a double-whammy in 1997. Perry injured his right knee playing the outfield against the Yankees in spring training. He underwent surgery again in early April. But when he started to rehab the knee late in the '97 season, he suffered a setback. Perry underwent a second arthroscopic surgery on September 4, 1997.

"My knees messed me up," Perry said. "It was one of those things where I wanted to get a chance to play.

"Injuries took away my developmental years—twenty-five, twenty-six, twenty-seven. I missed those three years. If a team can't count on you to play every day, they won't take a chance on you."

Perry became expendable. The Indians made him available in the November 1997 expansion draft. Despite his knee problems, Tampa Bay selected him in the third round. But the surgeries caused him to miss the 1998 season. Thus he was happy to start out the following season in Triple-A.

"In '99, I went down to the minors," Perry said. "And I was happy to play because I had been out of baseball two years.

"Everyone talks about how much money major league players make and how spoiled we are, but for the most part, we love to play the game. When I got a chance to play at [Triple-A] Durham every day in '99, I was happy."

Called up to Tampa Bay on May 6, Perry played sixty-six games, thirty-seven at third base, the rest of the season, hitting .254. He lost more than a month of playing time, again, with a left oblique strain late in the season.

But by just being able to play on a big league field, Perry was exposed to other teams' scouts, ensuring he'd have a future in the majors.

◆ ◆ ◆

A first baseman by trade, Herbert Perry was far from a Gold Glover at third.

"I try to make all the plays," he said. "I'm not flashy by any stretch. I don't go over there and jump and dive all around the place. I try to make all the routine plays.

"The biggest part of playing third is trust; trust your hands so you don't overwork your feet, and then you have to trust your arm to know you can make the throw no matter what angle you're at."

Perry made his fielding ability acceptable to other teams by the time the

Devil Rays started a long period of unloading veterans early in the 2000 season. He was placed on waivers.

Up on the South Side of Chicago, then–White Sox GM Ron Schueler had a third-base problem starting the 2000 season. Incumbent Greg Norton had continual defensive problems and wasn't hitting. Scanning the waiver wire, he picked up Perry, initially to provide depth at third, first, and left field.

But Perry hit well when manager Jerry Manuel started him at third. By June he was the regular third baseman, pushing Norton back to the minors. The White Sox were the surprise team of the American League. A 17-8 April and a 20-7 June that included domination of AL Central rival Cleveland and the hated Yankees, vaulted Chicago into first place. Perry was in the middle of the surge as one of his team's best clutch hitters. He was 20-for-60 in June, and then sported career monthly bests of five homers and twenty RBIs in July along with a .323 average for the month. On White Sox telecasts, nickname-monger Hawk Harrelson gave Perry a moniker that no one would have ever thought of back in Mayo: "The Milkman."

"Anytime we've won, you know Herbert's been involved in it," Manuel said at the time. "He's just a winning-type ballplayer, somebody you really need if you want to do well." The manager was on-target in his analysis. The White Sox were 27-12 when Perry drove in a run.

Perry's own quiet confidence as a hitter grew.

"I like fastballs, and when you're up there in the late innings, [for] most setup men and closers, their best pitch is a fastball," he said then. "With starters, it's a change-up and sliders.

"I like to hit early in the count. When they come in, they're trying to get ahead of you. It's his strength versus my strength. It's a pretty good matchup."

Always, always pushing him to succeed was his upbringing in Mayo.

"Your work ethic is huge up here," Perry said. "There are days when you don't necessarily feel like lifting weights or hitting early. That's when you start to slip a little bit. That's where the working background has a lot to do with success in this game. When you're going back, you can't quit. If you give up, you're dead. Sometimes it's hard to work at something when it's treating you as badly as this game can treat you.

"I really believe that for anyone who plays this game for any amount of time, it's your business and you have to treat it like you're punching your clock. You hate to break that rhythm. When I walk on the field, I walk differently than anywhere else. Your step has a little more spring to it. You're focused."

Perry ended the 2000 season hitting .308, the first regular White Sox third baseman to hit at least .300 since George Kell's .312 in 1955. And while Mariners pitching stifled almost all of his teammates in a three-game Division Series sweep, Perry was 4-for-9 with a double and an RBI.

The Perry family enjoyed even more good news in 2000. Chan finally made his big-league debut for the Indians August 5 against the Anaheim Angels. Except for a short demotion to Triple-A Buffalo, the younger Perry spent the rest of the season in Cleveland.

Both brothers knew, however, that good times in baseball usually cannot be bottled. Chan was on the move after the 2000 season, signing as a six-year minor league free agent with the Braves organization. Meanwhile, Herbert expected to repeat his success in his second straight starting season as a third baseman in Chicago. He signed a one-year deal to return to the White Sox.

Yet like many of his teammates, 2001 would be a downer compared to the American League Central title campaign of the previous season. Frank Thomas's torn tricep muscle, suffered while trying to field an early-season grounder, set the tone for a crippling series of injuries. David Wells, imported amid much controversy, broke down by midseason and never pitched again for the White Sox. Large portions of the pitching staff also were lost due to surgeries. New shortstop Royce Clayton barely hit half his weight in the early going, and didn't recover until it was too late. The lineup sputtered at times without Thomas.

After enjoying a season free of injuries in 2000, the old aches and pains returned for Perry. He began the season on the disabled list. Clayton's arrival at shortstop pushed Jose Valentin over to third while Perry was out. He would not be an everyday third baseman again in Chicago.

"I've always been a 'yes sir' or 'no sir' sort of person," Perry said at midseason. "I just try to do my job. I'm not very demanding. If a manager believes we're a better team without me in the lineup, I'm not going to go in and say put me in the lineup or I'll say something in the papers. When you see the struggles a coach or manager goes through to keep everyone happy, it's not an insult to put someone else out there."

But the injuries and sporadic play began to wear on Perry's famed even-keel, team-guy persona. He saw action in just 92 games, hitting .256 with seven homers and 32 RBIs. On the last day of the season, Perry came the closest—for him—to lashing out.

"If you lose your job, that's one thing," he said, "but if it's just taken from you . . . you can't play third base every third or fourth day in this league. This year I've always been the odd man out. There were some days where I didn't even feel like coming to the ballpark. That's a bad attitude, but I felt like I couldn't do my job. Then, again, I didn't have a job."

Jerry Manuel, who was full of praise for Perry just one year earlier, seemed to question his mental toughness as the 2001 season ended.

"There were a lot of times we wanted to play him and he was hurt," Manuel said. "There were times he played and asked out of the game."

On November 28, 2001, Perry was traded to the Texas Rangers for a player to be named later. Valentin and top prospect Joe Crede gave the White Sox plenty of protection at third base. Perry said he would not have come back to the White Sox in 2001 if he knew the season would have gone so disastrously.

"Playing baseball is just the field and the team," he said. "Texas is a good move for me. I really would like to turn it around to make this look like a mistake, and give me some motivation.

"The only time ownership talks about a player being loyal to the team is when they're really interested in signing them. There's less team loyalty to players than player loyalty to teams. The only time you hear them play the team-loyalty card is when they tried to re-sign Alex Rodriguez in Seattle, Ivan Rodriguez in Texas, and Cal Ripken, Jr., in Baltimore. They try to get them for less.

"If you're loyal to me, I'd be loyal to you to a fault. I didn't deserve anything to not play every day. Now, I'm playing the game for me. I'll play hard for whoever is paying for me. I really thought I could settle down and play in Chicago."

He may not be able to settle down in Texas, either. The Rangers made a considerable investment in 2001 first-round pick Mark Teixeira, the best college hitter in the amateur draft. Third baseman Teixeira's big league ETA was supposed to be sooner, rather than later. That means Perry could once again be on the move, trodding a well-worn journeyman's circuit around baseball.

But he would always find his way back to Mayo at season's end.

◆ ◆ ◆

Herbert Perry was raised a dairyman. But that didn't mean he'd stay one for life. Big league baseball has changed him, giving Perry financial security that eight hundred head of cattle could never provide. Edward Perry is taking over his son's dairy interests, although Herbert would always live on the old homestead. Family, after all, doesn't change in Mayo even if one member becomes semi-famous and affluent.

"I'm getting into the mini-storage business," Perry said one night early in 2002. "In the offseason, I work out and hunt.

"It's hard for people to dairy. Marriages end up different. My mom put up with a lot. I love cows, and will always work some with cows. There's good money in the dairy business, but you have to be there all the time. I'm not hard enough on [hired-hand] labor to get the work out of them if you let someone else try to do it. I get frustrated dealing with people, that I'd try to do it all myself. It's a seven [A.M.] to seven [P.M.] job."

Freed from herding cattle and supervising the daily milkings, Perry now will have to become a coach, following in Edward Perry's footsteps. It seems the baseball genes have been passed down to a fourth generation of Perrys.

Herbert and Sheila Perry have three children: Gabrielle, Ethan, and Andrew. The boys appear to be precocious in baseball, like their father.

"Ethan is a great athlete," Perry said of his ten-year-old. But he was particularly fascinated by Drew, who was not the prototypical "terrible two's" toddler in the summer of 2001.

"Here he was, two and one-half and twenty-six pounds, and he could hit a pitch thrown from thirty feet," Perry said, amazed. "Not many kids that age can pick up a ball and follow it from that distance. He's got a perfect swing.

"He was making up games and takes a bat wherever he goes. When he was one and one-half, every baseball player on TV was 'Daddy.'"

Pretty soon Ethan and Drew Perry will go out on the family property to envision themselves as big leaguers, this time not so far removed from the majors as previous generations of their family. There will be players to imitate and rocks to be hit to perfect a swing. And maybe the brothers will be able to do something significant in the game, like their father and uncle.

The baseball cycle begins anew in Mayo, just like the seasons of the year for the dairymen in a piece of Americana under glass.

14

THE NONCONFORMIST

Baseball is best enjoyed from a child's viewpoint. And, somehow, Turk Wendell never had to grow up, totally, as he ran to and from the mound as a successful reliever for the Chicago Cubs and New York Mets.

While many of his contemporaries squeezed the joy out of the game as it evolved into a cutthroat entertainment business, Wendell exulted in the very nature of competing. He almost communed with the game's spiritual aspects in much the same manner he did with Mother Nature in his other passion as an outdoorsman.

"The time I have the most fun is when I step on the mound to play," Wendell said. "When I get a chance to pitch, that's me, the fun, that's what it's all about. All the other bullcrap, the trades, the money issues, releasing guys, calling up guys, sending guys down, I can do without. All the other crap ruins the game of baseball. It gets frustrating, because I'm out there trying to have fun."

How Wendell displayed this eternal-kid's joy earned him notoriety as a character not cut out of a classic baseball scratchin', spittin', and swearin' mold. In the good ol' days he would have been called a flake for his on-the-field histrionics.

As a young pitcher he'd chew licorice and brush his teeth in the dugout, wave at his center fielder from the mound, and leap over the foul line on his journeys to his workplace. Later, after putting these eccentricities to rest, he'd proudly wear a necklace on the mound, festooned with animal teeth of various sizes, all seemingly shark-sharp. Teammates could enjoy his home-made wild-game casseroles in the clubhouse. His habits weren't superstitions because he wore uniform No. 13 for a long time; the supposed unlucky number simply had been available as a minor leaguer. He was fearless on and off the mound. On February 9, 2001, he flew with the Air Force Thunderbirds for seventy-five minutes in an F-16 fighter, pulling at its peak 9.4 Gs, the highest G-load anyone except a pilot has experienced.

But through all his quirks and unusual experiences, Wendell wasn't on the roster as a house jester; he was one of the game's best set-up men, possessing a fastball that jumped around the strike zone like some backwoods beast fleeing from the pitcher's bow and arrow. That earned him courtship from many interested teams in the 2000–01 off-season and a vow by Wendell, ever the unusual fella, that he'd play the last year of his contract for free. He eventually re-signed with the Mets for three years with the proviso that he could not play for free; it was against the rules.

"If they gave me a fair three-year deal, I'd give them a fourth year for free," Wendell said. "I don't really play for the money.

"I'm very fortunate to be able to step on the field every day. How many people can say they live their dream every day? Less than 1 percent of Americans can say they live their dream every day.

"It irritates me when I see guys take it for granted. I think they lose perspective over where they are, who they are. Money and fame can eat up a lot of people. I've seen guys make $3 million or $4 million a year, and live paycheck to paycheck. They live beyond their means. What do they think, that it's a never-ending supply of money? It's sad, but it happens. I try to talk to them, but you can only help those who want to be helped."

The half-decade transformation from character to cagey late-inning man made Wendell attractive to contenders at the trade deadline when the Mets tumbled out of the National League East race after the 2001 All-Star break. Ninety miles down the interstate, the Philadelphia Phillies got surprising mileage out of a kiddie-corps roster that had hardly experienced the barren seasons of the late 1990s at Veterans Stadium. The Phils had bullpen holes, and surprisingly got Mets GM Steve Phillips, a rival in their own division, to dispatch Wendell and lefty-specialist Dennis Cook to fuel their battle with the Atlanta Braves.

Wendell had the right attitude to help a youthful contender like the 2001 Phillies. He tried to build up some off-the-field camaraderie with the kids. And fresh from his World Series experience against the New York Yankees, he'd figure to give his new teammates plenty of confidence in the late innings, along with the looseness a certified baseball character brings to a clubhouse.

"Some days you're going to lose," Wendell said. "And when you turn around and cameras and microphones are in your face, you say, 'I sucked. I lost.' But tomorrow I'm going to bust my ass to be the best I can be again.

I respect that [attitude], rather than the guy who passes the buck and says so-and-so called the wrong pitch, or someone else made an error. Hey, you're human, you can make mistakes. You're gonna make mistakes.

"As soon as the game is over, it's over. Tomorrow is a new day."

But tomorrow never seemed to come for Wendell in the final two months of 2001. For the first time in his decade-long big league career, he endured a living hell. His competitor's personality compelled him to continue to take the ball while he mentally clamped down on a sore elbow. Thus his normally sharp-breaking stuff betrayed him. Wendell would give up one walk-off homer after another to tear the heart out of the Phillies' nascent pennant drive. Such performances, of course, attracted the attention of baseball's most unforgiving fans, a continually frustrated group of Veterans Stadium boo-birds that used to jeer even the heroic Mike Schmidt, who would have been treated like a god if he had played his home games in Wrigley Field or Busch Stadium.

The cycle would spiral ever downward. Wendell would fail, the fans would boo, and the pitcher's uncharacteristic dark mood would worsen. Hate mail seemingly exempt from the ecumenical national mood engendered by September 11 inundated Wendell's locker. The "crap" that Wendell could do without was enveloping his total being, and getting worse by the day. The joy of baseball was being wrung steadily out of Wendell's boyish persona that was being transformed into an embittered veteran. He couldn't hold his tongue any more, and couldn't keep it clean as he walked toward the shower after the Phillies' final game of 2001.

"Is the fuckin' season really over? Now I can tell these people I want to get the fuck out of here," Wendell said loudly and to no one in particular.

At thirty-four, he was merely getting a post-graduate course in baseball. If Wendell had to work hard to show he was a capable pitcher and not a clown years ago, he'd now have to prove something else all over again: that he was worthy of a franchise's trust and confidence come crunch time in the seventh, eighth or ninth inning.

Months later, as Wendell went for a drive with daughter Dakota through the hills near his Castle Rock, Colorado, home, his bitterness had cooled to a degree, but he was still agitated about the Philly fans. It apparently was the reliever's fate to never be 100 percent comfortable. His challenge seemed to be in recapturing the innocent-kid side of his personality to bring the joy that he always treasured back to his life.

♦ ♦ ♦

The set-up men who bring the game to the ninth-inning closer are increasingly worth their weight in gold. They're not rewarded statistically as of yet;

there is no Jerome Holtzman to champion the cause of "holds" as an official number in the manner that the dean of baseball writers had accomplished with saves starting in 1959.

But Wendell had hit the jackpot before the 2001 season with a three-year, $9.4 million contract from a Mets management buoyed over having played in the first crosstown World Series against the Yankees since the 1956 Brooklyn Dodgers. Over the last three seasons, he had harnessed what many experts had called the best moving fastball in the game. Wendell was 5-1 with a 2.93 ERA in 1998, then set a Mets record for appearances with eighty to go along with a 5-4 mark and a 3.05 ERA in 1999. Until he gave up a run in the 2000 Fall Classic, Wendell had been touched for runs by only the Braves in the 1999 National League Championship Series, out of the four post-season series in which he had appeared prior to facing the Yankees.

"I had a certain fondness for him," Mets GM Steve Phillips said early in the 2001 season. "He was in the first trade I ever made [August 8, 1997 with the Cubs]. He gives you an extraordinary effort every time every time he gets the ball. I wish I had twenty-five guys like him."

Despite his background growing up in rural western Massachusetts and his love for the outdoors, Wendell and wife Barbara had grown to love New York.

"Without a doubt," he said. "It's like the Sinatra song: if you can make it there, you can make it anywhere. And we made it there. The fans and media make you a better player. They don't expect anything less than perfect. You really mature a lot as a player and person dealing with that stuff on and off the field. If you let it get to you, you won't succeed there. But if you stay focused on your goal, every day, then you can thrive on it.

"I had always said to myself I'd never, ever want to play for the Yankees or Mets. I didn't like New York City. But it's probably the best thing that ever happened to my career. I tried to keep an open mind about it. I had a great time there."

No wonder the Wendells were skeptical about going to Veterans Stadium when Phillips decided to pull the plug on the 2001 season with a July 26 trade that netted the Mets two pitching prospects. Wendell tried to offer up some logic to his wife.

"I said, 'Hey, you were worried about it when I was traded to the Mets,'" he said. "It's an honor to be traded to a contending team, a team that wants you, that will give up young players for you."

Phillies GM Ed Wade and manager Larry Bowa believed Wendell and Dennis Cook would help on and off the field.

"These guys have done it in pennant races and in the World Series,"

Bowa said. "They're not going to be scared to take the ball. And they're not only going to help on the mound, they're going to help in the clubhouse, too."

And by early August, Wendell looked like he was fitting in, even though he already had blown a couple of crucial games. He tried to be a unifying force among the huge cadre of kids on the Phillies roster.

"Maybe I'd try to help on little things, and just getting the team a little more unified," he said in the quiet of a pregame clubhouse in Milwaukee's Miller Park two weeks after the trade. "I took a bunch of the rookies out to dinner. One of the guys here for three years said, 'This is pretty cool. It didn't happen before.' We'd have three or four team dinners in New York, pitchers' dinners. Usually you'll have cliques of Latins and blacks. I wouldn't expect someone who is totally opposite of me to hang out with me.

"I just try to bring more of a positive frame of mind to young guys. We lost a game in Colorado, and I was a pretty good contributor to the loss. Everybody had their faces hanging down. They were moping around the clubhouse. But the Braves also lost. I spoke up: 'Who cares if we lost a game; the Braves lost, too, and we didn't lose any ground.'"

The positive attitude extended—at the time—to the inevitable boos from Phillies fans.

"I really don't care. They can boo all they want," Wendell said. "They have a right to boo, especially as badly as I pitched. I have pretty much sucked since I was traded here. I'm not a person who would go out to a game and boo somebody. When I sit down and watch a game, I enjoy the game for what it is. I never understand why they'd yell obscenities and boo. But it couldn't be any worse than New York."

Could Wendell handle continued booing?

"Absolutely."

◆ ◆ ◆

Mark Fidrych is obviously the most direct spiritual ancestor to Turk Wendell's offbeat personality. "The Bird" was baseball's sensation of 1976, augmenting his sensational rookie Detroit Tigers season with one of the quirkiest characters around. Fidrych was a spectacle on the field, talking to the baseball, landscaping the mound before pitches and gesturing to his teammates, among other eccentricities.

A whole host of nonconformists, characters and outright flakes carried a long line of wacky tradition all the way through Wendell's debut in pro baseball in 1988.

"When you think of a sport, everyone doesn't walk the walk," Hall of Famer Fergie Jenkins said. "It makes a ballclub interesting."

Amazingly, the oddball personalities seemed to be concentrated among pitchers, Fidrych being perhaps the funniest.

There was Al "Mad Hungarian" Hrabosky and his menacing psych-out act on the mound that infuriated opposing hitters and fans, but delighted Hrabosky's teammates when he was in his Cardinals prime in the mid-1970s. Bill "Spaceman" Lee went against the baseball grain at about the same time, a real thorn in the side of Boston manager Don Zimmer.

Bill Faul, a Tigers and Cubs pitcher of the 1960s, used to try to motivate himself by playing a record in the trainer's room prior to games, in which a monotonic voice would keep repeating, "Low-w-w and aw-a-a-y, low-w-w and a-w-a-a-y." Teammates and media interpreted Faul's actions as self-hypnosis, and indeed as late as 1988 Faul was teaching hypnosis in the Cincinnati area. "There's a little sun in all of us," he said of his perception of an energy vortex in all humans.

"I thought the guy was nuts," Jenkins said of crossing paths with Faul in 1966. Catcher Randy Hundley thought worse, that Faul was a character out of a Dracula or Wolfman movie.

Bo Belinsky was a free spirit who seemed to believe in free love in the early 1960s. More precisely, he took a minuteman's stance toward his off-the-field pursuits. "Bo was a little different," said Jenkins, Belinsky's teammate on the Phillies. "He never wore underwear."

Cubs pitchers Bill Bonham and Bob Locker practiced yoga exercises out on the field in the mid-1970s with outfielder Pete LaCock, son of *Hollywood Squares* host Peter Marshall, until a reactionary management ordered the trio to do their thing out of sight of the fans.

The likes of Joe Pepitone, the first player to bring a hair dryer into the clubhouse, and funnyman Jay Johnstone were true characters as everyday players. But the biggest and brashest nonconformist—and he hates the word "flake"—was a center fielder/author: Jimmy Piersall. Still railing against what he perceived as Anthony Perkins's less-than-straight portrayal of him in the movie version of *Fear Strikes Out*, Piersall said he was an entertainer. He still is at age 73, via continued outlandish analysis on Chicago's all-sports WSCR Radio.

"What you did on the field doesn't make you a flake just because you don't live life according to the rules," said Piersall, whose coup de grace was running the bases backwards in celebration of his 100th career homer as a Met in 1963. Sitting on the monuments in Yankee Stadium and kicking fans who had run onto his territory in center field were among the other highlights of a wild career. Piersall said he was crazy, and had the papers to prove it after being hospitalized in a mental institution in 1952.

But Piersall claims that such individuality is being squeezed out of baseball by umpires' tight control of on-field behavior.

"There are no colorful guys now," he said. The umpires won't let them [be colorful]. The game can be very dull. Umpires are arrogant now, and they think the fans come to see them," he said. "They won't let you do entertaining things. When I played, they let you go [argue] for two minutes, and then you had to stop. They knew the individual players and how high-strung they were."

But there's still room in baseball for those who are different, who are visually and verbally demonstrative.

"It just depends on the degree," said pitcher Steve Trachsel, a teammate of Wendell's in Triple-A, the Cubs, and the Mets. "I like guys who show emotion. I think that's good. A guy who drops the F-bomb on the mound and the camera's on him, everyone gets upset. Hey, man, you've got to play this game with emotion. That shows you care. I'd rather see that than see a guy give up a game-winning homer and stand there, OK, oh well, let's walk off the field. If you're not upset, I think that's worse."

So Wendell was just what Dr. Trachsel ordered growing up. Examining Wendell's life, he may have been a nonconformist at birth. A precocious baseball mind, he told his mother at age three he'd be a player. Wendell would become a die-hard Red Sox fan in rural western Massachusetts, near the New York border. Loving both baseball and the outdoors, he refined his pitching and hunting skills at the same time. Wendell began earning notices in Wahconah Regional High School, then attracted scouts in earnest during three years at Quinnipiac College in Hamden, Connecticut.

"I felt more driven to pursue a dream," he said. "I just think I loved the game of baseball so much. I wasn't afraid to show people just who I was or that I wasn't afraid to fail."

Wendell had begun playing alongside older men on a semi-pro team at sixteen. "All the guys on the team were anywhere from eighteen or nineteen to thirty-five," he said. "I got a lot of heckling. I was very naïve. They had a lot of fun with me. I knew I was different than anyone else because I was playing at that level already."

Wendell's stuff was different than most everyone's.

"I realized my ball moved a lot," he said. "One time, my fastball started out on the outside part of the plate, then moved all the way across the plate. Before the [1988] draft, I talked to pretty much every major league team. I talked a lot to the Expos and thought I would be drafted by them."

Instead, the Braves took him in the fifth round. Their reviving farm system had a live wire on its hands. The carefree Wendell would start to act out his emotions on the field.

"What I would end up doing had nothing to do with superstition," he said. "You get into a routine, you're successful at it, you keep doing it. Baseball's such a daily grind, that the guys who succeed the most are the guys with a strict routine. It's just something early on that once you had a routine that works, you stick with it."

Assigned to Pulaski (Tennessee) in Class A rookie ball, Wendell began raising both eyebrows and smiles when he gave an inadvertent boost to oral hygiene nationwide by wielding a toothbrush in the dugout between innings.

"One day, I had a bad taste in my mouth, so I started brushing my teeth," he said. "I'm a big believer that if you don't feel comfortable, you're not going to play that well. The more comfortable you feel, whether it's a smell, a bad taste in your mouth, if you didn't take a shower, it's going to affect the way you perform—especially as a pitcher, when you don't get a chance to play as much as a regular player."

Wendell needed the regular teeth brushings, but not because of halitosis. An accompanying quirk was his chewing of licorice in the dugout, leaving his teeth bathed in a glaze of sticky, sugary residue.

"I just felt that I wanted to be a good role model for kids [instead of chewing tobacco]," he said.

Combined with other gyrations, gestures and jumping over the foul line, Wendell seemed a left-hander trapped in a right-hander's body. But the antics did not retard his upward progress in the Braves' farm system. He had a mixed-bag in the won-lost department, but impressed all with his stuff, even if his flakiness seemed to obscure his talent.

"I kind of got a kick out of it," Braves pitching coach Leo Mazzone said of watching Wendell in one of his early minor league spring trainings. "He meant well about everything. He was pitching well, too, and made himself into a prospect."

By 1991, Wendell seemed to be moving toward a shot at the Braves' rotation with an 11-3 record and 2.56 ERA at Class AA Greenville (South Carolina). Instead, he'd have to look for his opportunity elsewhere when the Braves traded him and lefty Yorkis Perez to the Cubs for pitcher Mike Bielecki and catcher Damon Berryhill on September 29, 1991.

A right-elbow stress fracture washed out most of Wendell's 1992 season. When he resumed pitching at Triple-A Iowa in 1993, Wendell raised the eyebrows of teammates in his new organization.

"At first, I wondered what does this guy think he's doing?" said '93

Iowa teammate Steve Trachsel. "I thought these things would incite the other teams to try to beat him. Is he trying to create attention for himself?

"But once he got on the mound, and got the job done, you're just saying as long as he can pitch, he can get away with it. It's the guys who do all that stuff and give up fifteen runs that you sit there and wonder."

Entertainer-turned-Cubs-minor-league-outfield-coach Jimmy Piersall did not take Wendell aside when he witnessed all his cavorting about at Iowa. Instead, he saw a kindred soul. "I thought it was great, like Fidrych," Piersall said.

Wendell got a mixed reaction from major-league opponents during cameo appearances with the Cubs in 1993 and 1994.

"Jumping across the line and doing some of his antics in back of the mound was cause for motivation at times for the hitters," recalled Todd Zeile, like Trachsel a Cubs and Mets teammate of Wendell's. As a Cardinal in 1993, Zeile remembered a sense of gratification that the animated Wendell failed on the mound.

In his earlier Mets years, Brooklyn-boy John Franco grinned at the sight of Wendell's act. "I don't think it fired us up or annoyed us," he said. "We all kind of found it amusing, something different. I don't think he was showing anybody up. I kind of enjoyed it. You need to have a guy like this. He should have been a left-hander. He does everything a left-hander should do."

But when new manager Jim Riggleman arrived on the Cubs scene for the strike-shortened 1995 season, Wendell's on-field persona would change—through a virtual mandate by the seemingly mild-mannered Riggleman.

"When Riggleman came over, he said that when he was on the Padres, they wanted to kick his ass," Trachsel said. "It was like that with other teams."

Riggleman told Wendell that he ought to be known for his budding talent on the mound, not the side stuff.

"The first conversation he had with me was that he wanted me to stop," Wendell said. "He said he wanted people to realize that I could pitch and have a good arm. He didn't want people to write about all the crazy stuff, that he wanted people to write about my arm."

The message got through.

"I just stopped," Wendell said of junking the flaky stuff with the exception of avoiding contact with the foul line, a common baseball superstition. "I think it's made me a better person. I've matured as a player.

"I want to be known as a pitcher, not a weirdo. It was never, 'Hey, there's that pitcher for the Cubs.' It was, 'Hey, there's the weirdo who brushes his teeth.'

"It was more the end of one thing, and the start of another."

Turk Wendell calmed down some of his antics at the request of his manager but still superstitiously refused to step on the baseline. *Steve Green/Chicago Cubs*

Coincidentally, Wendell's big league fortunes soared. After six scattered starts for the Cubs in 1993–94, Riggleman installed him in middle relief full-time in '95.

"I'd form a new routine as a reliever instead of a starter," Wendell said.

Statistically, he was inconsistent, but impressed the Cubs enough to keep coming back for more. When Doug Jones flopped as the team's closer midway through the 1996 season, Riggleman gave Wendell the chance to close. He had a career-high 18 saves with a 2.84 ERA.

"Riggs is the only manager I ever had who ever gave me a chance to prove myself, to prove to himself that I can pitch at this level," Wendell said. "Nobody else gave me a chance. That's the only thing that I regret about baseball, that nobody gave me a chance to prove myself as a starter. I'd get one start here, one start there."

Trachsel, whose 13-9 All-Star season in 1996 benefited from Wendell's set-up and stopper work, saw a cause-and-effect to the pitcher's increasing effectiveness.

"He was a good relief pitcher anyway," Trachsel said. "When he started to tone it down, he got more respect from other teams."

But stability on the job did not mean Wendell trashed his individuality. Without the toothbrush and licorice, he still was the most distinctive pitcher on the staff. His feats in the outdoors made great clubhouse talk and daily newspaper notes fodder. Wendell brought the outdoors to the ballpark, in more than just spirit.

His childhood in the sticks had made Wendell love the outdoors. He first ventured into the pristine woods near his Massachusetts home at eight. "It's so rural there, you could snowmobile clear through to Canada if you wanted to," he said back in 1996.

An avid bow-hunter, Wendell did not venture into the woods just for sport. He'd usually cook what he hunted.

"I don't even eat what I catch when I go fishing," he said. "I throw it back. But you can't hunt something, kill it, and throw it back. You don't shoot it and leave it there. I don't like that. Shoot it and give it to [poor, hungry] people who want to eat it if you don't eat it.

"Bow hunting brings a great sense of accomplishment. It's not about the kill, it's the whole hunt. I just like being out there, watching animals, and being a part of nature. I enjoy the tranquility of it all, the peace and quiet. You can see so many unique things no one else can.

"I [target] practice all summer long. You need a good aim. You can't wound the animal. I have to be sure that if I shoot at it, I kill it. I wouldn't be able to live with myself otherwise. It wouldn't be fair to that animal.

"People get the misconception that I [just] kill. That's not what hunting is all about. If it was killing, they wouldn't call it hunting, they'd call it killing. I have more love for animals than people can ever imagine. I go out and watch them all the time. I take pictures. I have a black-and-white darkroom. They intrigue me. There's a time and place for both watching them and hunting them."

Fans can witness an emblem of Wendell's journeys every time he takes the mound. As he became more prominent in relief, he took to wearing a necklace adorned with teeth.

From a distance, the necklace appeared to be some kind of shark's-tooth concoction.

"It's not a shark," Wendell said. "It's all trophies from hunting. Mountain lion, elk, wild pig, buffalo, deer, and turkey."

Why does Wendell wear it?

"Because it's mine," he said. "When I get a chance to put my uniform on every day, it's a symbol of all the hard work it's taken to get me to the big leagues. I never take it for granted. I never throw my uniform on the floor. The necklace is a symbol of the all the hard work I've put in off the field, another passion and love I have in life. This represents all the spirits of the animals and just my gratitude toward them for being able to harvest them.

"I'll add to it. The one thing I need to put on it was a bear. That would be it. There are black bears not far from my house in Colorado.

"The spirits of the animals are like me. I'm more like a free spirit. The animals are more like a free spirit. They live for the moment. They do whatever it takes to survive. That's kind of how I am."

Just like his on-field antics, Wendell earned more publicity early on for his hunting activities than his pitching, this time when he chased a deer through a car wash in a small Massachusetts town.

"It was 3:30 A.M., and I was out bow-hunting," he recalled. "This deer jumped out and smoked my truck. I pulled over. Another guy, a bakery guy, pulled over. The deer was flopping in the road. The guy said to put the deer out of its misery. I grabbed my bow, but the deer got up and ran off, staggered and fell. I tracked it to the car wash. I ended up putting the thing down for good."

Also an amateur cook, Wendell would share the products of his backwoods conquests with his teammates. Using a hamburger grinder and adding rice and corn, Wendell would prepare enough venison casserole to stock lunches for each Cubs homestand. Trachsel, pitcher Terry Adams, and then–pitching coach Fergie Jenkins, also an outdoorsman, would be first in line.

"I ate it all the time," Trachsel said. "The big day was when he came in with buffalo beef jerky. He brought in a box and it was gone in five minutes."

Wendell also impressed the real city-slickers in the Mets clubhouse.

"I've had some goose jerky, some deer jerky," John Franco said. "I'd taste some of it, but not all of it. He's got a good career after baseball, making jerky."

Moving to the Big Apple, three times the size of Chicago, in 1997 did not slow down Wendell's forays into the woods. He quickly scoped out some great hunting grounds surprisingly near the megalopolis.

Wendell said he could go twenty minutes up the road into Connecticut to break out his bow. Having a "blast" hunting out East, he knew that deer season opened September 15, turkey season started May 1 in New York. Even during the season, he spent almost all his spare—and waking time— hunting. He'd get up at 3 A.M. after a short nap to go to the woods, and would keep going until midnight at Shea Stadium. "I don't sleep much anyway," he said.

Wendell took Terry Adams bow-hunting while with the Cubs. In New York, his backwoods companions included Rick Reed, Rick White, and, surprisingly, Franco. Turkey legs and claws would be the souvenirs hanging in the locker at the ballpark. Franco even pressed Wendell into pest-control duty.

"I had a raccoon at my house in Staten Island, and I had Turk take care of it," he said.

The outdoors and its four-legged inhabitants never got the best of Wendell until, seemingly, one late January night in 2000 in the woods near his home in Colorado.

"I was hunting around Rampart Range with another guy," Wendell said. "I happened to shoot a mountain lion, fifteen miles back in the mountains and twenty miles from my house. It was too late to walk out of there after that. I wasn't lost. I spent the night [with his companion and the lion carcass]. I didn't know it was seventeen below zero."

When Wendell didn't come home and didn't call, his wife, Barbara, called the police. A search party was organized. But the pitcher said that wasn't necessary.

"I built a fire, cut down pine branches, and lay down on it," he said. "My wool outfit protected me. I was not at all frightened. Actually, I had a great time. I couldn't get a cell signal to tell my wife not to worry. Twenty-five people went out to search for me. After daybreak, I walked out of the woods, and they were standing around. I wouldn't have done anything differently."

Wendell continues to have no fear, of the conditions or of what four-legged creature he'll encounter.

"If you'd take every step in your life like it's your last one [like animals], we'd be a lot smarter in the things we do," he said. "They fear just about everything. A lot of times people are afraid to go in the woods because of a bear or mountain lion—they're afraid they're going to eat you. But all the times I've been in the woods, I've seen a bear just once."

Wendell offers just one bit of advice for fellow nature-lovers venturing into the woods: "Always bring with you a lighter."

261

But he had to remember that on the job, his task was to put out fires. No flammable pitches were welcome.

◆ ◆ ◆

The Turk Wendell who cavorted about the field while blazing trails around woods and waters was no superficial, flighty, Shallow Hal–type. He'd given thought to greater things than baseball.

A conversation about hunting in the clubhouse, for instance, drifted into the subject of gun control after another one of the school shootings that plagued America in the late 1990s. What came forth from Wendell's lower-decibel words was that this outdoorsman would be no poster boy for the National Rifle Association. Wendell reasoned that handguns had no use in hunting, thus their private ownership should be restricted.

He'd never endear himself to the lords of baseball, either. Wendell hates the politics that enmeshes the game.

He cited his own slow advancement to the Cubs in 1994 as an example.

"It was frustrating," he said. "There was a situation where I was pitching better than [right-hander] Kevin Foster at Triple-A. He got called up to the big leagues and I didn't. The manager came up to me and said, 'I know you're wondering what the hell is going on. Well, Kevin Foster was traded for Shawn Boskie. Boskie's pitching well and they have to justify the trade.' What can I do?

"There are lots of players in Triple-A and Double-A who could play in the major leagues and be very, very successful. But because of certain circumstances they don't get the chance. Look at Rick Reed. He was classified as a '4-A' player for years. He never had a chance to pitch on a consistent basis. [Bobby] Valentine puts him in the rotation, and they wondered why this guy was in Triple-A for so long. There are lots of stories like that. They get frustrated, get tired of it and quit. Or get hurt.

"It takes a unique combination [to reach the majors]. If you don't have Kerry Wood–like stuff, you have to have someone believe in you."

Then a player needs a sponsor, like in business or politics?

"That's a good way to put it," Wendell replied.

Fortunate to have the better part of a decade of big league service, Wendell seemingly is set for life financially. But he cautions that neither he nor any other big leaguer can take anything for granted.

"Every dollar of our paycheck goes into our bank account—it's invested," Wendell said. "All the money that I make off the field, signing appearances and such, is the money we live on. That's it.

"My kids will know what it takes to earn something. I'll provide them with everything they *need*. But the things they *want*, they will earn. That's the only way to teach them. I'm very protective of them, but they have to live their life and take their lumps. That's how they learn. That's kind of how animals learn. I'll do the best I can do, and hopefully that will teach them to make good and smart decisions in their life."

He would teach his children to treat others the way they wanted to be treated.

"I treat people with the utmost respect, and I want to be treated the same way in return," he said. "I want to let fans, especially kids, know that I'm a person just like they are. I won't come to the ballpark in a business suit with airs on. Instead, I come in jeans and a T-shirt. They'll look at me as more of a normal guy like their brother or dad or someone else."

Wendell does not like the image of money-grubbing players.

"People think you're an overpriced athlete," he said. "But they don't understand the average guy spends up to seven years in the minor leagues, making peanuts. He's already given up fifteen to twenty years of his life to the game of baseball. And if something happens to him in those minor-league stints, what does he have to show for it? Absolutely nothing.

"Then in the majors, he has to prove himself for at least another three to six years to prove his the best of the best to make a substantial amount of money. Then half of it is taken out in taxes. If you're making $1 million, $500,000 is taken off the top. Then you give your agent 4 percent of the $1 million. People don't realize so many have hands out taking bits and pieces of your paycheck. If you want to be a millionaire at the end of the year, you have to make $2.3 million to have $1 million in the bank at the end of the summer. What person in America has a concept of that? Nobody. They think if you make $1 million, you're a millionaire. If you make $500,000, you're thought of as being as rich as can be.

"The living expenses are enormous. I spend $3,500 a month on an apartment during the season. That's absurd, on top of a mortgage [for his offseason home]."

If Wendell had his way, the lust for money would somehow be purged from baseball. That's why he offered to play the final year of a four-year contract for free.

"Money is the absolute number one thing wrong with baseball," he said. "Money's ruining the game of baseball, from both the owners' and players' aspects. If I knew the answer, I'd be head of the union instead of Donald Fehr. I think baseball will survive, but I won't be around to see it.

"We would play this game for nothing. That's something guys lose sight of, the love of the game. That's something I try to find every day, whether it's the smell in the stadium, the smell of fresh-cut grass. It makes me reflect about a time when I was in Little League, Babe Ruth or high school ball. It keeps the flame and fire burning for the love of the game."

In a forgettable fall of 2001, for both the country and Turk Wendell, that flame began flickering. And the would-be kid on the mound for the Phillies would be hammered with adult-style frustration.

◆ ◆ ◆

Wendell seemed the perfect fit for a fledgling Phillies contender late in the 2001 season. He had long since buried his ambitions of being a fifteen- or twenty-game winner. He was content as a setup man without the statistical reward of saves. In every measure, his own and others, he was a perfect team player even while he was an individualist.

"I take things in stride now," he said earlier that year. "I'm a lot more relaxed. I've got a three-year contract, and I'm not fighting for a roster spot. To have that sense of security is a nice thing. If I have a bad two weeks, I'm not going to be sent down. It's one of the things that helps a player get over the hump and bounce back."

He would not brood over failure.

"You take the good with the bad, make the most of what's in-between," Wendell said. "You have a bad day, you figure out that you've had worse. Yesterday's long gone. Even if I went out and struck out the side, got the save or the win, it's gone. Today's a new day. The game's over. I've seen too many people dwell on the negatives. You've got to worry about today's game."

You didn't have to go hunting with Wendell nor sample his wild-game concoctions to get along with him.

"I get along with everybody," he said. "I'm kind of a quiet guy, too, more of a loner. I'll keep to myself. But I try to make the clubhouse homey. We're a family for seven and one-half, eight months. You learn that part of surviving is to make the most of every situation you're in."

If the Phillies wanted references on Wendell's status as a good team player, they need not have gone further than former Mets teammate Todd Zeile.

"He was great to my son," he said of Wendell. "A fun, lively spirit in the clubhouse. He plays with a great respect for the game. He's positive for any team he's on."

But there was one other factor that both Wendell and his teammates had left out, a quality that was another throwback to generations of previous pitchers. His love for baseball, desire to make the majors, and rugged outdoorsman persona had enabled Wendell to develop a high pain tolerance. He'd pitch with all the requisite aches and pains, and there would be no complaints. Not if one's job was on the line. He adhered to the classic pitcher's credo.

He had lost all but one month of the 1992 season due to a right-elbow stress fracture, but Wendell claimed he had pitched with the injury without even knowing it. He recovered, but all the years of warming up with the stress of throwing pitches that moved had taken a steady toll on his arm. He suffered what was later diagnosed as tendinitis, but did not tell anyone at the time he was hurting.

"I started hurting after the trade [to Philadelphia]," Wendell would admit in the off-season of 2001–02. "The dry humps hurt when you get up [in the bullpen] several times in a game, and don't pitch."

Wendell had blown games previously, like any heavily-used reliever. On April 28, 2001, while still a Met, he had served up a tiebreaking homer to the Cardinals' J. D. Drew in the seventh inning. Angered, Wendell then threw a pitch behind Mike Matheny, the next hitter, and was ejected.

In his first five appearances as a Phillie, he gave up walk-off homers to the Mets' Robin Ventura and the Giants' Andres Galarraga, did not retire a batter while being charged with three runs in a one-run defeat to the Rockies, and allowed two inherited runners to score on a double by the Giants' Marvin Benard in another close game.

"The freaking Mets looked like geniuses right now. They got rid of me just in time," Wendell said. To try to change his luck, he gave infielder Tomas Perez a Rolex watch to give up uniform No. 13, getting rid of another odd-ball number he had worn during his successful New York seasons: 99.

The number change didn't help. Neither did wearing his socks high in a fashion change from his usual cleats-hugging pants. By August 17, 2001, Wendell had been on the mound four times as the opponent's winning run crossed the plate to end the game.

"I feel like I'm in the movie *Groundhog Day*. I don't think I've ever been in a streak like this," Wendell said at the time. His ERA had ballooned to 10.13 in his first twelve Phillies appearances. In a game against the Diamondbacks at Veterans Stadium, he served up two homers in one inning. A chorus of boos erupted, and the first cracks in Wendell's even-keel emotional façade began to appear.

"I don't really care about the fans," he said. "I'm playing for the guys in this clubhouse and the organization."

Even with the twinges of pain, Wendell tried to improve his mechanics.

He worked with Phillies pitching coach Vern Ruhle on modifying his leg kick. He also tried to decipher the tale of the tape.

"I have a highlight video that I watch frequently," he said. "It's twenty successions of a slider that I like to throw for a strike. Then twenty fastballs in succession. Then sinkers, changeups, the way that I picture in my mind. In a game, the catcher puts down a sign, I immediately click to that visual."

But nothing worked. Wendell continued his downward spiral. And the usual Phillies boo-birds transferred their vituperation to print. Hate mail began descending on his locker at Veterans Stadium.

One letter was as repetitively profane as they come: "You suck, you suck, you suck, you suck, you suck, you suck, you suck, you suck, you suck. P.S. You suck."

A fan who identified himself as a Phillies season ticket holder threw the money issue at Wendell: "Unlike you, I'm not stealing a paycheck from my employer. I don't have a lot of money so I want to thank you for being sure I won't have to spend money on tickets to the playoffs."

Others wished bodily harm on Wendell: "Did you every think about wearing that necklace so that it punctures your jugular vein?"

"One guy said he wished I had been in the World Trade Center," Wendell said later.

Wendell gestured on the field, but it wasn't the goofy, harmless, Fidrych-style fun of 1988 to 1994. After being routed by the Braves in a September game, Wendell yelled and made what the *Philadelphia Daily News* described as a "dismissive gesture" toward a vocal fan in the box seats who wore a Philadelphia Eagles jersey.

"I don't care about the fans. Fuck the fans. And quote me," he barked at reporters after the implosion against the Braves. As he left the clubhouse, Wendell pulled on a Red Sox cap.

Perhaps Wendell had mixed it up in a battle he couldn't win.

"The whole Northeast [fan] mentality is pretty rough," said Rangers center fielder Doug Glanville, who lockered next to Wendell as a Phillie. "They're tough fans. You have to be careful with the fans. It's like everything is so tightly knit. It's an intensity that's in this part of the country. It spills into the arenas."

A day after the Wendell-fan confrontation, the pitcher submitted to X-rays. They came back negative. The diagnosis was acute tendinitis in the right elbow. He had thought he had blown out the elbow and needed "Tommy John" reconstructive surgery. Philadelphia reporters had asked him several times if his elbow was hurt, but he denied it each time.

"Maybe I was being too stubborn and too competitive," he said upon hearing the tendinitis report. "I like to go out and earn my money. If I say my arm is sore and I can't pitch or that I have to go on the disabled list, to me *that's* stealing money."

Wendell considered asking for a trade, which was his right having been dealt in the middle of a multi-year contract. But he failed to pull the trigger on that request through the winter of 2001–02.

The fence-mending between Wendell and the perennially frustrated Phillies fans would be difficult, at best. As he mentally tried to repair himself during the winter, he hardly sounded conciliatory.

"The Phillies fans are absolutely brutal," he said. "Without a doubt, they're worse than New York fans. New York fans have compassion for someone who busts his hump. I never got hate mail in New York.

"I'm going to make them eat their words and show them I can pitch. I've got bigger challenges down the road. There's not anything I can't overcome."

The boo-birds' impact was faint compared to a physician's prognosis early in 2002. All those times Wendell enthusiastically had taken the ball when he was tired had caught up with him. He had elbow surgery that caused him to miss the 2002 season. He'd have to wait until 2003 to settle his score with the fans.

Like so many Americans in 2001, Wendell had been forced to grow up all of a sudden. His final challenge would be to recapture that youthful, full-of-wonder view of baseball he had cherished.

As a throwback to generations of nonconformists, walking in lockstep with everyone else just wouldn't be Wendell. His most forgettable stretch of baseball had threatened to impose just that status on him.

15

THROWBACK TO
THE FUTURE

If you're a throwback, you've got to not only look the part, but also act it.

Mark Prior's got the visual image. Brush-cut hairstyle with a hat pulled low over his head. Socks that sprout high over calves that resemble tree trunks. An economical style that combines power and control.

But even though he's barely old enough to remember the first George Bush in the White House, Prior might as well have been straight out of the Eisenhower era.

"I consider myself a throwback, but I'm a new-generation one," the Cubs' phenom, all of twenty-two, said. "For me, throwback means guys who go out there every day, bust your butt and do what you gotta do to be successful. If it means you're not friends with the guys on the other side of the field, so be it. That's my attitude."

Prior got some high-tech training from pitching guru Tom House and arrived in the majors a highly-polished prodigy just past legal drinking age. But the heart of his makeup comes from learning the right way to pitch from the throwbacks who have gone before him.

"The guys I've always looked up to are old-school guys: Nolan [Ryan] and Roger [Clemens], Randy [Johnson] and [Curt] Schilling," Prior said. "[Greg] Maddux. All those guys are throwbacks."

Almost all of these role models combine raw natural ability with a keen baseball mind. Again, Prior is proceeding down a well-worn path.

"Everybody goes about their game differently," he said. "Schilling puts in two, three hours every day getting ready for his starts. Randy knows what he has to do. I think I'm a combination of both."

But many of Prior's contemporaries wouldn't believe they're a combination of anything, let alone define "throwback" or "old school." There is a discernable generation gap between the twentysomething baseball crowd and veterans in their thirties who prepped under authentic old-school types, having played in the 1970s and 1980s. They in turn learned how to play the game right and act the part of a professional from baseball figures who toiled prior to the free agency and arbitration era, when next year's paycheck depended upon this year's performance.

That brings it back to the age-old issue: money. The up-and-coming crop of players is perceived to have had it too easy in the pocketbook, too fast.

"Younger guys, they get too much stuff fed to them," said well-traveled outfielder Matt Stairs, who with his softball-player physique looks the part of a throwback. But Stairs also carries the throwback spirit in his blood, having gone through a wringer to which the latest crop of players would scarcely relate.

"They spent a year, a year and a half in the minors, come to the majors, and get everything on a silver spoon," Stairs said. "They get $10 million or $15 million [signing bonus] and they don't have the pressure of getting a paycheck of $600 every two weeks.

"Some guys come up and struggle as rookies, they let them go the whole year. When I came up ten years ago, you go oh-for-three games, your ass is going back to Triple-A. Guys come up, hit their first major-league homer, they flip the bat. That's the way they played in the minors."

Others wonder whether the young crowd realizes how to play the game right, considering the influences on them in a power-crazed game. Home-run hitters get the girls and the glory. Sixty or seventy homers in a season no longer is science-fiction. Hitting behind the runner and giving one's self up does not get you a hallowed place on *SportsCenter*.

"When you play that way, it's got to be installed in you from Little League, from your parents," authentic throwback Fernando Viña of the Cardinals said. "It's all about what you have in your heart. You run with that, do your role. My role is get on base, do what you can. Fans want to see home runs. Hitting a home run is a great feeling. Some guys are made for it, some are not. If not, you got to be a table-setter, and that's what I am. You got to play the role you know best."

Some of the warhorse baseball types who circulate throughout the game often cringe at what they witness. They don't believe many younger players eat, sleep and breathe baseball as before.

"Most of them respect the game," said Yankees scout Chuck Cottier, a former longtime coach and manager. "They just don't know how to go about it the way they used to. There's more money for them. They don't read as much in the box scores about other teams. It starts in the minor leagues. You used to read in the box scores about how your major league team did, so you could brag about the players at the major league level. Now some of these kids at the minor league level don't even know who's playing in front of them."

But the game of baseball somehow regenerates itself in the face of all adversities. Years of forgettable World Series and declining TV ratings seemed fated to continue at an accelerated pace less than two months after the generation-defining jolt of September 11. Yet the Diamondbacks and Yankees staged a Fall Classic that would have made the 1960 Pirates and Yanks proud. Less than a year later, the game seemed careening toward a fatal players strike that was avoided only at the last second, much to the disappointment of a cynical flock of strike-mongering media vultures waiting to swoop down on the game's carcass.

So it's the same concept with the newest group of throwbacks. A few like Prior seem to have been raised that way. Others grow into the part when they properly appreciate their place in the game and the ability to adhere to its traditions.

Four of the baseball's greatest young stars—the American League superstar shortstop quartet of Alex Rodriguez, Derek Jeter, Nomar Garciaparra, and Miguel Tejada—were cited by both Stairs and Cottier as possessing throwback styles. Yet it's another AL shortstop not gifted with the five tools of the foursome who draws most of the praise.

"I certainly think [David] Eckstein is a throwback-type of player, a Pee Wee Reese–type of guy," Blue Jays manager Carlos Tosca said of the Angels sparkplug.

The Reese comparison might be a stretch for Cottier, who feels the late Dodgers table-setter was more naturally talented than Eckstein. However, he'd take Eckstein's persona anytime.

"He's a little dirtball player that's not afraid to get dirty and knows how to play," Cottier said. "The biggest thing is, the young players in the major leagues now don't know how to play. He knows how to bunt, he knows how to run bases, he knows where to be on relays. He knows how to play the game."

Viña knows a plucky middle infielder when he sees one.

"He plays hard, goes at it and gives it all he has," he said of Eckstein. "Nobody ever gave him anything."

Also endorsing Eckstein as one of their favorite young old-schoolers were Stairs and Cardinals scout Mike Squires.

Alfonso Soriano of the Yankees may have had superstar numbers in 2002, but still operated from a hustling, get-dirty basis, said Tosca.

"He's a guy who looks for ways to beat you," he said. "If he has a bad day offensively, he'll try to beat you with his speed. He's not the prettiest defender in the world."

Third base is another position where a player often risks his health with line drives taking milliseconds to reach the position, along with all the diving and expeditions after foul balls into dugouts and box seats.

Tosca believed his prime 2002 rookie, Eric Hinske, will feel right at home at the position for years to come, and not just because he can flat-out hit.

"He's just a baseball player," Tosca said. "He's just a grinder. He doesn't mind getting his uniform dirty. He enjoys the whole gamesmanship of the game. I don't think he chews tobacco, though.

"What he is will probably be a George Brett–type of guy. A good hitter who will hit for power, and he'll be a good defender. Early on, he was kind of feeling his way through [at third]. Now that he's more comfortable, his defense is really improved. Our third-base coach, Brian Butterfield, helped him with that. We think he'll be an above-average defender and a middle-of-the-order hitter with power and the ability to walk. He's an excellent baserunner. He's got deceptive speed to steal bases, great instincts to steal bases."

"I just want to be a complete player, handle myself on field as best as I can," Hinske said. "I just try to play the game hard, be consistent every day and get my uniform dirty. If you want to call me that [throwback], fine."

Hinske could be joined at the hot corner by the White Sox's Joe Crede in a battle for future All-Star berths. Crede finally grabbed ahold of the position late in 2002 after several years of indecision by the Sox front office about when to promote him.

"A guy like Joe Crede, he spent quite a lot of time in the minor leagues, paying his dues and waiting for his chance, and never complained one bit," said Sox reliever Kelly Wunsch. "He played hard, never pouted about being in the big leagues. He's soft-spoken. He's paid his dues."

Crede has another young old-schooler in the lineup with him, according to infielder Jose Valentin, long a throwback with his value system and out-spoken nature.

"Aaron Rowand and the way he plays hard," Valentin volunteered as his favorite young throwback. "In the outfield, he likes to go through walls. He's always dirty. He plays a little bit like Kirk Gibson."

A player who almost became a White Sox in the offseason of 2001–02 in a trade vetoed by the Disney Company has been an old-schooler for years, according to Stairs.

"Darin Erstad is probably the all-time hustle guy," he said. "It doesn't matter whether it's 15-0 or 1-1, the way he plays the outfield, the way he doesn't give any at-bats away. I remember a game against us [the Athletics], it was 14-1, he dove in the gap and robbed [Jason] Giambi. It was an unbelievable play. He ran head-first into the wall in Anaheim. He made the play, threw the ball home and afterward suffered the injury."

A National Leaguer who now has experience running uphill at Minute Maid Park in Houston would be a worthy understudy to Erstad, Stairs added.

"Lance Berkman's got the goatee, he plays hurt, he dives for everything in the outfield," he said. "He impresses me the way he plays. I enjoy watching him play."

Making it a trio of center fielders is the Dodgers' Dave Roberts, according to Viña.

"Dave Roberts plays the game the way it should be played," he said. "He's a hard-nosed guy. He battles hard, lays bunts down, hits the ball the other way."

Meanwhile, Prior isn't the only pitcher who will be a certified old-schooler in 2010. Sox reliever Wunsch could be the epitome of the well-traveled southpaw by that date. With his near-underarm delivery, he'll always be in demand as a specialist who can get the tough left-handed hitter out in the seventh or eighth innings.

"I sure hope so," he said of being the proverbial eternal pitcher. But he probably won't take it as far and as long as Mike Morgan.

"I expect that to happen at some point in my career [moving around]. I'm not sure I'm going to play until I'm forty. This job is a grind, it's tough on family life, it's hard to be away from the family as much as we are. Five years from now it might be my philosophy [play until they tear his uniform off, á la Morgan]. It might not be ten years from now.

"I spent six and one-half years in the minor leagues. As long as I spent in the minor leagues, I'm not about to give it up at the least bit of adversity. I'll be like the pesty weed in the garden."

And, like countless others, Wunsch may wander the majors at some point, only to return to the White Sox.

"That's when you really know you went the rounds when you start showing up on the same teams again," he said.

In the short term, at least, Wunsch had the privilege of participating in "holds" for young Sox ace lefty Mark Buehrle. Along with the Athletics' Barry Zito, the pair of southpaws could inherit the mantle of "crafty left-hander" from Jamie Moyer.

"If you don't have the 'cheese,' you've got to find something else to do," Wunsch said. "These guys have used their abilities well."

On Buehrle: "He's got to be smart and throw pitches that move, and move them around the zone. He's not a guy who throws 95 and blows them by people. He has to be on, he has to be focused, he has to be into the game to be successful."

On Zito: "Just how he kind of carries himself. He doesn't strut, doesn't have any arrogance to him. He just goes out and pitches. He just flips that curveball over and over again. You don't see that many big over-the-top breaking balls these days. That pitch in itself is kind of a throwback. Now it's sliders and splitees and cutters. The looper doesn't show up that often any more."

Non-pitcher Viña nominates one of his Cardinals relievers as a throwback. "Mike Crudele is a battler, a gamer," he said. "He goes after it. Here, hit me or I'll get you. He's a smart pitcher."

That's the operational word, "smart." Baseball's the thinking man's game, and the thought process does not have to stop if you have a birthdate after 1975.

EPILOGUE

This book may be all about individuals who adhere to a "throwback" philosophy.

But none of them operate in the old-school baseball world in which stability was the byword and team rosters remained familiar to their fans for years on end. Free agency and the constant tinkering with payrolls, either to load up rosters or cut costs, dominate the sport's landscape. Rarely does a star come up through the farm system of one team and play with the same franchise until the end of his career.

Jim Thome proved that point once again. Seemingly fated to be a lifetime Cleveland Indian, Thome opted not to take a "hometown discount" for his new contract in late 2002. He took advantage of a spending spree by the Philadelphia Phillies—stocking up on talent in advance of their new stadium scheduled opening in 2004—to obtain an even more lucrative contract in the City of Brotherly Love. Thome dare not fail, considering the leather-lunged nature of Philadelphia fans.

Partially compensating for the addition of Thome's salary, the Phillies let Doug Glanville escape via free agency. Although Glanville had established himself as one of baseball's best defensive center fielders, his offensive production continued to decline in 2002. He opted to leave the city in which he had distinguished himself academically at Penn for hotter climes with the Texas Rangers.

As winter ebbed, the question of a lucky number thirteen team on Mike Morgan's resume was unresolved. Morgan had been a big part of the Arizona Diamondbacks' world-championship chemistry in 2001, but was consigned to a kind of baseball "taxi squad" for Arizona during much of the 2002 season. Released after the season, Morgan still wanted to pitch and checked into yet another spring-training invitation as a non-rostered player. But the invitation didn't come, putting before Morgan the stark truth that he may have to take his glove and his unique personality home for good to wife Kassie and their two daughters.

Craig Biggio, though, maintained a true old-school outpost in Houston. Staying with the Astros, he did move—to center field. Biggio endured the second position switch of his career to accommodate the arrival of free agent Jeff Kent at second base. Biggio is athletic enough to handle the move, and his football background will give him courage to charge up that unique incline in deep center at Minute Maid Park.

Greg Maddux toyed with the idea of leaving Atlanta, but ended up staying with the Braves. However, that famed ol' pitching gang at Turner Field was broken up with the free-agent departure of Tom Glavine after fifteen years in Atlanta.

INDEX

277

ABOUT THE AUTHOR

GEORGE CASTLE covers baseball for several Chicago-area newspapers. He also hosts the radio talk show *Diamond Gems,* heard throughout the Midwest.

Castle has followed baseball as a fan and media person since the 1960s, growing up in the right field bleachers of Wrigley Field and paying old-school prices as low as one dollar to get in. Grandfather Morris Zutz was the first-generation baseball fan in the family, sitting in the same bleachers to watch stars such as Hack Wilson.

Castle has written for a variety of national sports magazines, and selected and edited the tape for the Jack Brickhouse and Radio Hall of Fame sportscasters exhibits, as well as tributes to Jack Buck and Ernie Harwell, at the Museum of Broadcast Communications in Chicago. He lives in the Chicago area.